X

SPIRITS FINELY TOUCHED

HAROLD SKULSKY

SPIRITS
FINELY TOUCHED

The Testing of Value and Integrity
in Four
Shakespearean Plays

THE UNIVERSITY OF GEORGIA PRESS

ATHENS

Library of Congress Catalog Card Number: 74–18586
International Standard Book Number: 0–8203–0368–2

The University of Georgia Press, Athens 30602

Set in 11 on 13 pt. Intertype Garamond
Printed in the United States of America

To the memory of

SAMUEL SKULSKY

יזכור אלהים נשמת אבי מורי
שהלך לעולמו. אנא תהי נפשו צרורה
בצרור החיים. ותהי מנוחתו כבוד.

Contents

Acknowledgments

The first four chapters of this book appeared in different form in the following places and grateful acknowledgment is made to the publishers of these journals: *PMLA* for " 'I Know My Course': Hamlet's Confidence," 89 (1974): 477–486, and "Revenge, Honor, and Conscience in *Hamlet*," 85 (1970): 78–87; *Journal of the History of Ideas* for "Pain, Law, and Conscience in *Measure for Measure*," 25 (1964): 147–168; and *Shakespeare Quarterly* for *"King Lear* and the Meaning of Chaos," 17 (1966): 3–17.

I should like to thank the following for various good offices: Dr. Haviva Langenauer for the beautiful calligraphy that adorns the dedication; Mrs. Hilda McArthur for her unfailing professionalism in typing the manuscript; my teachers Douglas Bush, Herschel Baker, and the late Moses Hadas for the inspiration of the example they set and for their personal generosity to me over the years; my friend and colleague Vernon J. Harward for his manifold kindness and for the subtle and humane scholarship of the medieval lectures I have had the pleasure of attending for some years past; and Susan Skulsky for criticism and discussions that have helped me profoundly to speak my mind with greater clarity and finesse than I should otherwise have done.

Introduction

THIS BOOK is an attempt to study related varieties in Shakespeare's work of a particular kind of dramatic suspense. Since, as far as I am aware, the kind of suspense I mean has not yet been clearly identified as such, it will be useful to begin by distinguishing it from two others that are more familiar. In submoral suspense, we wish a character success on his own terms irrespective of whether those terms are as a rule morally acceptable to us. In moral suspense, we come to wish a character success on our terms rather than his because success as the character defines it is revealed as foolish or harmful in itself and threatening to the character's moral integrity; our new anxiety on his behalf thus begins with the fact that the character has proved capable of defining success as meanly as he does. What is ultimately at stake for us in this case is the sheer survival of the character as just that person who earned our sympathy at the outset.

Suspense of the former kind seems to be limited to crude romance or melodrama and is hardly to be found in a pure form in the Shakespearean canon. Suspense of the latter kind is generated in some degree by all four of the plays to be considered, though perhaps especially by *Hamlet* and *Othello*. It is in turn the occasion of a third or speculative suspense that is my main concern. In this case what we fear is that we shall be compelled by what the character does and suffers to give up as nonsense or fiction the premises on which, among other things, we ground our concern for his moral integrity. The disagreeable possibility begins to suggest itself that such premises have either no truth or (what is worse) no meaning. The premises I have in mind affirm in one way or another the dignity or coherence of the human condition—the sort of dignity or coherence Aristotle seems to envisage when he includes among affective requirements of tragic drama not only pity and fear but τὸ φιλάνθρωπον, the love of man.

For example, we may share the belief, implied or expressed by the

character or his associates, that moral principles like those that bid
for his allegiance purport to be statements of what is generally the
case; that their truth depends on qualities (for which the irreplaceable
names are "good" and "bad" or their synonyms) that generally mark
out experiences like pleasure, beauty, and love or their opposites; in
short, that it makes sense for the character to insist as literal statement
on the goodness of his ends and the rightness of choosing them.
Suppose, then, that it is borne in on us by the dialogue or action that
moral principles may not be generalizations after all but merely cries
or commands; that they are not false only because they are not true
either; that they are no less arbitrary, if more numerous, than
the rules of chess.

To take a second but related example, the character and we may
be reminded that even if such qualities as goodness and badness do
indeed occur in human experience, by that very circumstance neither
he nor we can have arrived at moral generalizations, and hence at
moral principles that can guide our behavior toward other men,
unless we can somehow observe other men's experiences. But now
suppose, once more, that it is borne in on us in the course of the play
that minds are inviolably private, a privacy we are only the more
conscious of when the fiction of an aside or a soliloquy lets the
audience, and only the audience, into their presumed recesses; that
the character has failed, and can only fail, to argue his way from the
behavior of others to other minds; that the celebrated insight
reserved to love turns out to be a chimera.

These two unpleasant doubts about morals and minds, suggested
and sustained by action and dialogue, are the related varieties of
speculative suspense I propose to study in *Hamlet, Measure for Measure, King Lear,* and *Othello.* I have chosen these plays because they
seem to invoke such concerns more richly and subtly and centrally
than others in the Shakespearean canon. In each of them our com-
placency is shaken by moral suspense and destroyed by speculative.
We may begin by wishing a character well by his own lights—Hamlet
in his quest for vengeance, Duke Vincentio in his deputation and bed
trick, Lear in his phantom inquest on justice, Othello in the kind of
love he asks of Desdemona and thinks at first he has won—but soon

we are troublingly aware how deeply that character is in danger of being corrupted or made monstrous by his own specious ideal. This posture of concern rather than censure is a triumph of the moral over the moralistic; the playwright masterfully denies us the luxury of righteous judgment. But there is another kind of luxury in which we can take refuge, and which must likewise be denied us if we are to be fully engaged; it is the sort of fundamental security to which speculative anxiety is the sobering retort. The playwright does not always abandon us to this insecurity. He sometimes allows us an eventual catharsis or affirmation. But as in other cases, it is not so much the release as the suspense that gives the drama its form and its power over the audience.

This book tests a hypothesis about how the emotional appeal of certain Shakespearean plays is modified by a particular kind of intellectual appeal. Others have explored similar hypotheses about Shakespearean plays, and it may forestall confusion to state at the outset some crucial differences between my own and kindred views.

It has been suggested by moralizing critics that Shakespeare's most engrossing demand on his audience is (a) to judge the acts of his characters with a view to (b) judging the characters themselves. In the Christian version of this approach, energetically defended by Roy W. Battenhouse,[1] an important part of the background of principles required for the first kind of judgment (on acts) is the articulate moral theology handed down to the sixteenth century by the great Fathers and Doctors of the Church. The reader will have noticed that moral suspense as I have defined it occurs when we find that a character's decisions threaten to be wrong and hence corrupting. So far, then, I agree with the moralists. Moreover, despite the doubt cast by Roland Mushat Frye, among others, on the historical relevance of patristic and Scholastic literature to an understanding of the finer points of Shakespearean ethics,[2] it is in my judgment very far from unhistorical to draw on such sources to clarify principles that are independently shown to be stated or implied in the text of the plays. This is so if only because the great sixteenth-century theologians themselves often simply mediate the opinions of their predecessors.

But some scholars would go a step further on grounds that seem to me eminently convincing: "The Homilies . . . —the one body of doctrine familiar to every Anglican from the time of Edward VI on—provide an admirably complete introduction to the full range of medieval exegesis. In them, every member of the Established Church would again and again, year after year, have heard some two hundred quotations from the Fathers, alluded to by name, encompassing all of their distinctive ideas."[3]

It is the second step in the moralistic program, the assessing of blame, that I would reject as a false direction in Shakespearean criticism. Vigilant captiousness collecting items for a verdict is too clearly at odds with the magnanimity of the tragic vision. What is perhaps equally to the point, it fails to do justice to the tragic ambiguity of the determinism that lies at the base of the Christian outlook. Shakespearean criticism has sometimes seriously misrepresented the facts of this matter, and it will be necessary to review them thoroughly before we consider their bearing on a critical posture of recrimination.

"With a rush of irony," one critic informs us, "the audience now realizes that Hamlet's moment was ideal for the total revenge he intended: death at the very moment Claudius was rejecting the call of grace and thus willfully choosing damnation."[4] Another critic reports: "Christianity taught that man as a spiritual being was endowed with the divine gift of grace, which he might store for his soul's salvation, exercise in his dealings with his fellow men, or decline from through sin, at his own free will."[5] But put thus crudely, neither account avoids the Massilian heresy whose repudiation by Augustine is common doctrine in the sixteenth century.[6]

It is too simple to say that free will rejects or declines from grace. Grace that saves cannot be resisted. Grace that can be resisted does not save. And the free will that is affirmed in the Augustinian tradition is not free from determination by God: "I shall confess that a man can [be sinless in this life] by God's grace and his own free will, as I do not doubt that free will itself belongs to the grace of God, that is to the gifts of God—not only to the end that it exist but that it be good, that is, be turned to doing the bidding of the Lord."[7] It is true that Roman Catholics of the sixteenth century would find in their Aquinas that predestination, like the providence of which it is a part, does not impose necessity on events considered in themselves. The sentence "He will not die in mortal sin," even of one predestined to be saved, does not express a necessary truth. But reading further they would find a sentence that does: "If he is predestined to be saved he will not die in mortal sin." Predestination is infallible, and has no cause but the will of God.[8] For Rome as well as Reform, the predicament of Claudius at his prie-dieu is filled not only with irony but with a terrible pathos: "O limed soul that struggling to be free / Art more engag'd!"[9]

In the orthodox view, then, free will (so called) consents to grace only by the will of God, and it resists grace only by enthrallment to sin. The occurrence of the term *free will* in theological contexts is thus not to be taken at face value. The will is freed from enthrallment to sin only by the gift of enthrallment to righteousness.[10]

The enthrallment to sin survives in the Reformation doctrine that the moral if not the intellectual depravity of human nature is total. According to Frye, this formula is misleading.[11] Unfortunately, there is little support for his attenuated version of the doctrine; it is not enough to say that man is unable to act so purely as to merit grace. All works that derive from postlapsarian nature, as Article 13 has it, "have the nature of sin." Calvin admits that a pagan's virtues are gifts of God, but only in their results, not in their motives.[12] If one discounts man's flickering reason[13] and "the special graces of God, which He bestows . . . on men otherwise wicked," virtues purely natural "must be considered worthless."[14] "Through sin," as Hooker says, "our nature hath taken that disease and weakness whereby of itself it inclineth only unto evil."[15]

According to Frye, Calvin "cites examples 'to warn us against adjudging man's nature wholly corrupted, because some men have by its promptings not only excelled in remarkable deeds but conducted themselves most honorably throughout life.' "[16] But this reading truncates the passage in question (*Institutes* 2.3.3). The examples do not warn us but merely "seem to warn us" against assuming man's total depravity. Actually the purity in a seemingly virtuous nature is not nature but grace, and "not such grace as to cleanse it, but to restrain it inwardly." Calvin's conclusion is that in such cases "God by His providence bridles perversity of nature, that it may not break forth into action; but He does not purge it within." Man's virtue, to paraphrase Isabella, is accidental and his vice a trade.

The great theologians tend to treat the misbehavior that results from this bondage as worthy of punishment, and one might be tempted to conclude that they are not determinists after all. Frye apparently means to draw this conclusion when he describes them as holding that "in terms of moral choice men could do what they willed to do, and were responsible for the results of their actions."[17] But this form of words is an accurate summary only because it happens to be consistent with determinism. That men could do what they willed to do has no bearing on whether their will in turn was in their own power, which Calvin for his part denies.[18] Like his great predecessors, Calvin believes in moral responsibility and in the usefulness of exhortation. But he insists that these beliefs do not conflict with unlimited predestination.[19]

We have already noted the ironic determinism in Aquinas's way of showing how God avoids imposing necessity on the will though He moves it by Providence. "It is not possible both that God should move the will toward something and that the will should not be moved. At the same time, the latter statement taken by itself is not impossible."[20] It is only in this trivial sense of not being internally contradictory that the will's resistance to divine motion is "not impossible." Aquinas's denial of necessity is thus contrived to do no damage to "the certainty of Providence, which does not fail of its effect."[21]

Battenhouse claims that there is a contrary tendency in Aquinas: "It is in the will's power, Aquinas explains, to give consent to an ignorant judgment, made by a reason which is impeded by an intensity of the sensitive appetite and a 'vehement and inordinate apprehension of the imagination.' "[22] But the freedom of will from appetite, imagination, and ignorant judgment would consist in the power to dissent as well as consent. And by the time Aquinas affirms this power he has already introduced qualifications that effectively undermine it.[23] "For the judgment and apprehension of the reason is thwarted because of the vehement and inordinate apprehension of the imagination. . . . The passion of the sensitive appetite is followed by the apprehension of the imagination. . . . So as a rule the passion of the sensitive appetite is followed by the judgment of the reason and hence by the will, whose nature it is always to follow the judgment of the reason."[24] For Aquinas the will of man is subject not only to the will of God but often to the lower instincts as well.

These, then, are the facts. I have dwelt on them at length because both Frye and Battenhouse, not content with recommending a theory of Shakespearean drama in which offending characters may be unequivocally to blame, go on to father their idea of blame on theological tradition. Thus Battenhouse: "May not a dramatist let us see, in each of the tragedies he exhibits, that the seeming dilemmas of the hero are in reality self-made ones? Only by persisting in a self-pleasing love does man's ignorance become fatal. An implicit positing of this explanation of human disaster, it seems to me, is what can distinguish Christian tragedy."[25] Frye is a little more explicit about the supposed merit of the theory itself: "Dramatic characters act in terms of practical choices, and both Shakespeare and his audience had to be able to agree that the stage characters were morally responsible for those choices. To such an understanding of moral responsibility, the theologians contributed unequivocal support: in terms of moral choice men could do what they willed to do, and were responsible for the results of their actions. Without some such understandings, the drama would lose direction and meaning."[26]

I have already argued that the assessing of blame sorts ill with the largeness of the tragic vision, and that the great theologians are very far from unequivocal in their support of free will, and hence of moral responsibility. In chapter 6 I shall try to show why free will itself, as usually defined, might well seem repugnant to reflective members of Shakespeare's audience, and be made to seem so by the terms in which Iago and others praise it. As for the "direction" and "meaning" of drama, I think these may be, indeed by default must be, accounted for on other principles. The ones I propose are moral and speculative suspense, especially the latter in the two forms I shall pursue in the studies that follow.

I have been raising objections to the sort of Shakespearean commentary, Christian or secular, that issues in verdicts like L. C.
Knights's on Hamlet: "Hamlet, with whatever excitements of his
reason and his blood, is a man who has given himself over to a
false direction of consciousness; and at each of the crucial points of
the action Shakespeare leaves us in no doubt of the inadequacy—
and worse—of Hamlet's basic attitudes."[27] Hamlet's excitements are
here dismissed with curious haste, as if such things were irrelevant to
whether a man has given himself over or been driven to bad courses.
But unfortunately for the whole enterprise of fixing responsibility,
Hamlet's excitements are not merely relevant. They are imponder-
able. Shakespeare's audience cannot be a jury and should not behave
as if it were. In theatrical judging at least, to condemn the actor of a
fault is the very cipher of a function, and to condemn the act is the
very essence.

Some enemies of moral criticism, however, would get rid of the
essence too—our discriminating concern that the hero (autonomous
or not) is doing the wrong thing. And here I must make common
cause with the moralists against a characteristic form of attack in this
vein: that moral judgments, even if they stop short of blaming the
erring character for what he does or becomes, are still imaginatively
and intellectually diminishing to drama. Harry Levin, for example,
makes three crucial points: (a) "singleminded dogmatism, since it
brooks no contradictions, can feel sure which course is right and which
is wrong"; (b) "moralistic commentary" turns its object into "a
dreary sequence of avoidable mistakes"; (c) the result of such commentary is that "Shakespeare's heroes, never rising to heroic stature,
are reduced to a parcel of delinquents, truants, and heretics."[28] But as
to the dogmatism supposedly inherent in feeling sure, it is at least
equally dogmatic to contend that the only means to such assurance is
to brook no uncertainties; one can also take thought, and surmount
them. And one can give the audience of one's play enough evidence
to do the same. On the second point, it is hard to see why unavoidable
mistakes about moral principle need fall outside the province of such
commentary. One can, with charity, "condemn the fault and not the
actor of it." Finally, to argue that a character is recognizably a

delinquent, truant, or heretic is not to deny that he rises to heroic stature. Heroes are not saints. The decisive issue of critical strategy is whether such arguments may sometimes be correct and esthetically relevant. To rule out this principle a priori is to incur at least the suspicion of dogmatism.

John Holloway's argument starts from the attractive premise that "before it is a source of insight great imaginative literature is a source of power." He suggests the content of this power adequately for our purposes by talking of such things as "varied emotional excitement," "exuberant repose," and a "sense of life-giving energy," and by informing us that such power is paralleled in daily life by "the outstanding and momentous experience."[29] On this basis he can proceed as follows: "No one can suppose that any moral insight, however rich and complex, invites this kind of response. . . . It is clear that our response to a great work of literature is of an altogether different kind. Thoughtful and interested attention, thankfulness for valuable knowledge, a desire to do this or that may be present, but are all peripheral." But this is to assume that "moral insight" must take the form of "a general statement."[30] It may take the form of applying such a statement; and the experience of applying it, for example to the actions of a character who offends against the stated principle, may be at once exalting and shattering in proportion to the gravity of the offence, the majesty of the offender, and the intensity with which one has been made to identify with the latter. Perhaps this mingling of distress and pride explains the phenomenon observed by Holloway, that in responding to the tragic hero "we enter deeply and compassionately into his or her predicament or ordeal, yet at the same time realize that its interest and value to us lie in its very extremity, and are unwilling to have it in any way abridged or mitigated."[31]

To be sure, it is hard to see how one can continue to think this experience momentous after reflecting that there is in fact no catastrophe and no issue of principle to worry about: the person whose wrong turning we are afraid of is imaginary, and we fear he will go the wrong way because we are sure which way is right. Since he is indeed imaginary one might be tempted to conclude by process of elimination that our concern for him is momentous only if we are not sure which way is right after all—only if we have been brought face to face with an impasse in our own morality. Hence Ernest Schanzer's proposal that some Shakespearean plays engage us by posing a moral problem that is either moot or insoluble. The problem "will inevitably take the form of an act of choice confronting the protagonist," and will be "presented in such a manner that we are unsure of our moral bearings, so that uncertain and divided responses to it in the minds of the audience are possible or even probable."[32]

It will be clear from the ensuing studies that I find no such moral antinomies in the plays to be discussed. I shall argue that what saves moral suspense in those plays from the limbo of the hypothetical and the truistic is the kind of suspense I call speculative. Schanzer himself seems to acknowledge this alternative possibility when he identifies the issue that exercises the Trojan council in act 2, scene 2 of *Troilus and Cressida:* "The only problem raised in this scene that may leave us in a state of doubt is not a moral but a metaphysical problem: What is value? Is it inherent in the object, as Hector maintains, or does it reside in the estimation put upon the object by the observer, as Troilus would have it?"[33] This last and not moral uncertainty is the kind of problem whose dramatization by Shakespeare will concern us in this book, though Schanzer's way of describing it suggests a misunderstanding that it may be wise to clear up before proceeding.

The issue between Troilus and Hector is not metaphysical. The question is not whether the property named by the word *value* inheres in the objects prized or in the eye of the prizer, but instead whether the word *value* is the name of a property at all (however subjective) or merely an empty counter used to give commands and expressions of will the prestige of statements. The problem concerns not metaphysics but meaning.

If I am right, then, what bothers us in these plays is that certain things we say may, as assertions, be absurd, not that they may be false. The quest for reassurance that they make sense is not therefore to be confused with the quest, attributed to Shakespeare by some critics, for the "comprehension" or "understanding" of life as these are defined by Holloway, for example: "These expressions point less to any sense of what are the basic values of life than to a sense of how, at the most radical level, life works . . . what kinds of actions we can expect to succeed, what to fail. . . . Shakespeare's comprehension of life in *Macbeth* is that he who starts like Macbeth is likely to proceed and end as he does."[34] This is an unpromising illustration of how Shakespeare's plays reflect the laws of life, for many usurpers avoid failure; the generalization holds only if "failure" is taken in the normative sense Holloway rules out as a source of dramatic energy. Nor is it easy to see the dramatic energy in morally neutral or merely descriptive laws of life even if we were to suppose that Shakespeare is in the business of projecting them.

The point of resemblance between my view and those represented by Schanzer and Holloway is that I too insist on the intellectual or cognitive dimension of our response to Shakespeare's plays. The point of difference is that what these plays call in doubt and sometimes succeed in vindicating is in my view neither the consistency of our moral principles nor the regularity of human affairs.

It is possible to hold, in contrast to all these views, that knowledge is indeed sought and sometimes found in Shakespeare's plays but that it cannot be analyzed because it is not knowledge in the usual sense. Thus D. G. James contends that "the universe of reason is not, I take it, exhausted by mathematics, science, and philosophy; and if we argue that this is so, we must see in Shakespeare's plays a rational treatment . . . of human conduct and human destiny."[35] But rationality, we are to consider, is not restricted to the intellect. *King Lear*, for example, "represents a great labour of knowledge: not indeed of understanding but of perception." In what sense can mere perception without understanding be knowledge? Shakespeare's "eyes, and not his . . . thought, must be the instruments of discovery. He will not resolve but behold. But, in what manner is possible to perception which will not suffer itself to be overintellectualized, he must yet probe and test; he must abstract and classify and separate out; he must simplify in something of the manner of an experimenter; he must not squint at his object, mitigate, and soften down."[36]

But it is clear that perception becomes intellection as soon as it carries on any of the processes in James's list, for they are the processes that define the intellect. A perception that "will not suffer itself to be overintellectualized" is simply one that will not suffer itself to carry on these processes to excess. And why the talk of excess, of "overintellectualization"? The reason is that though James is at a loss to name a cognitive process that is not intellectual he nevertheless wishes us to "allow the imagination as a form of genuine knowledge." Some faculty not prominent in doing mathematics, science, and philosophy must be laid under contribution if literature is to retain its importance: "We cannot, I take it, if we are committed to believing that literature is important, fail to argue that poetry . . . issues from a peculiar labor of knowing."[37] If literature offers us a kind of thought or knowledge offered in equal measure elsewhere, then in James's view it has no special claim on us.

But this is to assume that thought or knowledge is the end of literature, as it is of the other endeavors cited by James. If it is rather a means, among other means, to giving us a special amalgam of satisfactions, then it need not itself be unique to preserve the uniqueness of literature's claim on us. There will be no occasion to cast about (unavailingly in James's case) for a unique order of knowledge to dignify literature. This last is my own view. The concerns that I shall trace through certain Shakespearean plays happen to exercise philosophers as well as playwrights. But in plays they are not an end but a means to generating the effect I call speculative suspense.

To contend that the intellectual phase of Shakespeare's endeavor is a means and not an end is to dethrone it, and I must now try to show how this view differs from the views of those who would discount the intellectual phase altogether. One characteristic form of this position denies that speculative activity is to be found in Shakespearean drama on the ground that a *particular kind* of speculative activity is not to be found in it. Thus one is often told that "Shakespeare was not a philosophical poet: there is in his work no system, exposed or half-exposed, of what may rightly be called a philosophy."[38] Or again: "If we were to think that Shakespeare were merely arousing us— without satisfying us with a flat statement—it would be tantamount to admitting that Shakespeare was not a philosopher, and we cannot admit that."[39] But it is not a requirement of philosophical endeavor that it issue in flat statements, much less in systems. To admit, moreover, that Shakespeare attempts in his play of ideas to arouse us intellectually is to go some way toward placing him in a maieutic tradition that is impeccably philosophical.

The object of this kind of reasoning is, as in the case of the antimoralists, benevolent enough; it is to acquit the playwright of dogmatism. But reflection is not dogmatism. Neither is it dogmatic to arrive at tentative conclusions, as I shall argue Shakespeare occasionally does. Under the spell of this odd prejudice, some critics embarrassed to find affirmations in Shakespeare assuage their consciences by calling what they find by another name. Thus we are told that "tragedy never tells us what to think; it shows us what we are and may be";[40] though it is not clear how *showing* us what we are and may be differs in import from *telling* us what to *think* we are and may be. How else do we assimilate the state of affairs we are shown than as a thought? This false dichotomy is sometimes put as if it were technical and linguistic. Thus: "The total dramatic form . . . *is* rather than *has* a presentational rather than propositional meaning."[41] But whatever (if anything) it is to "be" a meaning *tout court*, there is surely nothing to keep a "presentation" from *having* a meaning as well, and nothing to keep the one it has from consisting of propositions.

Finally we may consider two versions of a simpler objection to critical focus on Shakespeare's dramatization of ideas. The general objection is that sustained intellectual seriousness and the concrete limits or function of writing for the theater do not mix. "It remains significant," argues one writer of this persuasion, "that there are these discrepancies [namely, of time-scheme, manner of dialogue, and assumption of fact in Shakespeare's plays], for they may lead us to expect to find contradictory 'meanings' juxtaposed in the plays."[42] A purveyor of grist for the King's Men is no stickler for coherence in detail. Another writer would have us remember that "Shakespeare acts not as moralist but as dramatist striving to please, that is, as artist, as poet. Is Shakespeare's greatness connected with his freedom from the meaning which students and men generally are prone to seek in art of every sort, thus reducing the giver of pleasure to the preceptor?"[43] The argument from negligence is a false induction. It ignores the likelihood that in a great artist the disregard for consistency in some things reflects an intense preoccupation with consistency in such other things as the pursuit of a theme. To be sure, that intense preoccupation may just as well be a striving to give esthetic pleasure. But the notion of such pleasure required by the second argument is too simple. It is, moreover, undermined by the argument as a whole. If all men seek meaning in art, then presumably they are pleased when they find it. If Shakespeare strove to please in his art, one way of succeeding was to offer a meaning. The likelihood that he did so is great in proportion to the comprehensiveness of the pleasure we suppose him to have striven for.

I have been trying to distinguish the approach to Shakespearean drama I have adopted in this book from three broad classes of approach to which it is in some respects akin: the moralist, the metaphysical, and the noncognitive. Moral suspense is not to be identified with the characteristic interest of moralizing critics. Speculative suspense is concerned neither with the phenomenon of the moral dilemma in particular nor with the order or orderliness of things in general. Finally, that the excellence of drama is not thought but power does not exclude the possibility that fullness of power needs intensity of thought. "Spirits are not finely touch'd / But to fine issues," Duke Vincentio informs us. To be "touched" here is primarily to be endowed, but it is also to be tested for one's endowment, and to be moved. By giving us reason to fear not only the moral death of a character but also the intellectual death of our own deepest convictions, the playwright sees to it that we and not only his creatures may in more than one sense be spirits finely touched, and to fine issues.

CHAPTER ONE

"I Know My Course": Hamlet's Confidence

THIS CHAPTER and the next are designed to support a single thesis. Put schematically, it is this. Hamlet is faced with a contradiction that he cannot quite ignore. Revenge is against his conscience, and yet he thinks it his solemn duty to exact it. In other words, he adopts the puzzling view that at least one evil act (not a means but an end) is obligatory. His unhesitating response to this puzzle is to cut the knot by proceeding as if (in general) the rightness or wrongness of an action had nothing to do with the goodness or badness of its human effects. Indeed, granted the alternative measures of rightness he tries, talk about "good" or "evil," or a "conscience" to measure them, would not make much sense. Hamlet's view, as it emerges, amounts to a despair of moral reason. The play ultimately discredits this view, partly by discrediting Hamlet, but especially by an intricate and powerful appeal to our heritage of moral sentiment.

The evolution of Hamlet's despair corresponds to the first form of speculative suspense I have distinguished—first, that is, in order of exposition, not necessarily of occurrence. In Hamlet's case, as it happens, our immediate concern is the accessibility of other minds. For the Prince is ready to act on his strange assumption (that evil per se may be a duty) only if he can catch the conscience of the King. And he might reject that assumption in any case if he had the penetration to measure the value of his actions by reference to the selves those actions touch. Thus, as it confronts Hamlet, the problem of other minds takes two forms: the use of present behavior to "detect" behavior of the past and future, and a compassionate intuition the exercise of which would be enough to belie Hamlet's despair. There remains the possibility that the problem can be solved in neither form. This subsidiary range of concerns will be the subject of the present chapter.

I shall be arguing that it is seriously mistaken to see Hamlet as something of a skeptic about our knowledge of other minds. But I should like to point out first that one can hardly be blamed for reading such a suggestion into his first extensive speech. What strongly tempts us in this direction is, not merely that Hamlet denies the possibility, even in principle, of plucking out the heart of his own mystery, but that he gives us no grounds for exempting other people's mysteries from the same iron law:

> QUEEN. Thou know'st 'tis common; all that lives must die
>   Passing through nature to eternity.
> HAML. Ay, madam, it is common.
> QUEEN.   If it be,
>   Why seems it so particular with thee?
> HAML. Seems, madam! Nay, it is; I know not 'seems.'
>   'Tis not alone my inky cloak, good mother,
>   Nor customary suits of solemn black,
>   Nor windy suspiration of forc'd breath,
>   No, nor the fruitful river in the eye
>   Nor the dejected haviour of the visage,
>   Together with all forms, moods, shows of grief,
>   That can denote me truly. These indeed seem,
>   For they are actions that a man might play;
>   But I have that within which passeth show,
>   These but the trappings and the suits of woe.
>   (I. 2. 72–86)

One must keep in mind, for the sake of the Prince's nomenclature, that the rhetorical tradition in which he has been reared assumes the validity of the science of physiognomy and hence of the literary *notatio*[1]—the description of a person's inward nature (or state) by means of outward signs that somehow unequivocally "denote" it. But at least in his own case, Hamlet argues here, *notatio* cannot succeed. "Forms, moods, shows of grief" cannot "denote *me* truly," or at least they cannot do so "alone." For such signs are "customary" and hence confined to what, as Hamlet has already willingly granted, is "common" or universal in human experience. And Hamlet's mind, by the very fact of being his, is not universal but "particular." To be sure, the Prince is careful to qualify the rigor of his negation; what signs cannot do "alone" they might still be able to do with help. But the qualification does little more than tantalize. The fact is that what Hamlet has within, in his uncompromising phrase, "passeth show." If we rule out clairvoyance, it is a mystery irretrievably beyond the plucking out. And the corollary, as we said, seems to be that other minds than Hamlet's, being equally unique and invisible, are equally enigmatic; and all attempts to penetrate them equally reduced to a futile indirection.

Whether and how far Hamlet himself accepts that corollary clearly makes a difference to his enterprise of hunting down the guilty mind and punishing its guilt. Skepticism on this score begets virtues of varying depth. If it extends only to the difficulty of predicting behavior, one would expect from the hunter humility and caution. If it includes the difficulty of achieving sympathetic insight, one would expect from the punisher a hesitancy to hate a priori and an exacting search for equity in the award of punishment—this last especially in view of Hamlet's dichotomy between the particular and the common. For even an exacting inquiry into the other mind may well be doomed if, as Hamlet seems to conclude, private experience and public sign are irreconcilable.

Some of Hamlet's countrymen, notably Polonius, have a professional stake in the general reliability of the public sign, and we must now discuss their theory and practice. In so doing it will be helpful to pause over a relevant fact of intellectual history. Authorities of preeminent importance to the Renaissance maintain that the other mind is indeed inaccessible.

The Secrecy of Mind: Rival Traditions

Granted such a conclusion, Polonius's theory of espionage—that one can "by indirections find directions out" (2. 1. 66)—is as much an object lesson in fatal arrogance as his personal claim to "wisdom" and "reach." For as we watch him plying the craft of "lawful espial" (3. 1. 32) it becomes increasingly obvious that one indirection can lead only to another: the bait of falsehood he teaches Reynaldo to

angle with is really good only for catching carps of rumor; the
conversation on which he and Claudius eavesdrop, and of which he is
so unhappy an interpreter, clearly does not interpret itself; and the
sickly disarray of Hamlet's visit to Ophelia has nothing to do with
love—if (as a Rosalind would add[2]) it ever does. The clues and
symptoms available to Polonius, in short, fail to vindicate the natural
history of human behavior that he so emphatically prefers to ethics
and first philosophy, to inquiring "*What* majesty should be, *what*
duty is, / *Why* day is day, night night, and time is time" (2. 2. 87–
88). And the preference is a hubristic prelude to the failure; rather
than waste his time in schoolboy "expostulation" on the what and
why of formal and final causality, the royal councillor has proudly
offered his employers a look at the how, an opportunity to "find out
the cause of this effect" by rehearsing a probable "declension" of
efficient causes:

> And he repulsed—a short tale to make—
> Fell into a sadness, then into a fast,
> Thence to a watch, thence into a weakness,
> Thence to a lightness, and, by this declension,
> Into the madness whereon now he raves
> And all we wail for.   (2. 2. 146–151)

To his undoing, Polonius does not distinguish in this regard between
physical principles and the human mind. Both are hidden, and changes
in either are heralded by natural signs, by a *notatio*, that will enable
us to "gather and surmise" the underlying reason (2. 2. 108); in
Hamlet's case, to

> *gather* by him, as he is behav'd,
> If't be th' affliction of his love or no
> That thus he suffers for.   (3. 1. 35–37)

And it is worthwhile to remember that when Polonius announces his
discovery of the "cause"—

> or else this brain of mine
> Hunts not the trail of policy so sure
> As it hath us'd to do   (2. 2. 46)

—his metaphor is as decorous for the pursuits of science as for those of "policy." For it is the figurative root of terms, like *indagatio, investigatio*, and even *methodus*, very dear to commentaries on the study of second causes.

To be sure, the only sort of evidence that can serve as a "trail of policy" will be, in Claudius's phrase (3. 1. 1), the "drift of circumstance." But as Claudius concedes, the councillor's "positive" assertions have never been wrong, and on this record Polonius declares himself willing to stake his life: "Take this from this, if this be otherwise" (2. 2. 156). The irony of the rhetorical forfeit is that Polonius will eventually be made to pay it in earnest, but rhetoric or not, the pledge that goes with it implies a confidence in the force of circumstantial evidence that rises to Faustian audacity:

> If circumstances lead me, I will find
> Where truth is hid, though it were hid indeed
> Within the centre.   (2. 2. 157–159)

In profundo veritas demersa. Even if the mouthless cave of truth in Democritus's apothegm were to be taken literally,[3] Polonius assures us, he would trust his "essays of bias" to guide him down to it; that the abyss in question is merely figurative is presumably an added reason for confidence.

What we are listening to, then, is far from simple rodomontade. The grandeur, by the standards of his age, of Polonius's folly can perhaps be best appreciated by seeing how a more prudent and orthodox contemporary handles the same old saw:

> And the great mocking-Master mockt not then,
> When he said, "Truth was buried deepe below."
> For how may we to others things attaine,
> When none of vs his owne soule vnderstands?
> For which the Divell mockes our curious braine,
> When, "Know thy selfe" his oracle commands.[4]

Selves, in short, are so difficult to apprehend that we are little the wiser about them when they happen to be our own. And in the human animal this difficulty is, if anything, compounded by the indulgence of a perverse talent. *Nemo non est dissimulator*, as the schoolboy tag has it.[5] Man the mimic of creation, after his Fall, becomes man the dissembler. "The heart," observes Jeremiah (17 : 9), "is deceitful above all things"—*inscrutabile* in the Vulgate—"and desperately wicked: who can know it?" Fittingly enough, it is the most versatile dissembler in the play who is most bitterly perplexed by the impenetrability of the human surface, and whose despair provides an eloquent foil to the hackneyed worldliness of his councillor:

> POL. We are oft to blame in this,—
>   'Tis too much prov'd—that with devotion's visage
>   And pious action we do sugar o'er
>   The devil himself.
> KING. [Aside] O, 'tis true!
>   How smart a lash that speech doth give my conscience!
>   The harlot's cheek, beautied with plast'ring art,
>   Is not more ugly to the thing that helps it
>   Than is my deed to my most painted word.
>   (3. 1. 46–53)

At least once, in his famous remark about style (2. 2. 90–91), Polonius's implicit faith in the outward sign betrays him into a strange confusion. For it is clear that brevity cannot be the "soul" of any wit of which tediousness could be called "the limbs and outward flourishes," and this not merely because brevity and tediousness are incompatible, but because both exist on a single plane: both, in fact, are "outward." The "soul" of an utterance, whatever it might be, is not its length. One can hardly imagine Claudius making the same mistake, haunted as he is, even in contexts that would seem to warrant it least, by the image of "the owner of a foul disease" who, "to keep it from divulging, let it feed / Even on the pith of life" (4. 1. 21–23).[6]

It is all the more surprising, then, to notice the same confusion in the King's account (2. 2. 5–7) of his nephew's

>   transformation; so I call it,
> Since not th' exterior nor the inward man
> Resembles that it was

—as if the change in the "inward" man were an object of direct observation rather than an inference from the "exterior." But one must bear in mind that the instincts of the two politicians were not very likely, after all, to be any further apart than their training; that Claudius's instructions to Rosencrantz and Guildenstern are of a piece with Polonius's to Reynaldo—to "gather" what they can from "occasion" (2. 2. 15, 16); and above all that during the Renaissance the commonplace *consentit cum mente color* enjoyed more than a proverbial currency.[7] It was corroborated, as we have mentioned, by the science of physiognomy; and the theorem of metaphysics that things unnatural are not long lasting was clearly applicable to mental states dissembled. The hypocrite who cannot be outguessed can safely be outwaited.

Moreover, it was possible, by embracing the Neoplatonic doctrine of the cosmic soul,[8] to go far beyond the pragmatic faith of a Claudius or a Polonius in the arts of the intelligencer. Like any other soul, that of the world was held to be present simultaneously to every part of her cosmic body, but especially to the bodies of other souls, with which last, by virtue of a common genesis, she forms a kind of sisterhood.[9] The joint possession of a transcendent soul accounts in the physical sphere for the latent attractions that underlie the art of magic, and in the cosmic sisterhood for the innate sympathy—Ficino calls it the *communio compassionis*—of all thinking beings.[10] Indeed, sympathetic affinity, not the movement of a physical medium, is the basis of all response or awareness, just as, according to Ficino, no intervening movement is presupposed when one chord vibrates of itself in reply to another, or when a mental image occurs at once and spontaneously to two good friends.[11] All acts of perception, by the grace of the cosmic soul, are acts of clairvoyance. And, as Sylvester's Du Bartas observes, since the cosmic soul contains the paradigm of all future events, natural, accidental, or voluntary, it is to her we owe our thanks for the gifts of those prophets

> Whose sight so cleerely future things did gather
> Because the Worlds soule in their soule ensealed
> The holy stamp of secrets most concealed.

The "prophetic soul" that dreams on things to come and inspires a man with second sight is ultimately not his alone; she belongs, in the phrase of sonnet 107, to "the wide world."[12]

But for much the greater part of Shakespeare's audience these speculations would probably have seemed worse than idle. The common parishioner would know that God alone can compel us, in Claudius's phrase, to give ourselves in evidence, and the educated man could add that not even the angels (except in the heterodox view of the Scotists) can penetrate the human conscience or the secrets of Providence.[13] As for the classical treatises on friendship, the rigor of their demands is badly compromised by the meagerness of their expectations. True friendship, says Aristotle, consists in loving not accident but essence.

> The serious man stands in the same relation to his friend as to himself, for the friend is a second self. Consequently one's friend's existence is desirable in the same, or nearly the same, sense as one's own. But it is because one is immediately aware of being good that existence is desirable, and that such existence is inherently pleasant. Therefore one must be immediately aware of one's friend's existence, and this would come about through living together and sharing discourse and thought.[14]

On the other hand, Aristotle makes it clear that the medium of exchange indispensable to friendship is appearance, and that it is a coin as liable to counterfeit as any other.

Cicero's parallel remark makes the problem even clearer: "Not only is simulation vicious regardless of its object, for it adulterates what is true and removes the criterion of it, but simulation of friendship is the most repugnant of all, for it destroys truth, without which friendship can have no meaning."[15] To make matters worse, a warranted love of self, as both authors repeatedly maintain, is the necessary paradigm for love of others. But a warranted love of self presupposes a just estimate—"virtue loves itself," says Cicero, "for it knows itself and understands how worthy of love it is"—and unfortunately, self-knowledge falls under an interdict that we have already encountered in considering some lines of Sir John Davies: the human mind, according to the regnant psychology, is capable of a purely reflexive act only by special grace; "the best sense with her reflecting thought / Sees not herself without some light divine."[16] The man in quest of friendship as the authorities define it is thus confronted with two problems that are formidable to say the least: the demand for intuition where only observation is possible and the vicious circle of ignorance that is generated by conceiving of the friend as a second self. And if friends cannot know each other, who can?

Hamlet as Spy: Unmasking the Hypocrites

We began by considering Hamlet's insistence that his state of mind, being as unique as what contains it, is no less ineffably private. On the strength of that passage one might expect him to be anything but cordial to his adversaries' faith in the technology of spying, much less to the a priori assurances of the Neoplatonists. But a harder look at the play as a whole disappoints this expectation. For the strange valediction with which it opens, to a sentinel relieved from duty "sick at heart," is no mere flourish. The hero of our play will be, not only a man who might have made a soldier, "had he been put on," and who has effectively been relieved of his vigil by the time we bid him farewell, but one also who, though he scorns to be troubled by "gaingiving" (5. 2. 226), admits in the very same breath "how ill all's here about my heart" (l. 223); who defies augury (l. 230) precisely because he is far from dismissing it; who characteristically "prophesies" that his dying wish will be granted (l. 366); and who, on hearing a suspicion dubiously confirmed, pays exclamatory homage to his "prophetic soul" (1. 5. 40). What these reflex utterances of the Prince's convey is something more intimate than a philosophy. It is a habitual confidence in his intuitive powers that is all the more telling for being casually expressed; a confidence that is clearly visible beneath the jocular Scotism of his rejoinder to Claudius:

HAML. For England?
KING.   Ay, Hamlet.

HAML. Good.
KING. So is it, if thou knew'st our purposes.
HAML. I see the cherub that sees them.

(4. 3. 48–50)

This easy sense of his own discernment colors the ideal of friendship that first appears in his sudden recognition of "Horatio!—or I do forget *myself*" (1. 2. 161). To forget Horatio would be to forget Hamlet for the same reason that claiming to know another's excellence, taken strictly, is a form of boasting: "I dare not confess that, lest I compare with him in excellence; but to know a man well were to know himself" (5. 2. 145–147). All that Hamlet can say without self-praise is that if any man is known to be well endowed ("known well"), that man is Laertes ("himself"). For the person one *knows* in the strict sense—and this is the basis of Hamlet's quibble—is oneself, in the first or second degree. Such a knowledge is pure introspection and therefore incomparably more certain than any mere report, however close to the source:

> I would not have your enemy say so,
> Nor shall you do mine ear that violence
> To make it truster of your own report
> Against yourself.   (1. 2. 170–173)

And the ability to elect one's *alter idem* seems to entail other powers as well. The soul becomes "mistress of her choice," Hamlet clearly implies, at the point where she can "of men distinguish" (3. 2. 68, 69).

It is, however, more typical of the Prince to refer the task (2. 2. 178–179) of picking his one honest man out of ten thousand to a faculty other than intuition. Neoplatonic *compassio* is nearer kin to charity than to spying, and Hamlet, like Othello (as we shall see), prefers spying. Perhaps to our surprise, he appears to be in very cordial agreement with Polonius's view that men's "adoption" may be "tried" (1. 3. 62); more than tried, he assures us in fact: "seal'd" with finality (3. 2. 70). Such trial, to be sure, is no business for amateurs: "You would play upon me, you would seem to know my stops, you would pluck out the heart of my mystery, you would sound me from my lowest note to the top of my compass; and there is much music, excellent voice, in this little organ, yet cannot you make it speak" (3. 2. 380–385). Guildenstern cannot pluck out the heart of a human mystery because he has not the "skill" (1. 378) of eliciting a significant response in the first place; he cannot make me speak because he does not "know my stops." And even if he knew them well enough to rival the superhuman virtuosity of Lady Fortune, the will to concealment would still remain for him to subdue or circumvent. If Horatio, then, by force of will is "not a pipe for Fortune's finger / To sound what stop she please" (3. 2. 75–76), Hamlet's mystery has little to fear from the tentative gropings of a Guildenstern.

On the other hand, the skill that Guildenstern admits he lacks, on Hamlet's premises, is very far from being a chimera. Its efficacy, in fact, is guaranteed by the ineluctable symmetry of the bond between body and mind. Hamlet makes his opinion on the matter very clear when he comes to consider a paradigm case of dissimulation, the histrionic act:

> Is it not monstrous that this player here,
> But in a fiction, in a dream of passion,
> Could force his soul so to his own conceit
> That from her working all his visage wann'd,
> Tears in his eyes, distraction in 's aspect,
> A broken voice, and his whole function suiting
> With forms to his conceit? (2. 2. 577–583)

Monstrous as it may be that the player can feign a passion, the fact remains that he does so only by generating in his soul "a *dream* of passion." Thus whenever his "function" is "suiting with forms to his conceit," one may safely take it for granted that those forms emanate from the "working" of a soul that has already been "forced" to the same "conceit." This occurs even when the display is "all for nothing —for Hecuba." What is vastly more to the purpose is that the player's response to a *genuine* motive and cue, as Hamlet goes on to insist, would be altogether distinct from the result of forcing the soul. And it was a commonplace that the same psychosomatic limitation on dissembling can operate quite as easily in the other direction. The seducer who pretends to be in love, says Ovid, is not after all so very dangerous; he will soon be what he pretends: "True will that love grow, which but now was false." By the same token a passion can be got rid of, says the physician of unrequited love, by the simple expedient of making believe one *is* rid of it: "Ape what thou art not, feign love shrunk to naught: / Thou'lt do indeed what thou hast done in thought."[17] Because of this reciprocity between the outward and the inward man, between "use" and "nature," it is wise to go through the motions of having achieved one's own reformation—to "assume a virtue, if you have it not" (3. 4. 160)—as a means to achieving it in earnest. "For," Hamlet assures his mother, "use almost can change the stamp of nature" (l. 168). No change in the human exterior, then, is ever quite meaningless. One can hardly wonder that Hamlet is emboldened by so hopeful a theory to rely at least as heavily as Polonius on the virtues of the diagnostic method.

Hamlet's interview with Rosencrantz and Guildenstern supplies an especially obvious example (2. 2. 291–322) of the principle of indirection involved: the discrepancy between the kind of information he purports to be soliciting from his schoolmates and the kind he ends by easing out of them. For his overt questions are patent throwaways. The first is "Were you not sent for?" But he quickly admits that he is already sure of the answer: "You were sent for; and there is a kind of confession in your looks which your modesties have not craft enough to colour. I know the good king and queen have sent for you." Hamlet now makes Rosencrantz's equivocal reply ("To what end, my Lord?") the basis of a second request for enlightenment: "That you must teach me." But he has no intention of having himself taught what he is already sure he knows. He spares them a breach of "secrecy" by speaking for them. Even here he forgoes an opportunity to test his assumption, for by exploring his loss of mirth with such memorable diligence he effectively avoids fulfilling his promise to tell them why they were sent for, and ends instead by changing the subject. What he really wants to know, of course, is whether they will "deal justly with me" by his high standards—whether their confession will be spontaneous or hesitant. Since he has been keeping an eye on them (as he tells us in an aside) he will have had all the answer he is after by the time he gets to his second question, and thus his final plea "If you love me, hold not off" is more verdict than exhortation.

It will be noted that the Prince attempts to lull suspicion by being, as Rosencrantz reports, "niggard of question; but of our demands / Most free in his reply" (3. 1. 13–14). Though, to be sure, he does not in fact lull suspicion—his interviewers have no difficulty in perceiving that there was "much forcing of his disposition" (l. 12)— his tactic of calculated loquacity is clearly far subtler than the frigid and obvious policy of noncommitment Polonius recommends to Laertes: "Give every man thine ear, but few thy voice; / Take each man's censure, but reserve thy judgement" (1. 3. 68–69). But once more, whatever Polonius's limitations as a theoretician for his son's benefit, his practice as explained to Reynaldo does not differ in essentials from Hamlet's. That practice, in a word, is to use a neutral generality—a dummy statement or question—as bait for the un-mentioned particular one is trying to elicit. By this method you are bound to come, in Polonius's phrase, "more nearer / Than your particular demands will touch it" (2. 1. 11–12).

As for any scruples that might have deterred the Prince from re-taliating so adroitly in kind—and he mentions none—there was no lack of ancient authority to remind him that the wisdom of serpents was not unworthy of the embattled Christian. Even so absolute a partisan of truthfulness as Augustine is brought to admit, in the course of his invective *Contra mendacium*, the permissibleness on occasion of prudently hiding the facts under a kind of dissembling, and Jerome gives some interesting precedents from Scripture.[18]

There is a twofold importance in this authoritative sanction of an art of dissembling. First, such a license tends both to spread and to sophisticate the practice, thereby compounding the problem of detec-tion; we should particularly expect an artist in sleight to be sobered by the mere fact of his own artfulness. Will this be true of the artful Prince? More important, the patristic sanction is grounded, not on an arbitrary double standard, but on what was felt to be a genuine moral distinction between acts of dissembling. The evil dissembler bends his wit and skill to others' mischief. The good, on the other hand, either devotes them to the benefit of others, even ultimately that of his dupe, or chooses the admitted evil of lying, with all its consequences, because this course is less evil than any of its alternatives. *Minus malum habet rationem boni*; the lesser evil is eligible under the aspect of a good. A Christian deceiver, then, cannot in conscience avoid the duties of justice and compassion implied by Jerome's comparison of justifiable dissembling with no less than the Incarnation. Will the Prince meet these requirements?

One of Jerome's examples, as it happens, is especially instructive on the issue of an antic disposition: the experience of David, who "was sore afraid of Achish the King of Gath. And hee changed his behaviour before them, and fained himselfe madde in their hands" (1 Sam. 21 : 12f). Beside such sacred warrant for craft, and especially for madness in craft, one must place two parallel accounts, almost equally celebrated, of secular history: Solon's pretended madness in Plutarch and Livy's relation of Lucius Brutus's valor at the court of the Tarquin, "covering discretion with a coat of folly."[19] The Renaissance was thus very well fortified by tradition against naiveté on this head, and Harington's Ariosto sums up the old apologetic faithfully enough in his defense of Bradamante:

> Then doth this damsell merit no reproofe
> That with Brunello (to all fraud inured)
> Doth frame herself to counterfeit a while,
> For to deceive deceivers is no guile.[20]

This morally anomalous form of guilelessness takes one form that is particularly worthy of note in view of the favor it finds with Hamlet. The following, from Holland's Plutarch, illustrates the gambit with a certain pungency:

> But that man may very easily find out the variable changes of a flatterer, as of the fish called the pourcuttle, who will but strain a little and take the pains to play the dissembler himself, making shew as if he likewise were transformed

into divers and sundry fashions. . . . For then he shall soon
see the flatterer to be inconstant, and not a man of himself . . . for that he receiveth always as a mirror the images
of the passions, motions, and lives of other men.[21]

Hamlet's refinement on this device is to fix on as amorphous or
subjective an issue as possible and then test the resistance to pressure
of his subject's opinions. In Osric's case the theme is the weather:

> OSR. I thank your lordship, 'tis very hot.
> HAML. No, believe me, 'tis very cold; the wind is north-
> erly.
> OSR. It is indifferent cold, my lord, indeed.
> HAML. Methinks it is very sultry and hot for my com-
> plexion.
> OSR. Exceedingly, my lord; it is very sultry,—as 'twere—
> I cannot tell how.   (5. 2. 97–104)

The famous cloud that the Prince assigns to Polonius (3. 2. 393–
402) is perhaps a more delicious exercise, for it allows the minister
to convict himself by his very adroitness at the game of graceful
recantation: "It is—backed like a weasel." Hamlet, in short, invites,
and may even tempt, us to greet his little experiments as so many
proofs of his acuity: "They fool me to the top of my bent"; Q.E.D.
But we are given little reason to cooperate; the competition in both
cases is pitifully unequal. Even Polonius grudgingly acknowledges
the disquieting *notatio* of old age whose physical items Hamlet later
calls to his attention with such relish:

> It seems it is as proper to our age
> To cast beyond ourselves in our opinions
> As it is common for the younger sort
> To lack discretion.   (2. 1. 114–117)

These victories over the stupid or the superannuated are suspiciously
cheap. As we shall see, they may be Pyrrhic as well.

We have been considering indications that Hamlet shares Polonius's addiction to the sort of worldly knowledge that went into the composition of many a Renaissance commonplace book, and that usually took the form of stereotypes not unlike the Theophrastan character. Surprising as this is, it is not entirely unprepared for. To be sure, we are not surprised at all to find Polonius, in his little aphorism on age and youth, using "common" and "proper" as synonyms, whereas we look twice when we come across kindred lapses in the young man who so eloquently insisted on the chasm between the "common" lot of "all that lives" and the irreducible particularity of his own bereavement. But the strangeness of these lapses persists only so long as we forget that the young man in question is a young scholar, if not a young pedant, and that if the old man pays homage to the ancient picture of the memory as a writing tablet in which "precepts" are "charactered" (1. 3. 58, 59), the "table" of Hamlet's memory is an even more ambitious receptacle for "all saws of books, all forms, all pressures past, / That youth and observation copied there" (1. 5. 100–101), and is in fact assisted by a physical article of the same studious description—perhaps the very one in which he is later discovered reading "words, words, words."

There is a double irony, then, in the spectacle of a man who sneers at "these tedious old fools" (2. 2. 223) and at the same time sees so clearly that the child actors who satirize their grown-up fellows "exclaim against their own succession" (2. 2. 368). Half of the irony, of course, is that the Prince's own "succession" is not to be. But the other half is that the old fool he exclaims against—the man who also went to "university" and also plumes himself on being a "good actor" (3. 2. 106)—is very much his fellow enthusiast of edifying generalities. There would, of course, have been no such irony and perhaps no tragedy, either, had Hamlet been less interested in the petty unmaskings possible to *notatio* than in the finer justice of the sympathetic imagination.

As we have seen, the *notatio* does not always fail Hamlet; as wit, certainly, he captures the trick of it no less adroitly than Overbury or the satirists:

He did comply with his dug before he suck'd it. Thus had
he, and many more of the same bevy that I know the drossy
age dotes on, only got the tune of the time and outward
habit of encounter; a kind of yeasty collection, which carries them through and through the most fond and win-
nowed opinions; and do but blow them to their trials, the
bubbles are out.   (5. 2. 195–202)

Hamlet has no difficulty in blowing the like of Osric to his trial,
and thus far perhaps is not to be blamed for expecting Gertrude to
see in the "outward habit" of Claudius a mystic resemblance ("like
a mildew'd ear," 3. 4. 64) to his secret crime, or for reasoning from
the elder Hamlet's manly form to his "wholesomeness"—though
none other than the ghost has already reminded him that "lewdness"
can come a-courting "in a shape of heaven" (1. 5. 54). Among
Shakespeare's more admirable people, after all, the belief in such a
relation dies very hard. "There is a fair behavior in thee, Captain,"
says Viola in *Twelfth Night*,

> And though that nature with a beauteous wall
> Doth oft close in pollution, yet of thee
> I will believe thou hast a mind that suits
> With this thy fair and outward character.

It may give us pause to notice how obliviously she undercuts this
will to believe by asking the Captain to help her "conceal me what
I am"; but when Antonio, later in that play, comes out unequivocally
for the opposite view—"Virtue is beauty, but the beauteous evil / Are
empty trunks o'erflourish'd by the devil"[22]—the circumstances plainly
inform us that disillusion itself may be illusory; Antonio is a victim,
not of mistaken character, but merely of mistaken identity. Hamlet's
optimism, for better or worse, is more tenacious; for even in disillusion he holds to the stereotyping faith of his tables. "Frailty thy name
is woman," and if woman's beauty is not a sign of honesty then it
must be a sign of the opposite: "Ay, truly: for the power of beauty
will sooner transform honesty from what it is to a bawd than the force
of honesty can translate beauty into his likeness" (3. 1. 111–115).

Hamlet's failures arise from the same hubristic optimism as his successes. It is especially ironic, for example, that the only outward show he thinks impenetrable—his own—augmented with the mask of an antic disposition, should be so easily pierced by his mighty opposite, and in a metaphor that signalizes the ultimate failure of Hamlet's one challenging effort at lifting his own mask:

> KING. Love! his affections do not that way tend;
> Nor what he spake, though it lack'd form a little,
> Was not like madness. There's something in his soul
> O'er which his melancholy sits on brood,
> And I do doubt the hatch and the disclose
> Will be some danger.   (3. 1. 170–175)

> QUEEN. This is mere madness,
> And thus awhile the fit will work on him.
> Anon, as patient as the female dove,
> When that her golden couplets are disclos'd,
> His silence will sit drooping.
>   (5. 1. 307–311)

Where Gertrude sees mere madness hatching dove's eggs, Claudius correctly awaits the emergence of a hawk. Hamlet's mimicry thus ends by failing of the total ambiguity that Ophelia's genuine madness achieves only too well:

>   Her speech is nothing,
> Yet the unshaped use of it doth move
> The hearers to collection. They aim at it,
> And botch the words up fit to their own thoughts.
>   (4. 5. 7–10)

But the subtler irony of this miscalculation is that the success of Hamlet's "disposition," independently diagnosed by both Polonius and Ophelia as "ecstasy" (2. 1. 102, 3. 1. 168), very nearly defeats the purpose of the Prince's interview with his mother. For it is precisely from her own "ecstasy" that Hamlet hopes to save Gertrude by an appeal to rational choice, or rather to sense, which

> to ecstasy was ne'er so thrall'd
> But it reserv'd some quantity of choice,
> To serve in such a difference. (3. 4. 74–76)

Yet after the ghost's interruption the Prince's own medical record catches up with him: how to prove that one's reforming zeal is not another of one's fits—"that I essentially am not in madness" (l. 187) —when one can think of no outward show "that can denote me truly"? There is nothing for it but to retract this last opinion. Hamlet proposes an impromptu series of tests:

> Ecstasy!
> My pulse, as yours, doth temperately keep time
> And makes as healthful music. It is not madness
> That I have utter'd. Bring me to the test,
> And I the matter will reword, which madness
> Would gambol from.   (3. 4. 139–144)

It is not reassuring that Hamlet's favored norm here should be the pulse of the very woman he has just convicted of "ecstasy"; nor are madmen exceptional in their reluctance to reword horrors. These tests of sanity are desperately inconclusive and, what is equally important, not at all atypical of Hamlet's usual standard of precision.

It would appear that tests may vary widely in sensitivity, and the "Mousetrap" once again is no exception, as Hamlet's own information on the subject should forewarn him. Trial by reenactment as it is defined by this information ideally consists in the circumstance

> That guilty creatures sitting at a play
> Have by the very cunning of the scene
> Been struck so to the soul that presently
> They have proclaim'd their malefactions.
>   (2. 2. 618–620)

By the specified criterion, then, Claudius's reaction will convict him if it involves a "present"—that is, an immediate—proclamation of guilt. Nor can Hamlet, on his own assumptions, be satisfied with very much less; for guilty creatures are not the only ones to be struck to the soul by "horrid speech" (l. 589). With something like *The Murder of Gonzago* at his disposal, for example, the declaimer of "Rugged Pyrrhus" would not only "make mad the guilty" but

> appal the free,
> Confound the ignorant, and amaze indeed
> The very faculty of eyes and ears.
>   (ll. 590–592)

In view of the indiscriminate potency of dramatic performance itself, Claudius's guilt must at the very least "itself unkennel in one speech" (3. 2. 86); if not, Horatio is told—if Hamlet is forced to settle for less—

> It is a damned ghost that we have seen,
> And my imaginations are as foul
> As Vulcan's stithy.   (ll. 87–89)

But—and this is the crucial point—Hamlet does settle for less, in advance; mere flinching on Claudius's part will serve for a death sentence as far as his nephew is concerned: "If he but blench, I know my course." Well before the actual performance, then, we find Hamlet effectively self-convicted, if not of a false and foul imagination, at least of a willingness to act on the devil's say-so with all the assurance of a celestial guarantee. And here one has to bear in mind the essential distinction between what Hamlet will accept as evidence, which does little credit to his desire for fairness, and what Claudius will eventually give him, which happens, no thanks to the Prince, to meet the standards he has been so ready to dispense with. It is interesting in this connection to observe that by the time the players are at work Hamlet has already adopted the less embarrassing assumption that "free souls" are impervious to the theater of cruelty: " 'Tis a knavish piece of work, but what o' that? Your Majesty, and we that have free souls, it touches us not. Let the gall'd jade wince, our withers are unwrung" (3. 2. 250–253).

Far from being troubled by uncertainties, then, Hamlet navigates through the moral night of Elsinore by the light of a "reach" and "wisdom" (2. 1. 64) in which he no less than Polonius has a firm if quite unwarranted confidence.[23] It is this confidence that induces him to spare Claudius while the latter is engaged in what Hamlet does not doubt is "the purging of his soul" (3. 3. 85). It is this confidence, for that matter, that animates his plea to Ophelia:

> Doubt thou the stars are fire,
> Doubt that the sun doth move,
> Doubt truth to be a liar,
> But never doubt I love.
>
> (2. 2. 116–119)

The logical form of this little poem is easy to mistake, so it is worthwhile to point out that the series of imperatives, like those of Donne's familiar "Song," embodies an a fortiori argument of the following type: (*a*) You might far more easily be unsure about *these* matters than about whether I love (in Donne's "Song," you might more easily catch a falling star than find an honest woman); (*b*) but it is impossible to be unsure about these matters; (*c*) therefore it is, if anything, doubly impossible to be unsure of my love. The second premise, of course, will not bear scrutiny. While it would indeed be a contradiction in terms to doubt—that is, to suspect—that truth is a liar, the other two statements are so far from being closed issues in this sense that they are (at the time of Shakespeare's writing) the subject of noisy disagreement among savants.

One recent writer contrives to save Hamlet from this intellectual gaffe by sacrificing his rhetorical point: the Prince is simply contrasting the indisputable fact of his love with the mere hypotheses of science.[24] But a Pyrrhonian Hamlet is effectively ruled out by his equation of physical knowledge with the maxims of pure logic; that truth is not falsehood was not a subject of inquiry, and was not open to dispute. *We* recognize that the equation is false, but the fact remains that Hamlet *makes* it. It is not Hamlet who sees the weakness of arguing that his love is at least as certain as a cosmology that is not certain at all. He sees no such uncertainty. If anybody does, it is the audience. Hamlet is not perplexed by these obscurities. We are.

The Mind of the Ghost: Hamlet's Inference

In more ways than one "The Mousetrap" is a crucial measure of the Prince's faith in his detective prowess: it must carry the burden of establishing, not only Claudius's guilt, but also the ghost's veracity and, *if Hamlet's reasoning is sound*, the supernatural provenance and authority of the demands it has made on him. To know Claudius's guilt, by this account, will also be to "know my course," and in both these senses Hamlet will eventually "take the ghost's word for a thousand pound" (3. 2. 297–298). And the stakes involved in the soundness of this reasoning are ominously higher than Hamlet's jocular estimate would suggest. Supernatural visitations are not social calls. The "intents" of such a visitant, as Hamlet's own greeting to the ghost clearly implies, are bound to be either "wicked" or "charitable" (1. 4. 42), and Horatio's spontaneous conjectures leave us in little doubt as to what order of wickedness or charity we are to expect: a ghost's exhortations can lead to "grace" for their listener and his country, or to damnation.

Immediately before his encounter with the ghost Hamlet holds forth sagely on the forces that spoil a man's good repute by "breaking down the pales and forts of reason" (1. 4. 28), but it is characteristic of him—perhaps tragically so—that the danger to his own "sovereignty of reason" (1. 73) needs to be pointed out to him by someone else:

> Why, what should be the fear?
> I do not set my life at a pin's fee,
> And for my soul, what can it do to that,
> Being a thing immortal as itself?

What Horatio fears for Hamlet's soul is a madness that will tempt its victim to "desperation" (1. 75) in the radical sense, a state of sin deadly in itself and deadly in the acts that grow out of it, of which suicide is not the only one Horatio apprehends; for it is important to note that when Hamlet compares himself to the Nemean lion and announces his readiness to "make a ghost of him that lets me" (l. 85), Horatio sees his premonition very near to fulfillment: "He waxes desperate with imagination" (l. 87). The errand of a revenant, then, is not mere wickedness or charity at random; when it troubles to come, it comes to save or to damn.

It is thus profoundly urgent that "The Mousetrap" be foolproof not only in its immediate result but in what Hamlet takes that result to imply. But once more there is every reason for us to suspect the validity of an inference from the ghost's veracity to its "honesty." Hamlet himself appeals to the relevant ethical objection in affecting to criticize the "slanders" of satirical wit on old men: "All which, sir, though I most powerfully and potently believe, yet I hold it not honesty to have it thus set down" (2. 2. 202–204). And it is hard to imagine that the devil will allow his distaste for telling the truth to get the better of him in the pursuit of more infernal dishonesties. To be sure, in a later play Shakespeare will have a character ask in surprise: "What, can the devil speak true?" But only to remind himself a bit further on of what everybody knows. As Eleanor Prosser points out in this connection, "Banquo knows from the first that truth may be 'the Devil's most insidious weapon' ":

> oftentimes, to win us to our harm,
> The instruments of darkness tell us truths,
> Win us with honest trifles, to betray's
> In deepest consequence.[25]

The outcome of Hamlet's theatrical venture, then, does not succeed in eliminating the possibility that the devil has indeed been at him, and "abuses me to damn me." Hamlet continues as before in need of "grounds / More relative than this" (2. 2. 632–633), but this time without knowing it. His inference from veracity to honesty is no mere lapse in his memory of lore about ghosts. It is rather a failure of logic and imagination. Like the Duke's bed trick in *Measure for Measure* (as we shall see), Hamlet's Mousetrap is a ruse whose inadequacy a more comprehensive moral and psychological imagination would have disclosed.

The playwright, by the way, does not proceed as if to a Christian audience the ghost discredits itself simply by being a ghost. We, and Hamlet, need to be put on our guard by various hints, including one that is purely Senecan and theatrical. The ghost of the archetypal Senecan prologue is a sorrowful agent of Nemesis, bringing fatal delusion on his descendants:

> To suffer paynes it seemeth wel my part,
> Not woes to worke: I am sent forth lyke vapoure dyre to rise,
> That breaks the ground or poyson like the plague in wondrous wyse
> That slaughter makes, shall I to such detested crymes applye
> My nephewes hartes?[26]

Were one to press Horatio's Roman hints and take his "prologue to the omen coming on" (1. 1. 123) as a technical description, the ghost's choice of a "countenance more in sorrow than in anger" (1. 2. 231) would be just the thing to give one pause. Why not more in anger than in sorrow, on an errand of justice without mercy? Hamlet, at any rate, interests himself busily enough, though to be sure *faute de mieux*, in precisely this kind of data: "Then saw you not his face? . . . What, look'd he frowningly? . . . Pale, or red? . . . And fix'd his eyes upon you?" These, indeed, are not inconsequential facts for an amateur of physiognomy and kindred arts, and the verbal suggestion of likeness yet to be penetrated, or likelihood yet to be appraised, chimes through the scene: "look upon his like again" (l. 188), "a figure like your father" (l. 199), "these hands are not more like" (l. 212), "it would have much amaz'd you—very like, very like" (l. 237). At least one of these "likes" inspires a positive suspicion: "these hands" do not bode well for resemblance as an earnest of identity.

It is worthwhile to stress the gullibility of Hamlet's immediate reaction to the ghost, despite the signs of danger. "Hamlet believes it to be a spirit—possibly good, but probably evil," says Eleanor Prosser, taking a contrary view:

> If it assume my noble father's person
> I'll speak to it though hell itself should gape
> And bid me hold my peace.
>
> (1. 2. 244–246)

And on "Thou comst in such a questionable shape / That I will speak to thee" (1. 4. 43–44): "The apparition is such as to invite question, but may it not also be 'open to question,' doubtful? Hamlet had so assumed until this very moment. He so assumes even as he determines to address the ghost as if it were in fact his father."[27] But these interpretations run counter to the apparent sense of the passages. Hamlet pictures hell as gaping, not to release the ghost, but to prevent Hamlet and the ghost from conferring; and he cites the "questionableness" of the specter's shape to justify, not hesitating to accept it, but so far accepting it as to ask it "What should we do?" (1. 4. 57).

Prosser also argues that "Hamlet's mocking tone, his almost taunting familiarity, could not be directed toward a spirit of health from Purgatory."[28] But the critic overlooks the possibility that the mockery is not at the expense of the ghost, but shared with the ghost at the expense of Hamlet's vainly inquisitive companions. The familiarity is inconclusive for the same reason. Hamlet warns his companions that he will put on an antic disposition (1. 5. 172) for the benefit of others, and it is not clear that present company is excepted. As for the general tone of exhilaration—"Hillo ho ho, boy. Come bird, come" (1. 5. 116)—it is surely the exhilaration of the falcon released. The hunt is on; Hamlet has his mission. We shall have to return to the overblownness of this sense of mission in the next chapter, but for our present purposes it is enough to point out that when Hamlet, in the absence of his friends, reacts to the ghost's lurid account of the murder, it is with an ardent and categorical vow (ll. 92–112). But we must now return again to the central issue of the ghost's vindictiveness. For the Prince eventually outgrows his initial gullibility, and in studying this later phase we must not fall into the trap of being, like Hamlet, so taken up with the ambiguity of the ghost's credentials that we miss the ambiguity of his demand.

The Mind of the Ghost: A Double Standard?

That demand itself is something of a Mousetrap, for Hamlet is more confident of its meaning than he (or we) can well afford to be, and what he makes of it, or the way he chooses to act on it—his failure to catch the conscience of the ghost—gives us our best opportunity to catch his conscience. In tracing Hamlet's response to the ghost's injunction the play offers us an exacting and ironic model of the diagnostic acuteness Hamlet affects but, precisely for lack of a commitment to equity and to the compassionate imagination, is debarred from achieving.

Though the ghost certainly calls for a revenge, it is notable that it leaves the kind of revenge up to Hamlet, with two reservations. The first—"taint not thy mind" (1. 5. 85)—seems to be the more difficult. One can "taint" one's mind either by corruption or by derangement; Horatio, we remarked, has already warned Hamlet against the two kinds of "taint" in combination. But if the ghost means its hearer to be free of both, it is posing a problem that is insoluble by its own admission. Claudius's deed may have been strange and unnatural, but the ghost has already informed us that even the best of murders is most foul—"murder most foul, as in the best it is" (1. 27). How does one reconcile this best (killing Claudius) with a mind free of moral taint, and with the ethos of a play that so splendidly reminds us, in its very first scene, of "Our Saviour's birth" (1. 1. 159)—a play that is resolutely and even technically Christian throughout?[29] As I shall have occasion to argue at greater length in the following chapter, the relevance of Christian teaching to the play is complex and would be open to serious question in any case without this steady Christian emphasis. With it, no such question arises. One can hardly be reminded of Christianity and be expected at the same time to forget the new dispensation: "Dearely beloved, auenge not your selues, but giue place vnto wrath: for it is written, Vengeance is mine: I will repay, saith the Lord" (Rom.

12 : 19). As has been recognized by Eleanor Prosser and Roy Battenhouse, among others, orthodox theology is perfectly clear on this point.[30] Retaliation for its own sake is God's unique prerogative, and even He exercises it only in hell.

Hamlet himself condemns man's usurpation of this prerogative quite emphatically: "I am myself indifferent honest, but yet I could accuse me of *such things that it were better my mother had not borne me.* I am very proud, *revengeful*, ambitious, with more offences at my beck than I have thoughts to put them in, imagination to give them shape, or time to act them in. What should such fellows as I do crawling between heaven and earth?" (3. 1. 123–130, italics added). Hamlet may well ask, on his interpretation of the ghost's instructions. But we must bear in mind that the ghost has said nothing about murder, and has neglected to define revenge: "But, *howsoever* thou pursuest this act" (1. 5. 84, italics added). We are not morally or critically bound to follow Hamlet's interpretation of this "howsoever."

The second of the conditions imposed on Hamlet aggravates the difficulty:

> leave her to heaven,
> And to those thorns that in her bosom lodge
> To prick and sting her.   (1. 5. 86–88)

Prosser's comment on these lines is suggestive: "And then: 'leave her to heaven.' The irony is surely the clue. Why Gertrude and not Claudius. . . . If Shakespeare did not intend the irony why did he so closely echo the familiar language of Christian exhortation—'leave them to heaven'?"[31] It will reward us to explore this suggestion. For despite the Prince's faith in his own perspicacity, he manages to act on a double standard of penal justice without noticing either his mentor's contradiction of the odd mixture of heaven and hell his mentor thereby exposes to view.

The kind of pricking and stinging that the ghost prescribes only for Gertrude happened, in the orthodox view, to be the essential ingredient in *any* equitable punishment. The principle that Christian punishment should correct the conscience, and hence return good

for evil, was so deeply ingrained in the penology of the canon lawyers that it had led to notorious excesses: "the civill lawes content
themselves ever with any excuse or colour in favour of the Delinquents, because when a fault is proved it punishes severely, but the
Canon Lawes which punish onely medicinally, and for the soules
health, are apt to presume or beleeve a guiltinesse, upon light evidence, because those punishments ever worke good effects, whether
just or no."[32] But the excesses only go to prove the fundamental
importance of the "medicinal" principle they abuse.

And the renunciation of merely vindictive punishment was no
less fundamental in the process of reforming English common law
during the fifteenth and sixteenth centuries.[33] When Shakespeare's
King Harry, in condemning his would-be assassins, disclaims all
desire for personal revenge and concludes by praying for their "true
repentance,"[34] he is implicitly serving notice that their punishment,
in inflicting bodily but not spiritual harm, will so far meet the mini-
mal demands of justice. All too few legal penalties, to be sure, were
corrective rather than retaliatory, and Shakespeare's Duke Vincentio
is doubtless acting out a utopian ideal when he defers the execution
of a homicide because the fellow is

> unprepar'd, unmeet for death;
> And to transport him in the mind he is
> Were damnable.[35]

But as we shall note at greater length in chapter 3, Vincentio's
utopianism is also his Christian duty, and a duty to which eminent
jurists of Shakespeare's time and country were increasingly sensitive.
If, as Hamlet apparently does, we accept an argument from silence,
the ghost is proposing an irreconcilable double standard: an anti-
christian punishment for Claudius and the better part of a Christian
one for Gertrude.

To make things more difficult, it is far from obvious that the
injunction to leave Gertrude to "those thorns that in her bosom
lodge / To prick and sting her" absolves Hamlet of active responsibility for Gertrude's spiritual health. How can someone be
left to the pricking of thorns if there are no thorns to prick? If, as

Hamlet suspects, Gertrude's heart is no longer "made of penetrable stuff" (3. 4. 36), he can hardly do justice to the spirit of the ghost's demand without finding something suitable to serve in lieu of thorns. His solution, of course, is to "speak daggers" (3. 3. 414) to Gertrude, a procedure that is clearly punitive in effect:

> O, speak to me no more!
> These words like daggers enter in mine ears.
> No more, sweet Hamlet!   (3. 4. 94–96)

But punitive, we notice, in the Christian or therapeutic way suggested by the most elaborate of Hamlet's explanatory metaphors:

> Lay not that flattering unction to your soul,
> That not your trespass, but my madness speaks.
> It will but skin and film the ulcerous place,
> Whilst rank corruption, mining all within,
> Infects unseen.   (ll. 145–149)

For Gertrude's complacent blankness at the outset is as unmistakable to us as it is alarming to Hamlet:

> What have I done, that thou dar'st wag thy tongue
> In noise so rude against me? . . .
>   Ay me, what act,
> That roars so loud and thunders in the index?
>   (ll. 39–40, 51–52)

Now, apparently for the first time,

> Thou turn'st mine eyes into my very soul,
> And there I see such black and grained spots
> As will not leave their tinct.   (ll. 89–91)

One begins to see that if Hamlet had adopted an attitude of laissez-faire toward Gertrude he would most assuredly have been "leaving" her, but not to heaven.

Hamlet's aim in putting Gertrude through her ordeal, in short, is Christian punishment, the kind King Harry endorses and Vincentio (though fitfully) provides for. If the ordeal does its work, Gertrude will be ready to take Hamlet's advice: "Confess yourself to Heaven; / Repent what's past, avoid what is to come" (ll. 149–150). But if the ordeal is to be effective—and the issue, one must always remember, is the health of his mother's soul—Hamlet has to run through all the necessary steps. To shirk the uncomfortable ones would amount to sentimental betrayal. He must make the falling off of Gertrude's will as graphically vivid to her as possible; pictures (l. 54) can point the contrast. She must be made to realize that sexual appetite is only as good as its object—that one "feeds" on a mountain but "battens" on a moor: and that what is corrupted in her is ultimately not her sense or judgment, which would be pardonable, but her will, which is not.[36] Her will in turn must be strengthened by an induced aversion, not to intimate relations as such, but to intimate relations with Claudius, who must be described as, not only physically repulsive ("nasty sty"), but morally repulsive as well ("a murderer and a villain").

If Hamlet is properly vehement and persuasive, he may hope to awaken in Gertrude the moral conflict that is the prelude to contrition. Hamlet does in fact realize this hope: "Oh, Hamlet, thou hast cleft my heart in twain" (l. 156). He manages to prepare Gertrude for contrition, and for the last and most difficult phase of her reclamation: the discipline that will help her to "throw away the worser part" (l. 157).

The Scholastic-Aristotelian tradition to which Hamlet is plainly an heir holds that vice and virtue are patterns not so much of uniquely deliberate acts as of generalized "habits"—tendencies, that is, to spontaneously good or bad behavior. Hamlet has already deplored the unholy coalition of nature and custom, humor and habit, in breaking down "the pales and forts of reason" in both men and nations, and o'erleavening "the form of plausive manners" (1. 4. 23–30). Traditionally the more painful specific against these influences is the corrective overcompensation Aristotle prescribes:

> One must strain oneself in the direction opposite to one's bias. For by inclining to the other extreme we shall arrive at the mean, as they do in straightening warped boards.

And one must by all means be wariest of the pleasant and
of pleasure herself. For of her we are not unbribable
judges. The attitude of the Trojan senators to Helen, therefore, is the very one we must take to pleasure, and in all
cases repeat their decree; for thus, by sending her away,
we shall err the less.

But such mortification of sense presupposes the strong will
Gertrude lacks. In such cases, according to the Stoics, a gradual
renunciation is more effective.[37] It is this latter program of withdrawal by degrees that Hamlet urges on Gertrude: the gradual substitution of the virtuous for the vicious habit, and hence ultimately
of virtue for vice.

> That monster, custom, who all sense doth eat,
> Of habits evil, is angel yet in this,
> That to the use of actions fair and good
> He likewise gives a frock or livery,
> That aptly is put on. Refrain tonight,
> And that shall lend a kind of easiness
> To the next abstinence; the next more easy;
> For use almost can change the stamp of nature,
> And either master the devil or throw him out,
> With wondrous potency.   (3. 4. 161–170)

Thus far Hamlet's tactics in the closet scene are quite respectably
ministerial. It is possible, of course, though not necessary, to suppose
that the Prince is carried away eventually by homiletic zeal and begins
to threaten Gertrude's sanity. Her three pleas for forbearance, we
notice, are each feebler than the last and all ignored; and the ghost
makes a point of worrying aloud that "conceit in weakest bodies
strongest works" (l. 114). On the other hand, the ghost has
evidently come to disapprove of Gertrude's being subjected to moral
conflict at all: "O, step between her and her fighting soul" (l. 113).
Indeed, its invisible entrance provides Gertrude with an ideal pretext
for making light of her son's preachments and relapsing smoothly
into the kind of smugness that has been endangering her soul.

Prosser concedes this point, citing the therapeutic benefit of self-knowledge, however painful. But when it comes to the active use of corrective pain, she seems to forget her concession: Hamlet "does not appeal to love or hope or contrition; he rubs her nose in her own filth—or rather the filth he sees in her."[38] If it is relevant to speak of Gertrude's need for repentance and salvation, then the filth can hardly be a creature of the Prince's morbid imagination. Like Prosser, L. C. Knights reluctantly concedes the therapeutic use of harsh candor, but then raises an objection to Hamlet's application of the therapy: "If with genuine, even with passionate, concern, you want to help someone in great need, someone in desperate ignorance of his true condition, do you, I wonder, say, 'This is what you are; see how ugly you look?' Well, perhaps you may; but certainly not in such a way that you seem about to make an aggressive attack."[39] But this argument is inconclusive at best. Knights's concession is none the weaker for being reluctant, and the speech in question (Hamlet's at 3. 4. 18–20) gives the lie to Gertrude's inference of homicidal intent on Hamlet's part. Moreover, the critic fails here to appraise Gertrude's interpretation in the light of his own general view that men in *Hamlet* (and by extension women too) are betrayed into error by something "in their own natures," in the present case by guilt.[40] The thesis of this chapter is that Hamlet suffers from a tragic delusion of insight into other minds. But the Prince would lose his tragic stature and our concern if he were simply incapable of acting in kindness. In the present case what he lacks is not kindness but sentimentality. Hamlet, in other words, is not so clearly in the wrong that we can safely ignore the overriding urgency of his appeal to Gertrude's "love of grace" (l. 144) and the impeccable therapeutic justification for vehemence in the face of apathy. A moral "ulcer" needs, not "unction," but the lance.

But again, if the Prince acquits himself well enough in the pastoral function at this point, he is not above betraying it elsewhere. Like the "ungracious pastors" Ophelia warns Laertes of after his own impromptu homily, Hamlet "recks not his own rede" (1. 3. 47, 51); for his understanding of the ghost's instructions commits him to the simultaneous pursuit of two irreconcilable codes of penal justice. For

Gertrude's benefit he must be "cruel, not unnatural" (3. 2. 413). To Claudius's undoing he must learn to be unnatural, to

> drink hot blood,
> And do such bitter business as the day
> Would quake to look on.   (ll. 408–410)

The curing of Gertrude's will compels him to "be cruel, only to be kind" (3. 4. 178), to resign himself to the lesser evil without which his mother cannot be rescued from an infinitely greater. The mission of revenge, on the other hand, must proceed in the opposite moral direction: "Thus bad begins, and worse remains behind" (l. 179).

And Shakespeare's play does not help the onlooker to forget where a Christian, for the good of his soul, is bound to stand on the matter of sentencing others—to forget, for example, that Gertrude's danger is not unlike his own, and that his will, but for the grace of God, must infallibly go the way of hers. Hamlet himself, oddly enough, is full of this counsel of charity:

> POL. My lord, I will use them according to their desert.
> HAML. God's bodykins, man, better. Use every man
> after his desert and who should 'scape whipping?
>
> (2. 2. 552–556)

He is well aware of the "vicious mole of nature" (1. 4. 24) whereby "we are arrant knaves all" (3. 1. 130–131). And he has strange company in this awareness; Claudius is not least pitiable when he speaks from what seems to be bitter understanding of the seduction he carried off with so little difficulty:

> There lives within the very flame of love
> A kind of wick or snuff that will abate it,
> And nothing is at a like goodness still;
> For goodness, growing to a plurisy,
> Dies in his own too much.
>
> (4. 7. 115–119)

Indeed, the kinship between Claudius's own disease of will and that of his wife bears witness to the clarity of Ophelia's mad insight that

"we know what we are but know not what we may be" (4. 5. 42–
43).

If Hamlet in his sanity had shared this humble and inclusive
awareness of the frailty of human resolve, his interpretation of the
ghost's injunction would perhaps not have been so dangerously
inconsistent. Or, given the inconsistency, his diagnosis of the ghost's
nature would not have been so favorable. A sense of equity and the
knowledge of other minds, here as elsewhere in the part of the
Shakespearean canon that we shall be surveying, are reciprocally
necessary.

From the Christian point of view Claudius's disease is not only
a terrifyingly adequate punishment, but a reminder that vengeance
taken on one sinner by another was damnable, not only for Paul's
reason: "he standeth or falleth to his owne master: yea, he shall be
established: for God is able to make him stand," but also for the
less charitable reason supplied by Paul's text: "Vengeance and recompense are mine: their foote shall slide in due time."[41] The
reminder depends on the special status accorded by Scripture and
tradition to the particular crime Hamlet thinks himself called on to
avenge: a brother's murder. Within the play the archetypal fratricide
begins to urge itself on us as a motif with Claudius's glaring error
in tracing natural death *"from the first corse* till he that died today"
(1. 2. 105, italics added). In the end it will emerge unequivocally in
the folklore of "Cain's jawbone, that did the first murder" (5. 1.
85).

But it is Claudius himself who brings into the open the latent
connection between what Cain did and the issue of human vengeance.
For fratricide, he reminds us, "hath the primal eldest curse upon't"
(3. 3. 37), and that curse quite specifically excludes human intervention. The divine object in marking Cain (Gen. 4 : 13–15) was
to proclaim that the avenging of Abel was a crime even worthier of
retribution that Cain's, as Lamech finds to his grief (4 : 24).[42] The
essence of Lamech's crime, according to the exegetes, is a deep
desecration of charity toward the branded sinner.[43] The pathetic
irony of Cain's divine safe conduct is given flesh in Agrippa
d'Aubigné's Renaissance version:

Il possedoit le monde & non une asseurance;
Il estoit seul partout, hors mis sa conscience,
Et fut marqué au front, affin qu'en s'enfuiant
Aucun n'osast tüer ses maux en le tüant.[44]

By forcing this kind of insight on us the French poem in effect
forbids us the luxury of self-righteous detachment, and the English
play does the same; what we see of Claudius's inner state makes
any simple condemnation very difficult:

> My fault is past. But, O, what form of prayer
> Can serve my turn? "Forgive me my foul murder"?
> That cannot be; since I am still possess'd
> Of those effects for which I did the murder:
> My crown, mine own ambition, and my queen. . . .
> Try what repentance can. What can it not?
> Yet what can it when one cannot repent?
> O wretched state! O bosom black as death!
> O limed soul, that, struggling to be free,
> Art more engag'd!   (3. 3. 51–69)

The ghost's antinomy is close to the surface here, for according to
moral theology, Claudius's despair is the nearest of kin to the
spiritual sloth from which Gertrude is rescued, just as her flattering
unction is the same kind he is doomed to use to worst effect: "We
love ourself" (4. 7. 34). Even after his point of no return Claudius
continues to draw our attention, if no longer his own, to the dilemma
of will in bondage:

> That we would do,
> We should do when we would: for this "would" changes
> And hath abatements and delays as many
> As there are tongues, are hands, are accidents;
> And then this "should" is like a spendthrift sigh,
> That hurts by easing. But, to the quick o'th' ulcer.
>   (4. 7. 119–124)

Clearly the ulcer in question is not the one Claudius is thinking of but the one Hamlet attempts to treat in Gertrude: spiritual paralysis.

It is, perhaps, no more than a Cain deserves. But Lamech's crime, we remember, was at least as deserving of God's anger as Cain's; "sevenfold" as deserving, in fact, since, as Sylvester's Du Bartas informs us, it does not respect

> The prohibition, and the threatning vow
> Of him to whom infernall powers doe bow:
> Neither his Pasports sealed Character
> Set in the fore-head of the murderer.[45]

And it is precisely this crime of Lamech's—interference with the workings of "the primal eldest curse"—that Hamlet has embraced as his duty. Clearly the memory of this curse does not help reconcile us to the vindictive half of the double standard Hamlet attributes to the ghost.

We have been arguing that, although a great deal has been made to depend on Hamlet's conjectures about what is going on in the minds of others, much reason has been given us to suspect Hamlet's confidence in his own powers of interpretation. Of these powers—that of behavioral prediction and (more crucially) of moral assessment—the mind of the ghost appears to be the crucial test. Indeed, it is typical of the Prince that he can pay lip service to the deplorable truth that "we fools of nature" are tempted by just such ghosts "to shake our disposition / With thoughts beyond the reaches of our souls" (1. 4, 54, 55–56) and yet so often be tempted to play the part of a fool of nature.

CHAPTER TWO

Revenge, Honor, and Conscience in Hamlet

HAMLET DISAPPOINTS the expectations aroused by his initial denial that private experience can be communicated. For it turns out that the only experience he was referring to was his own. He is perfectly arrogant about his ability to pluck out the heart of others' mysteries, even so special an Other as the ghost. And the contrast in principle between his ways of responding to the guilt of Gertrude and Claudius reveals some deficiency in that deeper penetration into alien mysteries whose fruits are compassion and equity. It is ironic that Hamlet's unwillingness to forbear the destruction of his enemy's soul, reflecting his lack of that deeper penetration, should be frustrated in the prayer scene by his false assumption that Claudius is penitent—hence by his very pretension to diagnostic acumen. We shall encounter again, in the spying activities of Duke Vincentio and Othello, a similar twinning of imperfect insight into other minds and imperfect grasp of the grounds of justice. In Hamlet's case these imperfections can hardly augur well for his success in making the solitary choice imposed on him by the ghost. For that being, with its evasive "howsoever" (1. 5. 84), has been disobliging enough to leave the task of defining revenge squarely up to the Prince.[1]

The play, by contrast, taken as a whole, is rather more obliging; for it illustrates two popular alternatives—the imperative of hatred and the code of honor, we may call them—either of which Hamlet might well choose. It will repay us to consider the light in which these are exhibited to Hamlet, and to us, before looking at the terms in which Hamlet eventually defines his mission, thereby resolving the ambiguity to his own satisfaction. We shall find, I think, that the Prince evolves a view of moral criteria that ominously resembles no view at all.

The Imperative of Hatred

Strictly considered, the imperative of hatred is not very aptly described as a law or criterion of justice, for its essential motive is not obligation but will, and the satisfaction it seeks is limited neither by turnabout nor, for that matter, by any other standard. Some classic discussions are especially helpful on this point. "In many circumstances," says Aristotle, "the angry man would take pity; the man who hates, in none. For the former wishes his provoker to suffer equally; the latter wishes his not to be." Aquinas inherits and elaborates this notion. Hatred consists in wishing evil to its object. When the object is human, therefore, hatred becomes a species of malice, the choice of evil for its own sake. But evil is indeterminate, and hence limitless. Moreover, Aquinas argues, "because hatred desires another's evil for its own sake it is satisfied by no definite measure of evil, for those things that are desired for their own sake are desired without measure." When it comes to malice, in short, one can't get enough of a bad thing.[2]

What hatred longs for is nothing less than the total destruction of the hated object and of all that can be identified with it. This "all," of course, will normally have its posthumous element. In a culture without a clear concept of damnation or of an immortal soul substantial enough to be worth the damning, the self may still be thought of as surviving, and vulnerable, in its lineal posterity. Aristotle's argument for a degree of misfortune after death is a celebrated case in point;[3] and the archetypal avenger in this sense will be a figure like the Virgilian Pyrrhus of the player's speech, for whom all Troy—"fathers, mothers, daughters, sons" (2. 2. 480) —is a single hated extension of his own father's murderer. The indiscriminate bloodymindedness of Pyrrhus's kind of revenge is faithfully reproduced in another Renaissance imitation, the brutal Rodomonte's atrocities at the siege of Paris.[4] Even in a pagan, Rodomonte's homage to grief was barely explicable to Ariosto, much less excusable. For Shakespeare's audience, one strongly suspects, a Christian prince of Denmark could obey the imperative of hatred only by forfeiting all claim to sympathy. It is instructively ironic, in this connection, that the passage in which Hamlet castigates his failure to speak out should be so closely parallel in cadence to the passage in which the player describes the only failure to act of which a votary of hatred is capable:

> Yet I,
> A dull and muddy-mettled rascal, peak
> Like John-a-dreams, unpregnant of my cause,
> And can say nothing.   (2. 2. 593–596)

> So, as a painted tyrant, Pyrrhus stood
> And, like a neutral to his will and matter,
> Did nothing.   (ll. 502–504)

But for the example of Pyrrhus, it would have been easier to agree with Hamlet's estimate of John-a-dreams. In the Greek warrior even hesitation is no sign of conscience, only of surprise at the shuddering of Troy, which

> with a hideous crash
> Takes prisoner Pyrrhus' ear. . . .
> after Pyrrhus' pause
> Aroused vengeance sets him new a-work.
> (ll. 498–499, 509–510)

Better to "peak" like a John-a-dreams who retains some moral awareness than be "roused" to the insensibility of a Pyrrhus.[5]

But the deeper irony of the passage exemplifies, as often in the play, the difficulty of penetrating the mind at the back of an utterance: where Hamlet, for reasons of dramaturgical symmetry cogently argued by Harry Levin,[6] may well be moved to tears because he sees in Priam "a dear father murder'd" (l. 612), and in Pyrrhus, consequently, the uncle who did the deed, the spectator with even a smattering of Virgil could probably be relied on to recognize Pyrrhus as the son of Achilles, "of a dear father murder'd," quite specifically bent on the "vengeance" (l. 510) for which Hamlet cries out (l. 610) at the turning point of his meditation on the

player's speech. And Hamlet himself reinforces the latter identification. For it is to this vengeance without bounds, vengeance by total
destruction, that the Prince at a crucial point commits himself.
The only difference is that the totality has been reinterpreted in a
new and terrible Christian sense:

> When he is drunk asleep, or in his rage,
> Or in th' incestuous pleasure of his bed,
> At gaming, swearing, or about some act
> That has no relish of salvation in't,—
> Then trip him, that his heels may kick at heaven,
> And that his soul may be as damn'd and black
> As hell, whereto it goes. My mother stays.
> This physic but prolongs thy sickly days.[7]
>
> (3. 3. 89–96)

To achieve Claudius's damnation Hamlet must hope to surprise his
enemy, and fix him forever, in a state of moral deformity. Here
again his aim is in accord with the classic description of hatred:
"Anger aims at pain, hatred at evil; for whereas the angry man
wants awareness in his victim, to the man who hates, it makes no
difference. All things painful are things of which we are aware. Of
the greatest evils, on the other hand, we are least aware, such as
being unjust or idiotic; for the inherence of evil is not painful."[8]
Hamlet wants his uncle to suffer the pains of hell; but the fullest
infliction of evil on Claudius will, in the moral dimension at least,
require his insensibility. His soul must grow as black as his destination.

Hamlet is devoted, at this point at least, to the death of his uncle's
soul; and the devotion is not ennobling. His idea of mercy as a physic
to prolong disease is as grotesque a parody as any we shall find in
Measure for Measure of the medicinal function traditionally ascribed
to equitable punishment, a function performed by Hamlet himself
in rebuking his mother. And it need hardly be added that Pyrrhus's
rage bears no resemblance to any rule of conduct that would make
it even tolerable to the audience. For if vengeance beyond the grave
has nothing in common with classic penal justice, it is equally ir-

reconcilable with the straightforward evening of scores prescribed by
the Old Testament: "The reuenger of the blood himselfe shall slay
the murtherer: when hee meeteth him, he shall slay him" (Num.
35 : 19).[9] No lying in wait, here, for the murderer's soul. Indeed,
from the Christian point of view, even Laertes' promise "to cut his
throat i'th' church" (4. 7. 127), however sacrilegious, is less of a
sin against the Holy Ghost than Hamlet's object in *not* cutting
Claudius's throat at his *prie-dieu*. And there could be little doubt
in the pious mind where such desires originate. As the good Sir
Thomas Browne observes: "Our bad wishes and uncharitable desires
proceed no further than this Life; it is the Devil, and the uncharitable
votes of Hell, that desire our misery in the world to come."[10]

And the affinity between Hamlet's aims and Pyrrhus's is not only
disagreeable but a little out of character. For the Prince, in his directions to Polonius on the treatment of the players, has revealed that
he is no stranger to the precept of charity, and his rejoinder to
Laertes—

LAERT. The devil take thy soul!
HAML.   Thou pray'st not well.
(5. 1. 282)

—shows him quite capable of deploring a malign purpose like his
own. More than this, on reflection he comes near to seeing the
similarity: "For by the image of my cause I see / The portraiture of
his" (5. 2. 77–78).[11]

In view of the "portraiture" Hamlet himself claims to have
recognized, there is something rather ominous about the result of
Laertes' single effort at penetrating another mind. For Laertes is
forced by Ophelia's madness to botch up her words to fit his own
thoughts (4. 5. 10), as Hamlet is, to a degree, by the ghost's
ambiguities; and his conclusion is the same: "Hadst thou thy wits
and didst *persuade revenge*, / It could not move thus" (ll. 168–169,
italics added). A little later Ophelia presents her brother with a
symbolic appeal equivalent to the ghost's "adieu, adieu, adieu,
remember me"; Laertes is given "rosemary, that's for remembrance;
pray, love, remember" (ll. 175–176). But what is to be understood

by remembrance, in both cases, is an open question, and Ophelia's speech, at least, leads one of the two aspirant revengers to an unwarranted conclusion; for in the excitement of "botching up" what he wants to hear, Laertes contrives to ignore the only words his sister utters that have any clear bearing on the issue he ought to be facing: " 'God 'a' mercy on his soul!' And of all Christian souls, I pray God" (ll. 199–200). An odd way to "persuade revenge," or even to suggest it. Especially the insatiable revenge of which Pyrrhus is a type, the revenge that, in Claudius's ironic endorsement, "should have no bounds" (4. 7. 129).

The Code of Honor

But one need not, perhaps, go quite so far as Pyrrhus. There is always the possibility of being prompted to revenge, not by anarchic hatred, but by fidelity to a code of honor coolly indifferent to the emotional excesses of the aggrieved party. Such indifference would be distinctly more rational than the imperative of hatred—if it did not extend to the nature of the grievance itself. Laertes, for example, finds no embarrassment at all in claiming to be undecided whether Hamlet's plea of innocence, though valid in *nature*, may still be unacceptable to *honor*:

> I am satisfied in nature,
> Whose motive, in this case, should stir me most
> To my revenge; but in my terms of honour
> I stand aloof, and will no reconcilement
> Till by some elder masters of known honour
> I have a voice and precedent of peace
> To keep my name ungor'd. (5. 2. 255–261)

Such an anomaly, oddly enough, is in perfect accord with the definition of honor laid down by such courtly "masters" as Laertes might be expected to consult. By this definition honor does not inhere in the intrinsic merit either of action or of agent; instead it is a quasi-legal fiction regulated by analogy with the law of property and, to a degree, of commercial credit. "There is no difference,"

Possevino tells us, "between someone who presses for his honor and someone who presses for his goods, or for anything else he owns."

This fiction is reflected in the debt of *duello* to the terminology of Roman law; thus the challenger in a cause of honor is the *actor*, the plaintiff in a suit for the restitution of alienated property, and the person challenged is the *reus*, the defendant in such a suit. Since the commodity under litigation is fictitious and possession is nine points of the law, the author of the graver insult both dispossesses his rival and imposes on him the burden of proving his right of ownership. Normally, turnabout will be sufficient "proof," but the sole exception is revealing: when a man has been given the lie, he has effectively been debarred from answering in kind; he has lost his credit, and his assertions will not pass current. "The dishonored are powerless to dishonor." In this case the *actor* has no recourse but to shift the balance of injury in his own favor by outgoing his enemy: "Verbal insult is removed, and one's opponent burdened, by giving the lie; the lie is removed by the slap; the slap by the blow; and the blow by death." But even with injuries that lend themselves more readily to a clarification of the truth—"che hanno pruova sufficiente"—outgoing will obviously be the more effective remedy; so much so that in Possevino's account the inadequacy of turnabout is virtually taken for granted. The victim of a blow will remain in the unenviable position of a plaintiff or would-be creditor "until he has taken away the injury received *and inflicted another more serious*" (italics added).

Thus the logic of the gentleman's code leads to the same kind of infinite regress as the longing of hatred. In both cases the successive actions at "law," the oscillations of the burden of "proof," will continue until the winner secures his honor by inflicting on the loser an injury that cannot be overgone. Our grievance, in Laertes' words, "shall be paid by weight / Till our scale turns the beam" (4. 5. 156–157). Striking a balance will not serve, or not so well. Laertes, it would seem, is amply justified in drawing a sharp distinction in "terms" between the law of honor and that of nature.[12] Indeed, the law of honor provides a schematic model of that indifference of codified rule to intrinsic moral criteria—to "natural equity"—which we shall find exploited for troublingly comic effect in *Measure for Measure.*

If honor has its jurisprudence, it has its economics as well, and for the same reason: what is being contested is an alienable commodity. This view, it should be understood, cannot be written off as mere cynicism, like Falstaff's "I would to God thou and I knew where a commodity of good names were to be bought."[13] On the contrary, it is, as we have seen, the basis of the code, unmistakably if tacitly acknowledged in the imagery of Hal's pledge to his father:

> Percy is but my factor, good my lord,
> To engross up glorious deeds on my behalf;
> And I will call him to so strict account
> That he shall render every glory up,
> Yea, even the slightest worship of his time,
> Or I will tear the reckoning from his heart.[14]

Hotspur's accumulated honor is the "commodity of good names" that Hal will proceed to "engross," and when the time comes the loser will fully agree with his rival that "budding honors" are the kind of thing one can "crop": "I better brook the loss of brittle life / Than those proud titles thou hast won of me." The same sort of Renaissance assumption underlies the messenger's announcement to the discomfited Sacripante in *Orlando Furioso* (1. 70): " 'Twas Bradamant that hath borne off from thee / What honour in the world soe'er thou hast won."[15] In the words of sonnet 25:

> The painful warrior, famoused for fight,
> After a thousand victories once foil'd,
> Is from the book of honour razed quite,
> And all the rest forgot for which he toil'd.

Thus honor, in the chivalric sense, is far from a contemptible prize; but it is equally far from recommending itself as a criterion of moral choice.[16] And Laertes' endorsement, clearly, does little to recommend it. On the other hand, Laertes is merely pretending to confine his vindictiveness within the limits of the gentleman's code.

Young Fortinbras lives by the code, and his career is consequently a fairer gauge of the standing in the play of honor as a standard for conduct.

In Shakespeare's Denmark honor is for better or worse a young man's game—and one suspects for worse, if what the characters have to say about youth is any indication. "Youth to itself rebels, though none else near," says Laertes (1. 3. 44). In youth, Hamlet agrees, "compulsive ardour gives the charge" (3. 4. 86). Polonius warns us, with some reason as it turns out, of Laertes' "savageness in unreclaimed blood" (2. 1. 34). And our first news of Fortinbras —"of unimproved mettle hot and full" (1. 1. 96)—is scarcely more reassuring. Like Pyrrhus, Laertes, and Hamlet, Fortinbras too has a father to avenge. His "enterprise," we are clearly informed (1. 99), has no legal or moral basis; it is purely an affair of honor. And when by good fortune he is thwarted in it, he simply chooses another path to his goal: "to employ those soldiers, / So levied as before, against the Polack" (2. 2. 74–75). It is this expedition that inspires Hamlet's remark on the discrepancy between the intrinsic unimportance of an "argument"—a patch of ground or even an eggshell will do—and the importance one can confer on it by engaging one's honor in its defense. "Rightly to be great," he contends,

> Is not to stir without great argument,
> But greatly to find quarrel in a straw
> When honour's at the stake. (4. 4. 53–56)

That is, to stir without great argument is admittedly *not* to be rightly great, but on occasion to find quarrel in a straw *is* to be so; because whenever honor's at the stake a straw *becomes* a great argument. Far from condemning the greatness thus conferred as frankly arbitrary and factitious, Hamlet holds up the "delicate and tender prince" (l. 48) as a model of decisiveness, not least because his "divine ambition" (l. 49) has made him impervious to scruple; his spirit "makes mouths at the invisible event" (l. 50)—including "the imminent death of twenty thousand men" (l. 60).

In this lack of scruple, and in the relativity of the value to which he has dedicated himself, Fortinbras anticipates the disastrous position taken by Troilus, another of Shakespeare's "delicate and tender princes," in the debate of the Trojan council (*Troilus and Cressida* 2. 2). Troilus, too, speaks for "manhood and honour" (l. 47) against "reason and respect" (l. 49); he, too, thinks of value as a fiat of the "particular will" (l. 53). What is especially instructive about the later play, however, is that it troubles to specify the crucial objection to the young man's code, namely that will as such cannot make "a free determination / Twixt right and wrong" (ll. 170–171) because decisions are free only as they are "true" to objective grounds of preference, grounds that cannot be willed into and out of existence; "pleasure and revenge," Hector warns, "have ears more deaf than adders to the voice / Of any true decision" (ll. 171–173). It is characteristic that Troilus's code of holding unconditionally to resolve (as we shall have occasion to remark from another angle in connection with *King Lear*) is demoralization thinly disguised as idealism. In the ensuing action the self-congratulatory stubbornness he has substituted by default for intrinsic standards of value and order betrays him into an irrationality so thorough that it obliges him to repudiate the law of identity, the "rule in unity itself" (*Troilus* 5. 2. 141), rather than take back his word:

> O madness of discourse,
> That cause sets up with and against thyself,
> Bi-fold authority, where reason can revolt
> Without perdition, and loss assume all reason
> Without revolt: this is, and is not, Cressid.
> (ll. 142–146)

To be sure, such absurdities, at least in the form given them at Troy, are not invincible at Elsinore. Even Hamlet, who is positive that honor can of itself exalt an argument and impart a rightful greatness to the arguer, pointedly declines to build his whole case on it. A source of greatness it may be; but it is also, paradoxically, "a fantasy and trick of fame" (4. 4. 61). Unlike Fortinbras, Hamlet has "excitements of my reason" as well as of "my blood" (l. 58).[17]

Honor and Suicide

But the whole point of the speech in which these phrases occur is that reason is susceptible to diseases, notably "bestial oblivion" and "craven scruple," of which scruple is at present much the more dangerous to Hamlet; for in his view any further exercise of reason on his part will inevitably consist in the morbidity and cowardice of "thinking too precisely on th'event." So far, at least, Hamlet might well say (with Troilus) that "reason and respect / Make livers pale and lustihood deject." Indeed, in an earlier speech he does say something very like this, and without any ambiguous deference to the "excitements of reason." Moreover, the context of this earlier remark puts honor, as an antidote to cowardice and "craven scruple," in a very odd light.

The premise of Hamlet's best-known soliloquy is that the very process of living entails what is degrading to a "noble mind" (3. 1. 57), a servitude of whips and scorns, of grunting, sweating, and bearing fardels, from which such a mind will naturally choose the only possible deliverance—to die. The distinction between choosing death and suffering it, or choosing to risk it, would seem to be clear enough, but in the course of his meditation Hamlet finds an opportunity to be quite specific:

> For who would bear the whips and scorns of time . . .
> When he himself might his quietus make
> With a bare bodkin?[18]   (ll. 70, 75–76)

The recommended course, clearly, is suicide, and the terms of Hamlet's introductory "question"—whether suicide or its contrary is "nobler in the mind"—are the familiar terms of the venerable debate between pagans and Christians over the *honestas* or *magnitudo animi* of that act. Hamlet is simply taking the pagan view that suicide is, to use Augustine's report of the opposition, *honestas turpia praecavens*, the *turpia* being summed up in the Prince's metaphors from the abasements of slavery.[19] It is the same view as Horatio, whose Stoicism Hamlet so much admires, will try in vain to live up to at the end of the play: "I am more an antique Roman than a Dane." At that point the Prince will assume that the reward of suicide is "felicity" (5. 2. 358), but in the present soliloquy he is not certain, and his uncertainty enables him to argue, not only that suicide is "nobler in the mind" than the baseness of continuing to live, but also that those who are ignoble in this sense are acting out of simple cowardice. The self-slaughter that was dismissed in Hamlet's first soliloquy as no more than a forbidden escape from the world is, by contrast, presented here as an act of honor, of taking up arms against the world's afflictions. It is this argument for the honorableness of suicide, especially in the dramatic context Shakespeare provides for it, that adds yet another obstacle to his audience's imaginative acceptance, not only of honor, but of revenge as well.

Hamlet argues that, all other things being equal, suicide would be the choice, not merely of the "noble mind," but of any mind that appreciated the full misery of the human condition. But all things are not equal. Suicide is possible only to those who are not cowards, the others being put off by "the dread of something after death" (3. 1. 78). Of this "something" Hamlet has just lately received some privileged information; "after death," of course, comes punishment for ill deeds done in our "days of nature" (1. 5. 12)—in Claudius's case, Hamlet hopes, eternal punishment. And punishment is a thing one would not dread but for a faculty that Hamlet here calls "conscience" and elsewhere dismisses as "scruple": the practical reason or moral sense one of whose functions is consciousness of ill doing. Indeed, as Hamlet goes on to explain, it was to enforce a thesis about conscience that he brought up suicide in the first place. For suicide is only one, though a notable one, of many cases in which conscience plays a contemptible role. It simply illustrates the principle Hamlet has in mind:

> *Thus* conscience does make cowards of us all;
> And *thus* the native hue of resolution
> Is sicklied o'er with the pale cast of thought,
> And enterprises of great pith and moment

With this regard their currents turn awry,
And lose the name of action.
(3. 1. 83–88, italics added)

It is necessary to stress the syntax here: the referent of "thus" is Hamlet's reflection that fear of the beyond "puzzles" the suicidal will. That puzzlement, of all things, is what Hamlet chooses to illustrate his thesis that thought inhibits action. Of course this association of ideas might be dismissed as a strained inference of the critic if it were an inference at all. But it is not. The connection is explicit, and the immediate relevance of Hamlet's general admonition to the speaker's own affairs is conspicuously supplied by his most recent commitment.

Suicide is, to be sure, an enterprise of great pith and moment from the pagan viewpoint Hamlet is adopting, and he may well see it for the time being as very near the top of his agenda. But he must of course absent him from that great man's goal awhile. The "enterprise" that has highest priority is revenge; it is on behalf of his vow to the ghost that Hamlet fears the conscience that "makes cowards of us all"—the "craven scruple" of which his encounter with Fortinbras's army will once again seem to accuse him. But by inviting the audience to see an analogy between suicide and revenge, in the joint opposition of these two enterprises to cowardice and conscience, Hamlet is ironically subverting his case. For he has put his mission in what the play consistently shows to be very bad company indeed.

The fitful inquiry into the circumstances of Ophelia's death that occupies much of the fifth act of our play would be strangely otiose if it did not serve to drive home one point of crucial relevance: that even if a prospective suicide had no other trespasses to plague him with "the dread of something after death," the act of suicide itself would be trespass enough. Laertes' remark that his sister has been "driven into desperate terms" (4. 7. 26) anticipates the central issue, for the mortal sin of which suicide is an irrevocable expression is the sin of despair. "There is nothing worse, then when one envieth himselfe";[20] that is why the Everlasting, as Hamlet himself admits, has "fix'd / His canon 'gainst self-slaughter" (1. 2. 131–132).[21] And

Horatio had been speaking more as a Dane than an antique Roman when he warned Hamlet that the ghost might tempt him to suicide, and that the cliff itself might overcome him with "toys of desperation" (1. 4. 75).

It is precisely this theme of damnation through despair that the question of Ophelia's death refuses to let out of our sight, and the theme strikes us with all the greater clarity for the unresolved ambiguity of Ophelia's guilt or innocence. To this ambiguity the gravedigger's malaprop interrogatory, breaking the silence at the beginning of the fifth act, is a fitting prelude: "Is she to be buried in Christian burial that wilfully seeks her own salvation?" (5. 1. 1–2). The second clown offers one possible answer: "If this had not been a gentlewoman, she should have been buried out of Christian burial" (ll. 26–28). Gertrude has already suggested another: Ophelia made no attempt to save herself because she was "incapable of her own distress" (4. 7. 179). The priest is uncertain, but inclines to the grimmer view.

> Her death was doubtful;
> And, but that great command o'ersways the order,
> She should in ground unsanctified have lodg'd
> Till the last trumpet.   (5. 1. 250–253)

Laertes, perhaps too stridently, decides for salvation:

> I tell thee, churlish priest,
> A minist'ring angel shall my sister be,
> When thou liest howling.   (ll. 263–264)

And Ophelia's "maimed rites" (l. 242) are equally ambiguous: to Hamlet they

> betoken
> The corse they follow did with desperate hand
> Fordo it own life.   (ll. 242–244)

And indeed we learn from the priest that they are not the same as are accorded to "peace-parted souls" (l. 261). Yet she has been buried in hallowed ground, and, as the second clown informs us, "the crowner hath sat on her, and finds it Christian burial" (ll. 4–5).

All this is scarcely designed to invite us to decide for ourselves; the evidence is far too inconclusive. But it does serve to prevent the audience from consigning to limbo even for a moment the doctrinal inhibitions they will have to suspend in order to make the most of a purely sensational play of revenge. And the elaborate comparison Hamlet has already made between suicide and revenge makes it doubly difficult to avoid following Hamlet's destiny with the same order of anxiety as we guess at Ophelia's. If Hamlet does not hesitate, his audience has the better reason to hesitate for him.[22]

Honor vs. Conscience

For, despite his reticence on the point, the ghost has solemnly intimated that Hamlet's mission threatens in some sense or other to taint his mind (1. 5. 85); and now if ever Hamlet's danger is upon him: when he ventures to equate conscience with cowardice he virtually puts his audience on notice that his encomium of suicide and kindred enterprises is a convention not of plot but of characterization—a plague sign of taint in its ultimate phase. As Prosser has pointed out, the espousal of libertinism, as dramatic shorthand for villainy, can be illustrated in a grosser form from a much earlier stage in Shakespeare's career. Here, from *Richard III*, is Clarence's murderer-to-be on conscience: "I'll not meddle with it; it is a dangerous thing; it makes a man a coward" (1. 4. 137–138). His infamous employer carries less 'conviction in maintaining the same opinion: "O coward conscience, how dost thou afflict me" (5. 3. 179). But he maintains it all the same: "For conscience is a word that cowards use, / Devis'd at first to keep the strong in awe" (ll. 309–310).

As part of a "mirror" for magistrates, the import of this detail is that the tenacity of Crookback's creed is itself a part of his doom.[23] But the status of conscience in our present play is, if anything, far more sacrosanct. For Hamlet has arrayed against it suicide and revenge, that is, offences against that part of the law of reason which is also notably revealed in the law of God; and as partner with

Scripture in that revelation, conscience is virtually an operation of grace. Laertes' consecration to revenge, which is perhaps noisier than Hamlet's if not more complete, makes this point very clear:

> To hell allegience! vows, to the blackest devil!
> *Conscience and grace*, to the profoundest pit!
> I dare damnation. To this point I stand,
> That both the worlds I give to negligence,
> Let come what comes; only I'll be reveng'd
> Most throughly for my father.
>
> KING.   Who shall stay you?
> LAER. *My will, not all the world.*
>
> (4. 5. 131–137, italics added)

In exalting will above conscience Laertes merely echoes without euphemism Hamlet's preference of "the native hue of resolution" to "the pale cast of thought."

But, as it turns out, conscience of some sort or other cannot be dispensed with, for an "honour" that erects will into law is no more amenable to persuasion than the lawless imperative of hatred. If we exorcise conscience we shall sooner or later be forced to assume something else of the kind. This is the irony of Claudius's appeal to Laertes in a later scene: "Now must your conscience my acquittance seal" (4. 7. 1). It is also the irony of the new, robust "thoughts" that Hamlet has substituted for "godlike reason," and for the thought whose pale cast seemed to him so sickly in his earlier soliloquy: "O, from this time forth, / My thoughts be bloody, or be nothing worth" (4. 4. 65–66). If Hamlet is urged on by "excitements of my reason *and* my blood" (l. 58, italics added), it is at the same time oddly difficult to tell the two sources of excitement apart.

It is as well to forewarn the reader at this point that in each of the plays to be studied we shall encounter a similar negation. This is not the last time we shall be invited to consider that there is no criterion of moral value and no faculty for guiding action that does not consist either of spontaneous will or of the command that expresses a will imposed from without. This is not the last time, in short, that we shall be invited to assent to the trivialization of reason and conscience. On the other hand, if reason and conscience can decay, honor and the gentleman's code can be redeemed, as Hamlet redeems them in odd lapses from vengefulness. The model of the "gentleman" to which he appeals in asking pardon of Laertes (5. 2. 238) is not the model Claudius praises in Laertes (4. 5. 148) in preparing to seduce him to an act of treachery. And the "honour" Hamlet commends to Polonius is so far from the ordinary code of gentlemen as to be indistinguishable from Christian charity: "Use them after your own honour and dignity. *The less they deserve, the more merit is in your bounty*" (2. 2. 556–558, italics added).

The Will of God

By the Prince's own standards, it would seem, revenge is an indulgence of the fallen will, and the honor that claims to control it, for all its legalism, is will all over again. Hamlet embraces revenge in its extreme, but with honor, as we have observed, he is not wholly satisfied; it is "a fantasy and trick of fame." An alternative sanction, however, is not easy to find; against revenge as against self-slaughter the Everlasting has fixed his canon. And the ambiguity of the ghost's origin, even more than that of its words, compounds the difficulty: if revenge is a counsel of the devil, as the faith testifies, and the ghost is a spirit of health, as the Prince eventually concludes, the anomaly of Hamlet's position achieves cosmic proportions. In this respect his invocation is prophetic indeed: "O all you host of heaven! O earth! What else? / And shall I couple hell?" (1. 5. 92–93). Later on he will not find it necessary to ask whether he is "prompted to my revenge by heaven and hell" (2. 2. 613); and this last is the "coupling" on which Hamlet's final interpretation of his role seems to depend.

To be prompted by heaven *and* hell no doubt verges on contradiction in terms. But in fact it is not unorthodox to allow that heaven may on occasion issue the same command as hell; and in accepting

responsibility for the death of Polonius Hamlet remembers what
such a supernatural entente usually means:

> For this same Lord,
> I do repent; but Heaven hath pleas'd it so,
> To punish me with this and this with me,
> That I must be their scourge and minister.
>
> (3. 4. 172–175)

A scourge of God, according to a familiar tradition of Christian
historiography, is a man divinely ordained to make an example
of his fellow sinners by means proper enough to God, to Whom
vengeance belongs, but ordinarily fatal to the soul of the agent. In
addition to this essential requirement, which is all that is strictly
entailed by the metaphor itself, many familiar types of the scourge
exhibit such adventitious traits as "religious antinomianism," "ambition, robbery and tyranny, cruelty, magnanimity, and invincibil-
ity."[24] Though Hamlet clearly finds no such array of traits mirrored
in his killing of Polonius, his application of the essential concept is
precise. Heaven has diverted Hamlet's murderous intent to its own
use, and it is only the use he repents of, not the intent. These are
the signs of a scourge—unwitting service and impenitence—and
Hamlet draws the appropriate conclusion. In the same way, Hal's
"inordinate and low desires," "barren pleasures," and "rude society"
are quite enough to satisfy Bolingbroke that his son is a "revenge-
ment and a scourge for me," marked out by God's "secret doom"
(I Henry IV 3. 2. 4–17). The tragedy of such a decree is that there
is little in an instrument of torture for even its Master to love;
Tamburlaine himself is the "hate" as well as the "scourge" of God.
To be elected a scourge, in the end, is to be bound to the violation
of one's own moral being, and it is no wonder that Hamlet thinks
of this role as a punishment.

But by assuming that the punishment emanates from God Hamlet
is virtually acknowledging that he deserves it, and this acknowledgment has persuaded some critics that he must be thinking back to
a particular offense.[25] The line of inquiry has not been successful;

of the two acts that Hamlet might be taken prima facie to regard
as offensive to heaven, neither has anything like the proper qualifications.[26] And this is not surprising, for no history of actual guilt need
be postulated to justify God in electing a scourge. This point needs
emphasis, for it is crucial to our inquiry to see that the notion of a
scourge presupposes a notion of justification, and of moral criteria,
as vacuous as its counterparts in the imperative of hatred and the
code of honor. But here the vacuity is far more threatening. For it
is hidden at the root of the scheme of things.

The language in which the theory of the scourge was couched is
often ambiguous, but it is a serious perversion to construe it as flouting
the common doctrine by limiting God's choice to those who are "already so steeped in crime as to be past salvation."[27] No guilt is so great
as to overcome divine mercy, which, like all divine attributes, is
infinite; indeed, it is precisely for blaspheming against this truth
that despair is traditionally branded, in the words of Chaucer's
Parson, as a "synnyng in the Hooly Ghoost," a disease to which even
Claudius knows the antidote:

> What if this cursed hand
> Were thicker than itself with brother's blood,
> Is there not rain enough in the sweet heavens
> To wash it white as snow? Whereto serves mercy
> But to confront the visage of offence?
>
> (3. 3. 43–47)

And if there is no such thing as sinning too much to be saved, there
is, correspondingly, no such thing as sinning too little to be damned;
"man," as Article 9 has it, "is very far gone from original righteousness, and of his own nature inclined to evil, so that the flesh lusteth
always contrary to the spirit; and therefore in every person born
into this world, it deserveth God's wrath and damnation." Hamlet
is plainly aware of this fact: "Use every man after his desert, and
who should scape whipping?" And Hamlet's views, we must bear
in mind, are solely in question here. Heaven, in short, is in no man's
debt either for reward or for punishment. In both justice and mercy

God's will is unconfined. The ultimate reason why a particular sinner is chosen a scourge is quite simply, in Hamlet's words, that "heaven hath pleas'd it so."

As conceived by the Prince, the divine pleasure currently in prospect—atrocity and perdition—is not merely arbitrary but intolerably bleak. Does Hamlet allow himself no small ration of hope? It has been suggested that when Hamlet says he is "scourge and minister" the latter term somehow denotes an alternative to the former.[28] But this proposal has more good will in it than grammar; a conjunction is a very strange way to add an alternative. What we have here is ordinary hendiadys; Hamlet will be the kind of minister who scourges. A more substantial consolation is held out by the Prince himself on his return from the sea, when he expresses a new reverence for the "divinity that shapes our ends" and, by implication, a serene confidence that a providential opportunity will, in the "interim," make "dear plots" unnecessary (5. 2. 6–11, 73–74, 231–234). The resolve to play a waiting game, to be sure, dates from his sparing of Claudius (3. 3. 89–95); but the serenity and the theological inflection are new, and they do not sound like a man expecting to be damned.

Moreover, on reconsidering Claudius's offenses Hamlet no longer doubts that it is "perfect conscience / To quit him with this arm" (5. 2. 67–68). And far from being damned for usurping divine vengeance, Hamlet now thinks it

> to be damn'd,
> To let this canker of our nature come
> In further evil.   (ll. 68–70)

The rehabilitation of conscience, the statesmanlike appeal to the public welfare, and the clear implication that Hamlet no longer thinks himself damned would appear to suggest that he has repudiated the role of scourge. At closer quarters, unfortunately, two of these indices cancel each other out and the third can be otherwise accounted for.

The same conscience that refuses to let Claudius "come in further evil" raises no objection, a few lines earlier, to its owner's gratuitous murder of Rosencrantz and Guildenstern: "They are not near my conscience, their defeat / Does by their own insinuation grow" (ll. 58–59). But, as Hamlet seems to concede, Rosencrantz and Guildenstern were clearly unaware of their complicity in his attempted murder,[29] and insinuation is not a capital crime. Hamlet showed himself well aware of this last when he repented of killing Polonius, another "intruding fool" who "made love to his employment"; indeed that inadvert crime was what persuaded him of his election to the unenviable office of scourge.

This falling off in the tenderness of Hamlet's conscience, taken together with the double standard conveniently applied by that faculty, should perhaps remind us that a Shakespearean character who invokes conscience in a doubtful cause is at least as likely to be perplexed in the extreme as to have regained his moral bearings. Othello too, at the lowest ebb of his moral awareness, argues that he must kill to prevent his victim from "coming in further evil": "Yet she must die, else she'll betray more men" (5. 2. 6). But the difference between the two cases of rationalization is as instructive as the parallel; Othello's disavowal of vindictive impulse may (as we shall see) be suspect, but he does offer Desdemona the respite that is indispensable to Christian execution:

> If you bethink yourself of any crime
> Unreconcil'd as yet to Heaven and grace,
> Solicit for it straight. . . .
> I would not kill thy unprepared spirit;
> No; heavens forfend! I would not kill thy soul.
> (ll. 26–28, 31–32)

It is crucial to recognize that Hamlet, *despite* his new serenity, the fresh endorsement of his conscience, and his princely if intermittent concern for innocent bystanders, has not disavowed his intention to kill the soul of his enemy. Indeed, the health of his victims' souls has come to worry him so little that he sends even Rosencrantz and Guildenstern "to sudden death, / Not shriving time allow'd" (5. 2. 46–47). It is a commentary on his argument from statesmanship that he should fail so spectacularly in the end to avoid "coming in further evil" to the amount of three additional deaths, and that the assassination of Claudius should be so far removed in spirit from solemn execution.

By sinning against the Holy Ghost, Hamlet continues to play the part of a scourge. To see why he no longer expects to be damned for it we shall have to refer again to that view of God's absolute sovereignty which, as we saw earlier, underlies the very notion of a human scourge. In such a view the moral law is simply a creature of divine will subject to revocation by that will at any time. Sometimes even a patriarch, as Augustine explains, might abrogate the ordinary law of God by God's extraordinary command—*ad personam pro tempore expressâ iussione*. In performing such a command the patriarch is like a sword that yields its assistance to him who wields it—*adminiculum gladius utenti*.[30] And the only difference between the deed of the sword and the deed of the scourge is that the latter ends in damnation.

In the Middle Ages the theory "that the heroes of the old covenant had a special command, or revelation from God," when their conduct "ran counter to the prevailing Christian ethics" was elaborated by Scotus, and passed on in substance to the theologians of the Reformation; though, like Scotus, Luther and Calvin denied that such dispensations can recur in the latter days.[31] Hamlet is not so cautious. Not conscience ultimately but the "divinity that shapes our ends" (5. 2. 10) condemns Rosencrantz and Guildenstern to a death by treachery in whose smallest detail, Hamlet is quite sure, "Heaven" was "ordinant" (1. 48). Like Tamburlaine—or the patriarchs, for that matter—Hamlet is performing what is "enjoin'd me from above." But like the patriarchs he will not be damned. The degradation of the idea of conscience has resulted, as in other plays we shall study, in a degradation of the idea of Providence; but here the latter degradation is characteristically accompanied by Hamlet's hubristic faith in his flair for plucking out the heart of another's mystery. It would seem that the quest for a satisfactory way of defining his mission has inspired the Prince to a new flight of clairvoyance: what the mind of the ghost has withheld Hamlet reads in the mind of God. And what he reads—in dread at first, and later in tranquillity—is naked will beyond good and evil.

The Noble Mind O'erthrown

In pursuance of his vow Horatio eventually offers his hearers an index to his projected relation of Hamlet's career in revenge:

> so shall you hear
> Of carnal, bloody, and unnatural acts,
> Of accidental judgements, casual slaughters,
> Of deaths put on by cunning and forc'd cause.
> And, in this upshot, purposes mistook
> Fall'n on the inventors' heads.
>
> (5. 2. 391–396)

"Plots and errors," as he sums things up, lie behind the present "mischance" (ll. 405–406). We have seen Hamlet elbow-deep in the plots, and he has not been notably innocent of the errors. Claudius, to be sure, has been guilty "of carnal, bloody, and un-natural acts," and both he and Laertes of "purposes mistook / Fall'n on the inventors' heads." But this does not absolve their opponent "of accidental judgements, casual slaughters, / Of deaths put on by cunning and forc'd cause." Horatio will no doubt proceed to excuse the latter: that is why he has deferred his felicity. But if he intends to go further, and justify them, his list is perversely calculated to obscure the fact.

It seems from what we have been saying that the inglorious bleakness of Horatio's summing up simply ratifies an assessment that the play itself, by degrees, has already recommended to us. The painstaking gradualness of this preparation needs to be stressed. For we have been told in effect by some critics, notably Eleanor Prosser, that the playwright might well have spared his pains, in view of the broad consensus in Renaissance Christendom on the wickedness of revenge. This consensus included "preachers, moralists, and the majority of the Shakespearean audience," and it is reflected in various passages in the Shakespearean canon: "The mass of evidence would seem to deny categorically that Shakespeare's audience viewed blood revenge in the theater as a 'sacred duty.' " We must after all discard the notion "that the Elizabethan checked his morality at the door of the theater and that we should too."[32]

Yet aside from the implausibility of so elaborate and subtle a dramatic effort to tell an audience what it began by taking for granted, our attention has recently been drawn to the occurrence of "a large number of revengers in Elizabethan narrative literature who are clearly not meant to be seen as villains."[33] Of these, indeed, "many are presented as heroic and praiseworthy,"[34] and this group significantly includes the hero of Belleforest's *Historie of Hamblet*.[35] The investigator, moreover, usefully points out the inherent weakness of inferring latent popular sentiment on a moral issue from a public literature dominated by "preachers" and "moralists": "The rational approach to the question of revenge, which usually means the official approach, is what appears in print, rarely the confused emotional attitudes."[36] There is no reason, we may add, to suppose that similar underground confusions cannot occasionally have invested suicide, too, with a kind of nobility, as in Sir Thomas Wyatt's unqualified tribute to the last act of Cato the Younger.[37]

The same point needs to be made about the prepossessions of Shakespeare's audience on the subject of ghost lore. From Prosser's account it might well appear that the source of the Prince's undoing lies no deeper than a mysterious unfamiliarity with some commonplace precautions on this head.[38] Forearmed against heterodoxy in the speech of a ghost, the Prince need never have resorted to a play designed, among other things, to exclude the possibility that "the spirit that I have seen may be the devil" (2. 2. 627–628). Yet there are grounds, which we have considered and shall return to, for thinking that Hamlet's fundamental mistake in theology or pneumatology is far less trivial. Meanwhile, we must rest content with pressing what seems a conclusive objection to the view that Hamlet's tolerance of a vindictive ghost is to be recognized at once as an elementary error of fact.

Prosser herself admits that her interpretation would have gained by Horatio's support.[39] But surely one must go further. The thesis that the hellishness of a vengeful ghost is a foregone conclusion for Shakespeare's audience is immeasurably weakened by the failure of the loyal and scholarly Horatio to remind his friend of this elementary sign of danger, as he does with alacrity of some others (for example, 1. 4. 69–74). For, as Prosser well says, Horatio is "a norm figure throughout; his word is to be heeded"[40]—and, by the same token, his silence as well.

If Hamlet is to retain a genuine tragic dimension, and if the play's elaborate ironies at the expense of revenge are to be seen as other than gratuitous, we must retrieve Prosser's discarded hypothesis. We must admit the possibility that the Elizabethan playgoer stood ready to suspend his moral disbelief, if only to enjoy sensational effects without the molestation of scruple. In the case of Hamlet, however, some such admission is required not by sensationalism but by what appears clearly to be the moral design of the play.

Let us assume, then, that what Shakespeare's audience paid for was a hectic afternoon of lurid action; for this, at the outset anyway, is what they got. The necessary thrill was provided by the morally neutral question of *modus operandi*: what grizzly end will Hamlet think up for the villain? And it was clearly necessary that the question remain morally neutral if the thrill was not to be spoiled. But it is not long before Shakespeare spoils it, or rather replaces it with a new question and a new order of suspense. For when the Prince asks himself which of two alternative courses more befits a great soul— which is "nobler in the mind"—he compels us to recognize him as a serious moral agent and (if we have not already begun to do so) to worry about him in a new way. The new worry, indeed, is nearly the opposite of the old; we worry lest Hamlet betray his commitment to the faculty of "noble mind" to which he pays such high tribute: the "apprehension" as of a god (2. 2. 317), the "large discourse" (4. 4. 36), the "fair judgement, / Without the which," as Claudius agrees, "we are pictures, or mere beasts" (4. 5. 85–86). "Discourse of reason," as Hamlet's training prepares him to understand its practical function, is not merely a prudential, but a moral faculty as well—though he assumes that a degree of morality may be expected even of "a beast, that wants discourse of reason" (1. 2. 150).

There is thus a disturbing irony in the spectacle of an "antic disposition" that moves Ophelia to recall "what a noble mind is here o'erthrown" (3. 1. 158). For the "noble and most sovereign reason" (l. 165) whose decline we are to be shown is not the prudential acuteness in which Hamlet increasingly takes pride, but the "nobility," the "conscience," the right reason that this very pride will slowly submerge. The Hamlet whose fall from grace we may well regret is not the tactical improviser who cries out: "O, 'tis most sweet, / When in one line two crafts directly meet" (3. 4. 209–210), but the man even his enemy thinks of as "most generous and free from all contriving" (4. 7. 136), the humane prince whose gorge rises at the cynicism of the gravedigger tossing about the remains of the dead: "Did these bones cost no more the breeding, but to play at loggats with 'em? Mine ache to think on't" (5. 1. 99–101).

It is difficult to recognize in this man the very different figure that is discovered preparing to "lug the guts into the neighbour room" (3. 4. 212), or, for tactical purposes, playing hide-and-seek with them later on (4. 2. 32–33). And it is difficult to reconcile the Hamlet who protests in one scene that he is "not splenitive and rash" (5. 1. 284) with the advocate of "rashness" in the next (5. 2. 7). Last and most important, it is difficult to reconcile the Christian and the man of charity with the avenger. Or rather, it is disturbing to *have* to reconcile these things. For the worser part is always threatening to prevail.

As we have seen, Hamlet's quest for a definition of vengeance traces a development. The strain of moral ugliness in his character, on the other hand, does not; in this case it is the revelation only that develops, from one expository test to another more exacting. This is true of the vanity of intellect that concerned us in the previous chapter. And it is true of the mindless activism that is paradoxically combined with it, and that concerns us now. Shakespeare sets the stage by showing us first a Hamlet oppressed not only by grief but by the frustration of the desire to act. The options immediately

before him are only two—to stay in court or return to university—
and but for his mother's preference there is little of moment to
choose between them. It is surely for this among other reasons that
the uses of this world have become weary, stale, flat, and unprofitable to him (1. 2. 133). His ennui is cosmic because the garden of
this world needs weeding (l. 135), but above all because he is not
the gardener. It is a world over which Hamlet lacks even the power
of open criticism, much less of action: "break my heart, for I must
hold my tongue" (l. 159). What Hamlet later confirms, in short, is
already obvious enough. The Claudius he despises at this point is not
only the heir to his father's bed, but in large measure the wearer of
the Prince's own diadem—the Claudius who had the temerity to
pop in "between the election and my hopes" (5. 2. 165).

Hamlet is blithely frank about these old hopes. By his own
flippant confession he is by nature not only proud and revengeful
but ambitious (3. 1. 125), and in the submissive appeal with which
he first greets the ghost we can already glimpse the moral indis-
criminateness of that ambition: "What should we do?" (1. 4. 57).
It is a plea for release, any sort of release, from a chronic and galling
state of unemployment. This release, as it turns out, is the essence of
the ghost's insidious gift to the Prince, for "every man hath business
and desire" (1. 5. 130); and now at last, for worse or better, so has
the Prince. The difference is that Hamlet's business and desire are as
cosmic as the ennui to which they are the timely antidote.

The world, after all, is possessed by things rank and gross in
nature (1. 2. 136–137). It is a prison in which Denmark is among the
worst of many confines, wards, and dungeons (2. 2. 249–253). The
"age" is "picked" (5. 1. 151) and "drossy" (5. 2. 197) with false
refinement and with customs more honored in the breach than the
observance (1. 5. 16). "Forgive me this my virtue," goes the Prince's
sardonic apology;

> For in the fatness of these pursy times
> Virtue itself of vice must pardon beg,
> Yea, curb and woo for leave to do him good.
>
> (3. 4. 152–155)

The sarcasm of this apology recoils, significantly, coming as it does from one who "could accuse me of such things that it were better my mother had not borne me" (3. 1. 124–125). But the speech is also significant for its anger at the "pursy times" that condescend to be redeemed by Virtue like Hamlet's as if they were doing their benefactors a favor.

Now it may occur to us that the rankness, grossness, and restrictiveness of the world are matters beyond redress, or at least beyond redress by the vengeful killing of a Danish usurper. And it may appear that the drossiness, pickedness, fatness, and pursiness of the age are in reality the story of all ages after the Fall of man. These perennial vices are not among the "ten thousand lesser things" (3. 3. 19) that may be affected by the mere fall of princes, and yet the latter is all Hamlet has in mind at the moment: the ghost's "commandment all alone shall live / Within the book and volume of my brain" (1. 5. 102–103). Whatever its merits the revenge is surely no panacea.

The crucial point, however, is that the Prince thinks or speaks otherwise. He is unwilling to set limits to the importance of the business he is about. This last, by his account, will include in its range no less than the "time" he so assiduously mocks and exposes. The duty of revenge is, to be sure, a "cursed spite." But there remain, for the frustrated activist, certain consolations: Hamlet not only has a mission, it is a mission he was providentially born to; it is necessary, ultimately, because "the time is out of joint"; and by accomplishing that mission the Prince will quite simply redeem the time. He, apparently alone, will set it right (1. 5. 189–190). It is, then, not surprising that Hamlet's first inclination is to accept the ghost as honest; there is something in the way of purpose and glory to be gained thereby.[41]

This self-inflation is one aspect of an ingrained contentiousness that grows, if anything, more compulsive and dissonant as the play goes on. It emerges harmlessly in Hamlet's owlish triumph over "philosophy" (1. 5. 164–167), in his affected nonchalance on hearing the latest gossip from his friends ("It is not very strange"

[2. 2. 380–385]), in his victorious contest of inkhorn words with Osric (5. 2. 117–137). More seriously, it appears to be the dominant motive in his immediate response to the news of Ophelia's death, a response that begins with self-proclamation—"this is I, Hamlet the Dane" (5. 1. 280–281)—and degenerates rapidly into the duel of elegiac prowess to which he challenges Laertes ("Woo't weep? Woo't fight? Woo't fast? Woo't tear thyself?" [1. 298]). For in obedience to his gladiatorial reflex Hamlet will not permit Laertes to "outface" him in mourning (1. 301); he takes not Laertes' indignation but his grief and its "bravery" as a provocative act (5. 2. 78–79). Even in his bereavement, if one can call it that, Hamlet is, perversely, the irrepressible contestant.[42]

The arrival of a patient Hamlet in the last act, then, brings no change for the better in his shallow competitiveness. Claudius's conspiracy in this act depends on the truth of his earlier report that Laertes' reputation as a fencer

> Did Hamlet so envenom with his envy
> That he could nothing do but wish and beg
> Your sudden coming o'er to play with him.
>
> (4. 7. 104–106)

The fifth act may offer us a serene Hamlet, but it also confirms and refines on this earlier anecdote. The bulk of his conversation during the match consists of tactics aimed at his opponent's morale. Ironic self-deprecation, for example:

> HAM. I'll be your foil, Laertes; in mine ignorance
> Your skill shall, like a star i'th' darkest night,
> Stick fiery off indeed.
> LAERT.   You mock me, sir.
>
> (5. 2. 266–268)

(The "ignorant" Hamlet is indeed mocking. He has, of course, been "in continual practice" and is convinced he will "win at the odds" [ll. 220–222].) And, before the third encounter, some candid taunting of the loser:

> Come for the third, Laertes; you but dally.
> I pray you, pass with your best violence.
> I am afeared you make a wanton of me.[43]
>
> (ll. 307–310)

Hamlet's new serenity, then, is so far from announcing a new access of moral insight that it easily coexists with the old habits, and with the very ideal of ennobling action that Hamlet has apparently entertained from the beginning: the duel. The same voice that reveled earlier in the "sport" and "sweetness" of intrigue (3. 4. 206, 209) is more than faintly audible in the later celebration of "the pass and fell incensed points / Of mighty opposites" (5. 2. 61–62).

The theme of Hamlet's development, or rather disclosure, is intellectual talent debauched in the service of intellectual vanity, and of a mindless activism. Given the theme, his final self-indulgence is what one might expect: a retreat from deliberate choice to that notorious *asylum stultorum*, divine Providence. The course to be sanctified from this point on is, conveniently, the now familiar "rashness" or "indiscretion" (5. 2. 7, 8). Our ends are shaped in any case by the event itself, or (farther off) by an invisible hand. We may therefore roughhew them how we will, in the faith that the event itself will in retrospect answer the nagging question, "What should we do?" Hence the deaths of Rosencrantz and Guildenstern need not come "near my conscience" (l. 58). Hence, when it comes to the death of Polonius,

> Hamlet does it not, Hamlet denies it.
> Who does it, then? His madness. If't be so,
> Hamlet is of the faction that is wrong'd.
> His madness is poor Hamlet's enemy.
>
> (ll. 247–250)

Prosser has suggested that the first of these lapses is not Hamlet's but Shakespeare's, who "did not finish clearing up the traces of revision,"[44] and that the second is not a lapse at all, but in effect a paraphrase of Romans 7 : 20: "Now if I do that I would not, it is no more I that do it, but sin that dwelleth in me." The Prince's overture to Laertes is, in short, "a confession, not a disclaimer, of sin."[45] But to take the second point first, the Pauline analogy does not hold. "Sin" implies guilt, if not intent; "madness" excludes both. Victimized by a convenient madness, Hamlet, unlike Paul, is by his own account simply "of the faction that is wrong'd." As for the alleged incompleteness of Shakespeare's revision in the former case, it is, if true, a stroke of luck. We can do without this additional evidence that Hamlet has erected irresponsibility into a code, but the pattern is clearer with it.

The sole evidence for the thesis that Hamlet has changed, has grown in wisdom as he proceeds through the play, is his resignation to Providence. Once we notice the way that resignation is used— as a license and not a deterrent to malevolent caprice—the thesis of his growth collapses. Hamlet acknowledges, to be sure, that his enterprise may be interrupted by death, which is inevitable: "If it be now 'tis not to come; if it be not to come it will be now" (5. 2. 231–233). But the intelligence that men's undertakings are subject to outrageous fortune is surely not new to the man who wrote,

> Our wills and fates do so contrary run,
> That our devices still are overthrown,
> Our thoughts are ours, their ends none of our own.
> (3. 2. 221–223)

In his tribute to the "special Providence in the fall of a sparrow" (5. 2. 230–231) Hamlet sees that he may not be permitted to do the deed that he has a little earlier called "perfect conscience" (1. 67). But there is no evidence that after a mere 173 lines he somehow no longer sees it as perfect conscience and is no longer on the watch for his opportunity. Indeed the evidence goes the other way: "The interim is mine, / And a man's life's no more than to say one" (5. 2. 73–74).

Prosser notes that Horatio, "our sturdy norm character, assures us that flights of angels shall sing Hamlet to his rest,"[46] but it is again crucial, given the myth of a redeemed Hamlet, to point out that Horatio does no such thing. His farewell to the Prince is a prayer, which the audience will no doubt wish to second. But Hamlet's achievement of eternal glory remains, as it should be, uncertain. According to the common doctrine, the Book of Life is in any case closed to us on earth. And Hamlet's worldly fate is no more an invitation than Ophelia's to musings about his otherworldly destination. Such musings would be a distraction from two issues far more to the purpose; whether another's conscience can ever truly be "caught," and whether conscience as such is reducible to will or decree.

But the pattern of Hamlet's spiritual career belies a sentimental optimism. The tragedy of Hamlet, as far as it involves what I have called moral suspense, is a tragedy of spiritual decline arrested only, if at all, by the brief madness of the Prince's last anger. We are relieved in some degree, perhaps, by the reflex violence of an act that would be abhorrent to us if it were deliberate—if it were, that is, the frigid act of hatred we and the Prince have been waiting for.

"Yet have I something in me dangerous, / Which let thy wiseness fear" (5. 1. 285–286). The irony of this advice is that its author never takes it himself. In the pride of his intellect, he hopes to find his unknown duty by seeking what is immeasurably less known: "For what man knoweth the things of a man, saue the spirit of a man, which is in him? euen so the things of God knoweth no man, but the Spirit of God" (1 Cor. 2 : 11). The vision of deity that results from this quest, as we have seen, is blasphemously partial; it sacrifices infinite goodness on the altar of infinite might. And the vision of duty that results from this warped vision of God is equally troubling to the onlooker—not least the onlooker who, like many in Shakespeare's audience, was committed by the teaching of his church to visions uncomfortably close to these.

If the story of Hamlet recalled no such visions and commitments but simply left us in considerable doubt about the integrity of its hero, then it would lose an essential claim to our continuing interest. It is not hard to find the moral principle under which Hamlet may stand reproved. It is very hard, if not impossible, to find a reason in turn for not assigning to that principle (as does Hamlet) the status of something like a mere imperative. There is a limit to the seriousness with which we can go on worrying about the demoralization of a fictitious character. There is no limit to the seriousness with which we can go on worrying about the demoralization of the idea of morals itself. It is in this sense only that the story is not contingently but necessarily "about" its audience. Hamlet's effort to trace the rightness of his decision to an emotion, an arbitrary code, and a divine decree is compelling because we are not and perhaps can never be sure he is looking in the wrong place. This is the ground of the dramatic effect I have called speculative suspense.

If this kind of suspense is indeed the source of the play's universality, then we have another reason for rejecting the view that what disturbs us most profoundly in Hamlet is his defiance or disregard of an accepted rule of conduct or assumption of fact. For the rule or assumption is itself on trial. Hamlet has put it there. To be sure, one of the ways in which Shakespeare brings us to disapprove of Hamlet's choices is to remind us at various points of our background of rules and assumptions. In this way he keeps us from exercising our prerogative, as spectators, of hypothetically suspending our disbelief in the rightness of revenge or the good intentions of vengeful ghosts. So far Battenhouse's general approach is persuasive: "Hamlet's bits of Christian language are important as evidence of canons he is bypassing in his yielding to self-pleasing imagination. Since he is not utterly without knowledge of the Christian rule, but impetuously overlooks it, his persistence in revenge is a fault of his own seeking."[47] But to the extent that our ultimate criteria are mere "rules" or "canons," we are left abjectly defenseless as soon as Hamlet forces us to proceed from finding fault with his morals to finding fault with his view of morals. Indeed, our moral judgment loses its cogency. For we have in effect conceded his most disturbing premise: if the principle Hamlet "bypasses" or "impetuously overlooks" is essentially a canon or commandment, what is to prevent the Rulegiver from exercising His prerogative of setting His rules aside?

The same premise weakens Prosser's case against a purgatorial origin for the ghost: "The visitation of a dead soul would indeed require a miracle, but the Catholic believed that on extraordinary occasions such a miracle might be granted."[48] Why should not

Hamlet think of himself as confronted with just such an occasion? In the same vein Battenhouse argues that "it is quite impossible, theologically, for the ghost's abode to be anywhere other than hell. Souls in a Christian Purgatory are holy souls genuinely repentant of their sins, and inspired with charity."[49] But again if the ground of charity is merely a rule, then it is subject to arbitrary redefinition by the Giver of the rule. And here the orthodox tradition is not reassuring. The gate of Dante's hell was wrought by the First Love as well as the other persons of God, and Dante informs us elsewhere that it is impious—that is, wanting in charity toward God—to exercise charity toward those who suffer His judgment.[50] The exclusive right of vengeance belongs to a God Who is Love. What is to prevent His purgatorial minister from mediating love in this extraordinary sense?

But this is the impasse to which Hamlet brings us by appealing to a revised notion of conscience in support of his right to betray Rosencrantz and Guildenstern and his duty to dispatch Claudius. It is perfectly true, as Battenhouse argues, that in this appeal Hamlet "has substituted a make-believe conscience."[51] But Hamlet goes significantly further and informs us that the data of this new faculty are the commandments of God. The sanction against following his "perfect conscience" is damnation (5. 2. 68) and the treacheries that are "not near my conscience" are of divine inspiration (1. 48). These two claims of Hamlet may well be wrong in fact; the disturbing possibility is that they may be right in principle.

In this respect Hamlet resembles his near contemporary at Wittenberg, John Faustus. Both are guilty of errors of presumed fact—in Faustus's case that there is power of which God is not the source, in Hamlet's that God grants dispensations from the moral law in the latter days. And both share equivalent assumptions of principle that we mightily hope may be in error—in Faustus's case that to be as God all one need be is omnipotent, in Hamlet's that the sole measure of right for God and man is the will of God. The errors of fact are far less formidable than this error of principle, if it is an error. It is the position that most Christian theologians have tried, not always with full conviction, to disavow. "For God," as Hooker insists, "worketh nothing without cause. All those things which are done by Him have some end for which they are done, and the end for which they are done is a reason of His will to do them."[52]

Hooker might well insist on the existence of reasons for divine acts of will. The view he is countering undermines not only the rationality of God but the rationality of morals. In the two plays, the heroes' position is discredited, if at all, by its fruit. The aspirant to omnipotence without direction becomes a servile master of revels for the Emperor Charles. The worshiper of the God of Will without Reason becomes morally callous and randomly destructive. These dramatic proofs are ad hominem and circular, since it is precisely the standards they appeal to that are in question; and Shakespeare at least will go on (in *King Lear*) to improve on them. But two things deserve to be emphasized in mitigation of their weakness. First, that it is the genius and perhaps the glory of dramatic proof that it addresses itself, as richly as it can, ad hominem. Second, that the theme of Hamlet's flawed integrity and his failure would seem to be, not the theme of the play, but an essential commentary on it. The hero's corruption unmasks his wrongness; this subordination of moral to speculative suspense or to its relief is the secret of *Hamlet*'s powerful unity.

On the strength of what has been said thus far, it seems fair to conclude that *Hamlet* is deeply involved with two philosophical concerns that we shall be tracing in three other Shakespearean plays: the accessibility of other minds and the existence of rational grounds for moral choice; concerns that the play treats as intimately connected. The hero has chosen to repudiate his earlier notion of conscience as a faculty for assessing the intrinsic value of his actions and their consequences; for him in the end conscience is simply a faculty for perceiving and following the will of God. This latter task, however, is no more easily discharged than the other tasks of psychological detection that the Prince undertakes in the course of the play. We are thus given a mixed verdict on the central issues: the achievement of a reliable insight into the minds of other people, at least on the loveless level of surveillance on which Hamlet has proudly chosen to operate, has been shown to be insuperably difficult; but the meaningfulness of intrinsic value and of the faculty that perceives it has been triumphantly vindicated. For Hamlet comes dangerously near to losing our sympathy precisely by ignoring this faculty, and by proceeding as if good and evil were mere labels issued by the caprice of a sovereign will. The verdict of the play to which we shall now turn will deny us even this last consolation.

CHAPTER THREE

Pain, Law, and Conscience in
Measure for Measure

THERE IS LITTLE in *Hamlet* to suggest that it is designed to raise lingering doubts about the existence either of rational criteria of justice or of a genuine faculty of conscience to perceive them. For one thing, the Prince confirms his fall precisely by abandoning his faith in their existence. For another, we are strengthened in our own faith by insistent reminders of a Christian outlook that runs counter to Hamlet's version of piety, an outlook in which God's prohibition of suicide and revenge is simply the highest authority and sanction, but not the reason, for the wrongness of these acts. In the present play, by contrast, hornbook verities are less helpful. It is not clear that to demand punitive measure for measure need be to seek, like Pyrrhus and Laertes, an eye for an eye, or that the legal laxity with which the play ends is indeed the charitable alternative to the legal cruelty with which it begins. We are, I shall suggest, abandoned here from first to last to a state of philosophical emergency, at the mercy of threatening ambiguities.[1] The emergency begins when a vexatious issue of principle is imposed on some articulate and ostensibly dedicated citizens of Shakespeare's Vienna. It will be our main business to define the issue at stake as precisely as we can, and then to try to explain why the poet finds it necessary to settle matters with a practical joke.

Measuring Justice: "Common Law" Is "Common Right"

Claudio has been found guilty of anticipating the rites of marriage. The capital punishment demanded for this offense by ancient Viennese law is nearly obsolete, but Judge Angelo, a precisian, resolves to pass sentence according to its letter. The judge is motivated

by two convictions. First, a sentence is to be justified solely by appeal
to law as the ultimate authority and definition of justice; the offense
in question "is so, as it appears, / Accountant to the law upon that
pain" (2. 4. 85–86). And that is that. A judge does not make
decisions, he hands them down as the "voice of the recorded law"
(2. 4. 61); and consequently, if the code states as fact that Claudio's
offense is to be regarded as equivalent to murder, Angelo feels no
obligation to justify this estimate beyond restating it:

> It were as good
> To pardon him that hath from nature stol'n
> A man already made, as to remit
> Their saucy sweetness, that do coin Heaven's image
> In stamps that are forbid.   (2. 4. 42–46)

As if to erase all suspicion that he has some extralegal justification
for assenting to this particular law, Angelo assures the convict's
sister with emphasis that "it is the law, not I condemn your brother"
(2. 2. 80).

The second point is that the only "rational" requirements for a
fair punishment, in Angelo's view, are uniformity and accuracy in
carrying out the law. The bare fact that a judge who passes a valid
sentence happens himself to be guilty of the offense he is punishing
cannot conceivably invalidate the sentence; that is a non sequitur if
ever there was one. The solution is to follow the logic of the situation
and punish the judge in the same way; never to reconsider the ap-
propriateness of the punishment itself:

> I not deny,
> The jury, passing on the prisoner's life,
> May in the sworn twelve have a thief or two
> Guiltier than him they try. What's open made to justice,
> That justice seizes. What knows the laws
> That thieves do pass on thieves? . . .
> You may not so extenuate his offence
> For I have had such faults; but rather tell me,

When I, that censure him, do so offend,
Let mine own judgement pattern out my death,
And nothing come in partial. (2. 1. 18–31)

Duke Vincentio, who is supposed to be abroad but has actually
remained in Vienna incognito to study the case, seems to favor his
judicial deputy's views. Since law defines justice, impartiality and
invariance are a judge's sole duties: "If his own life answer the
straitness of his proceeding, it shall become him well; wherein if he
chance to fail, he hath sentenc'd himself" (3. 2. 269–271). A judge
who spares himself is, to be sure, a partial judge, which is one form
of tyranny:

Were he meal'd
With that which he corrects, then were he tyrannous;
But this being so, he's just. (4. 2. 86–88)

A lawgiver who revises his laws is inconsistent, which is the only
other form of tyranny:

Sith 'twas my fault to give my people scope,
'Twould be my tyranny to strike and gall them
For what I bid them do. (1. 3. 35–37)

We notice that the Duke does not mention the inherent justice of
the legal punishment itself; for him as for Angelo, justice is identical
with law.

It is remarkable how close these reduced notions of justice and
reason are to the prevailing sentiment of English common lawyers at
the beginning of the seventeenth century. The law of England, asserts
the redoubtable Sir Edward Coke, is "the golden metwand, whereby
all men's causes are justly and evenly measured."[2] Hence common
law, common right, and golden rule, as he repeatedly argues, are
absolutely synonymous, and we are to be duly cautioned that "no man
must be wiser than the laws; for no otherwise thriveth the common
weal but in the summer of the laws' authority." There is no very
scrupulous acknowledgment in this kind of thinking of that crucial

distinction between "common" principle and "particular" case to which Hamlet fitfully subscribes on our first encounter with him. The higher law of reason is not reason itself in its autonomous, concrete activity. It is simply the common law exalted on high. "Before it was higher law it was positive law in the strictest sense of the term, a law regularly administered in the ordinary courts in the settlement of controversies between private individuals." Ultimately common law defines guilt, much as for the later Hamlet honor defines the "greatness" of an "argument" or cause; and with the same effect in both views of draining moral principle of declarative force and conceding it only the force of an imperative.[3]

As for the role of conscience or practical reason in administering justice, "causes . . . are not to be decided by natural reason but by the artificial reason and judgment of the law."[4] A judge's conscience, says Coke, is purely a function of legal scholarship; and a judge's discretion can consist only in "conscientiously" executing the discriminations of right and wrong dictated by law. In short, Coke's "artificial reason" is one with Angelo's fundamentalist rigor in interpreting laws. In the choice of punishments, both men maintain that "novelties without warrant of precedents are not to be allowed,"[5] for the integrity of the moral order as they conceive of it demands that the tradition of the courts be invariable. As for the judge who hands down a correct punishment that happens to be applicable to his own private conduct, the common sense of common law is precisely Angelo's: "What appeareth not, is not, and in this case it appeareth not before process at law."[6]

Now we must bear in mind that on this view individual moral alternatives cannot accredit themselves. There is no such thing as intrinsic merit; if there were, common law would not be common right by definition, as Coke maintains. Obligations "bind" by falling into the classes determined by the revealed will of society—or of divinity; for, of course, a Christian jurist who subscribed to this view of the moral standard would still be "bound" to acknowledge a set of imperatives more august than the common law; but to be consistent he would have to hold that God's law too is a pure *placet* or imperative,[7] and that once more the faculty involved in passing judgment is not conscience or reason but logic, the intellectual shadow of pure obedience:

> We see it familiarly in games of wit, as chess or the like; the draughts and first laws of the game are positive, but how? merely *ad placitum*, and not examinable by reason; but then how to direct our play with best advantage to win the game, is artificial and rational. . . . Such therefore is that secondary reason, which hath place in divinity (as well moral as mystical), which is grounded upon the *placets* of God.[8]

Bacon's "secondary" or "artificial" reason is clearly the same as Coke's. So that in our play Angelo's conviction that the ancient law of the "Viennese" courts is beyond criticism—is "all-binding" (2. 4. 94) and "most just" (2. 4. 52)—has illustrious endorsement, not only in the current political theory of English common law as the supreme arbiter of legislative justice, but also in the Calvinist reduction of right reason to an acquiescence in the Will of wills. We shall see that the analogy of God's *placets* does not escape at least one citizen of Shakespeare's Vienna.

Measuring Justice: Common Rights and the Merits of the Case

On the other hand, a law that equates careless love with murder, we should think, will inevitably have its critics. Angelo's opponents might well insist that it is par excellence the duty and dignity of a judge to use his judgment, where warranted, to draw the moral distinctions called for by concrete human predicaments, and to modify or abrogate the law accordingly. Active justice is a retail, not a wholesale, business.[9] Regardless of the law, urges Angelo's colleague Escalus, "Let us be keen, and rather cut a little, / Than fall, and bruise to death" (2. 1. 5–6). Under the aegis even of a very good law, as he complains, "some rise by sin, and some by virtue fall, / Some run from brakes of vice and answer none; / And some" —like Claudio—"condemned for a fault alone" (2. 1. 38–40).[10]

To avoid these injustices, law must be not merely carried out but applied with discretion.

But the penal law in question is not a good law. Its badness, in fact, is ludicrous, and the scandal, the mocking and persistent irony of the play, is that nobody in Vienna who enlists our particular concern and admiration speaks vigorously, or speaks at all, or seems in the least sensitive, to this cardinal point. For it is a question here, not of an exception to a generally benign law, but rather of a law that is generally destructive, and of course no less destructive in Claudio's case than in any others we can readily imagine. It is thus perplexing to note that Isabella, when she pleads for her brother, appeals, not to equity in the sense of moral reason, but to equity in the narrow and irrelevant sense of mitigating circumstances.[11] To compound the perplexity, these are mitigating circumstances that smack of the grossest favoritism. "Great men may jest with saints," she argues;

> 'tis wit in them,
> But in the less foul profanation. . . .
> That in the captain's but a choleric word,
> Which in the soldier is flat blasphemy.
> (2. 2. 127–128, 130–131)

At the same time, the possibility of attacking the law itself is strangely ignored. It will repay us to set in its historical context this possibility—the notion of legal fairness to which the onlooker is apt to turn at once, and on which most of the leading citizens of Vienna are, like Isabella, silent to the point of exasperation.

Measuring Justice: Natural Law vs. Natural Justice

The principle of equity (that the justice or injustice of an act is not strictly a function of positive law but is somehow inherent in the "nature" of the act itself) is subject to two classic interpretations, both current in the Renaissance, and each in its own way relevant to the Viennese mutterings against Claudio's penalty.[12] It is not surprising that the continental architects of the more familiar version, being

for the most part professional lawyers, agree with Coke and Angelo
that the standard of justice is law, in fact a hierarchy of laws—although their laws, unlike Coke's "golden metwand," are required
to be capable of justification and, unlike Angelo's ascetic revival,
are not merely imposed by force on alien matter: everyone somehow
or other harbors a tendency to exemplify the appropriate "natural"
law. Not all of the natural laws are equally inclusive, however, and
this is why there is always the possibility that an apparently deviant
act is not really a violation of the moral law in its most explicit form.
Moreover, not all the natural laws are equally binding, so that there
is nothing to prevent a complex piece of behavior from simultaneously exhibiting one step that is forbidden by a rule, and another step
that is enjoined by a second and more important rule.

On this very popular interpretation, every law, to be sure, has a
reason, but the difficulty is that the "reason" can be only another
law. This circumstance puts the potential critic of positive law in
a glass house. To assure us that the "justice" of nature, like that of
convention, is lawful is unhappily not at all the same as proving that
the law of nature is just, or any more just than the law of Vienna,
say; and this latter assurance is the kind on which the case against
Claudio's sentence ultimately depends. What is more, to avoid the
absurdity of an infinite regress of exceptions perpetually generating
laws to justify them, advocates of natural law must specify at least
one principle that has no exceptions—and not a mere tautology at
that, like "it is right to do good, wrong to do evil." Aquinas makes
a characteristic attempt to accomplish this without doing violence
to the facts of concrete moral experience. He argues that, whereas
one can refuse to return goods entrusted and yet be just, one cannot
conceivably steal without injustice; some duties are absolute. On the
other hand, he is candid enough to admit that theft for survival is
not a clear-cut case of injustice; to do what is unjust in the abstract
is not always to act unjustly.[13] Stealing is essentially unjust only in
relation to the crime, not to the criminal.

An appeal, then, to equity from the rigor of law is particularly
ill-advised when it seeks its credentials in legalist or deductive notions
of justification. Law so treated is a closed system whose magic circle

of fiat remains unbroken, even should all creation choose to obey it for eternity. The eternal whim of an infinite multitude is still a whim. And consistency is a "value" many conventional and arbitrary scales of value can fabricate equally well. Traditional measures of what in the main constitutes justice, so urge the proponents of equity, must themselves be measured from time to time by a direct examination of their actual moral consequences. For an "absolute" or a priori moral principle may betray us into injustice at any time. That the principle derives from Nature rather than from Vienna hardly insures us against the tyranny of its absoluteness. This is to flee from one sort of Angelo into the embrace of another.

But if natural regularity or order is not the essential fact of moral life, what is? The second traditional presentation of the evidence for equity is the notion of good as a simple quality. Aquinas's influential commentary is worth summarizing in this connection. The "goodness" of an experience, however complex the experience, is something simple that accidentally attaches to it, like a dash of taste or color in a total apprehension. Good laws are made by consulting our own and others' "internal sense" to find out what courses of action have invariably favored and hence will most probably favor the increase and diffusion of this special ingredient of experience in the community. Since value is a distinct element and does not have to be associated with any other experience or activity, a good law ("right" as opposed to "improvised") is a measure only of probable justice. The immediate experiences from which laws are drafted are individually self-certifying; by comparison moral generalizations, laws, are aptly enough described, Aquinas argues, as empty. In the majority of cases direct experience is not readily available to a judge, and here law is, of course, an indispensable ethical guide. But when there is danger of serious injustice, we ought to try to consult our interior sense.[14]

Logical inference, then, is not the only function of human reason. In fact, it may be the most trivial and least humane. The dictamen of ethical reason, at any rate, is at its source not law but direct experience. The classical Roman "equity" inherited by Erasmian humanism was often, to be sure, either a legalist appeal from the text of a law to its intent, the latter considered as invariably just, or a demand like Angelo's for evenhandedness in applying laws—"equal laws in equal cases." But when Erasmus echoes Cicero in warning against the lawful injustice of prosecuting to the limit of the law, or suggests that civil law cannot safely be accused of violating the law of charity without careful reference to the particular deeds to which the civil law is addressed, it is clear that law is to be regarded not as command or postulate but as contingent generalization, and therefore capable of failing either in some cases or in most. Reason, operating on experience, especially on a sympathetic understanding of the experience of others, is the utimate source and the ultimate arbiter of law—provided we are not to succumb to the despair of abandoning the humanist view for Angelo's.

In the light of our consideration of Renaissance equity we may define two senses in which we are entitled to expect equity to be protected from the Viennese law against fornication and its precisian minister. We are entitled to expect reasonable compatriots of Angelo to draw the necessary distinctions in gravity among acts that fall indiscriminately under that law's censure, and we are entitled to expect them also to point out the bizarre injustice—not the mere strictness—of the stipulated punishment. In both cases, moreover, we must bear in mind that what hangs in the balance, as in *Hamlet*, is not merely the rescue of Claudio but the vindication of our own confidence that there is a rational criterion of value.[15]

Punishment: Corrective Pain

The question posed by Claudio's fate in *Measure for Measure* involves, as we have seen, antagonistic views, one articulated and the other blatantly ignored, of the relation of justice to law and order. Since, however, the specific law at issue is a penal law, it remains to be seen how the controversial sentence meets or fails to meet the divergent requirements for punishment projected by the two schools of juridical thought. In precisely what terms does one go about appealing to reason from Angelo's legalism?

The justification for the legal infliction of pain is clearly stated for the partisans of equity in Lord Ellesmere's agenda for the court of Chancery in the early seventeenth century: "The office of the Chancellor is to correct men's consciences for frauds, breach of trusts, wrongs, and oppressions, of what nature soever they be, and to soften and mollify the extremity of the law, which is called *Summum Jus*."[16] Equitable punishment, then, true to its origins in the ecclesiastical tribunals of canon law, is supposed to correct consciences;[17] to be just, pain must reform, and it reforms by a kind of imposed spiritual renovation. To be sure, the traditional (Scholastic-Aristotelian) argument suffers a bit by a dubious analogy to the regulation of trade. Satisfaction derived from inflicting injury is thought of as excess benefit or usury. In correcting consciences, the evil of pain, which is by definition a mere subtraction of good, simply neutralizes the "profit"—the disproportionate fulfillment of will. Of course, the idea of gratified malice as a kind of benefit was bound to occasion discomfort to Christian thought; and Aquinas admits that in penology the commutative principle is not so readily apparent: "minus est manifestum."[18]

Yet for all its dangers, not the least being the possibility of defending torture, the fact remains that the therapeutic tradition of penology aims at destroying the criminal bent in the individual conscience, and is duly sensitive to the precise degree of distortion in the will being remedied. So that what Lord Ellesmere calls "mollifying" the excesses of law is not to be construed as a relaxing of strict justice; in Isabella's words, "lawful mercy is nothing kin to foul redemption" (2. 4. 112–113). Pity, says Aquinas, is no doubt an effusion of feeling, but genuine forgiveness remains a function of reason.[19] The *Nicomachean Ethics*, he reminds us, expressly warns against the inequity of the judicial precisian; and with good reason, for this vice consists in "pursuing justice for the worse, that is for punishment. . . . Legal punishments are intended, not as ends in themselves, but as a kind of medicine for sins."[20] As such their just application requires the benevolent insight into other minds that Hamlet (as we have seen) exercises in ministering to Gertrude and betrays in hunting Claudius's soul to the death.

It is abundantly clear, then, that the Duke, disguised as a kind of prison chaplain, is reflecting, not only the spirit of the sacrament of penance, but the tradition of juridical equity when he speaks of the inmates as "afflicted spirits" and asks to be told "the nature of their crimes, that I may minister / To them accordingly" (2. 3. 4–8). In the same way, his identification of this ministry with "common right" is the measure of his hostility, as priest, to the conception of ethics underlying Angelo's identification of common right with law. Indeed, the Duke's confessional instructions to Julietta on how to "arraign" her "conscience" (2. 3. 21) go a step further, by rejecting punishment outright, at least as an essential means of correcting conscience. True repentance is never directed to the punishment—"which sorrow is always towards ourselves" (2. 3. 32) —but to the nature of the crime; to the punishment itself the attitude of the penitent should be, not pain or remorse, but joyful acceptance: "I do repent me, as it is an evil," as Julietta responds, "and take the shame with joy" (ll. 35–36). But this line of thinking is not properly a justification for punishment at all. We shall have to return to it at a later stage of our argument.

Punishment: Deterrence

On the other hand, the traditions of common law and Puritanism could not very well accept this accommodation of penalty to person. Part of the reason was a theory of political freedom that, here as often, blurred into an ethic of submission:

> The individualization in practise which was permitted by the canon-law conception of searching and disciplining the conscience was wholly alien to the Puritan. For above all things he was jealous of the magistrate. If moral questions were to be dealt with as concrete cases to be individualized in their solution, subordination of those whose cases were decided to those who had the power of weighing the circumstances of the concrete case (and individualizing the principle to meet that case) might result. His idea of "consociation without subordination" demanded that a

fixed, absolute, universal rule, which the individual had
contracted to abide by, be resorted to.[21]

In short, submission to the tyranny of law means freedom from the
caprice of tyranny. To preserve this freedom, a convicted man, like
Claudio, must be held to his word and forced to meet the letter
of his corporate bond, the law of the land. Only secondary reason,
as we have seen, is relevant to the fulfillment of this bond. Appeal
to primary reason or conscience or sympathetic insight is an invitation
either to compromise or to loss of franchise. By default, then, the
sole function of penal law for a precisian like Angelo is to maintain
external order.

A favorite account of this function among the play's legalists is
the perennial one that threats are the sole means of keeping the
players at the game. Without the rod, law is "mock'd" (1. 3. 26–27),
and it is precisely the obsolescence of fear that the Duke and his
deputy are allegedly seeking to prevent by making an example of
Claudio (1. 4. 63–68). On the foregoing assumptions, the only
criterion applicable to an instrument of deterrence is whether it succeeds; but does it?

The play offers several tests. One of these involves the fact that
the deterrent principle extends to the act of deterring itself. For
example, if deterrence works, a judge who is subject to the laws he
administers will be deterred by his liability to prosecution from administering a given law with strictness; mercy, for legalist and cynic
alike, can always be written off in the play as a reflex of guilt. If
it had been up to the Duke (who, to be sure, is responsible only to
God) the old law would never have been revived, according to the
libel of the naturalist Lucio: "He had some feeling of the sport; he
knew the service, and that instructed him to mercy" (3. 2. 126–128).
And the Duke in turn bases his stratagems on the assumption that
Angelo, at any rate, will be instructed to mercy by "some feeling of
the sport": "When vice makes mercy, mercy's so extended / That for
the fault's love is the offender friended" (4. 2. 115–116). Even
after his disillusionment, and while pretending ignorance of Angelo's
guilt, he falls back on this axiom:

> If he had so offended,
> He would have weigh'd thy brother by himself,
> And not have cut him off. (5. 1. 110–112)

The school of mercy is vice, "the fault's love"—a view that is the legalist or cynical equivalent of Isabella's appeal to mercy: "Ask your heart what it doth know that's like my brother's fault." (This equivalence, among other considerations, makes it advisable to reserve our judgment about that appeal.)

But deterrence proves to be a very inadequate pragmatic justification for penal law; as it turns out, its victims are liable to fears even more imperious than the threat of law. Private revenge may sometimes seem likelier than public. Granted, Angelo did have qualms on first making the acquaintance of his own frailty; he went as far as to plan a reprieve for Claudio on the pretext of the purely contractual authority of law:

> O let her brother live!
> Thieves for their robbery have authority
> When judges steal themselves.
> (2. 2. 175–177)

But as events prove, a vice instructs to mercy only until some other vice betters the instruction. Angelo on second thought unlearns his lesson with alacrity:

> He should have liv'd,
> Save that his riotous youth, with dangerous sense,
> Might in the times to come have ta'en revenge.
> (4. 4. 31–33)

There is, moreover, the possibility that Lucio and his more august colleagues have not been cynical enough. Fear is not always the strongest motive. Pompey the bawd seems to have a truer, if less sophisticated, estimate of how Viennese fear compares in urgency with Viennese lust, for example: "If you head and hang all that offend that way but for ten year together, you'll be glad to give out a commission for more heads" (2. 1. 251–253). And as a matter of fact, the common-law apologists for penal severity in the early seventeenth century apparently did not take the argument from deterrence very seriously. "True it is," says Coke, "that we have found by wofull experience, that it is not frequent and often punishment that doth prevent like offenses. . . . And it is a certain rule, that *Videbis ea saepe committi quae saepe vindicantur.* Those offenses are often committed that are often punished, for the frequency of the punishment makes it so familiar as it is not feared."[22] Yet in the very same paragraph the jurist can turn around and demand "that Pardons be very rarely granted." Punishment for the common lawyer and perhaps for Angelo is apparently not so much a practical measure as an end in itself, the retaliation of an "angry law" (3. 1. 207). But a law capable of "anger" bears a suspicious resemblance to the mercurial sovereign from whom it was designed to protect us. We shall need to consider whether in the play, as in some contemporary speculation, law proves to be simply a tool of sovereign power. If so, and if sovereign power likewise countenances no intrinsic criterion of right, we are back once again at the mercy of naked will, individual will this time rather than corporate.

Punishment: Power and Law

The Puritan was the more eager to submit to the full power of law because it was, after all, predictable power and not violence. But even law, Angelo confesses, may erupt after years of dormancy: "The law hath not been dead, though it hath slept" (2. 2. 90). The Duke himself admits as much; the lawful exercise of power *can* have something unpredictable or tyrannical about it (1. 3. 36). Is this fluctuation of judicial policy essential, or are these sudden scourges in the name of maintaining authority an abuse of authority? Claudio poses the dilemma for us at the very outset:

> Whether it be the fault and glimpse of newness,
> Or whether that the body public be
> A horse whereon the governor doth ride,
> Who, newly in the seat, that it may know

He can command, lets it straight feel the spur;
Whether the tyranny be in his place,
Or in his eminence that fills it up,
I stagger in.   (1. 2. 162–169)

If the tyranny is indeed *in* his place, if power is a form of horse-manship and society the mount, there can be very little solace in contemplating the legality of the spur.

If the Duke has a definite opinion on the subject, he is con-spicuously reluctant to commit himself. Almost his very first words are a modest evasion: "Of government the properties to unfold / Would seem in me to affect speech and discourse" (1. 1. 3–4). To be sure, in the ensuing "speech and discourse" he defines the problem clearly enough:

... let them work. The nature of our people,
Our city's institutions, and the terms
For common justice;   (ll. 10–12)

but how are they to work? What is the relation of "common justice" to "art and practise" (l. 13)?

As for the Duke's scattered confidences about his own office, each of them is a little essay in equivocation. He has, he says, conferred on Angelo "all the organs / Of our own power" (1. 1. 21–22); the deputy is plenipotentiary, his power is "absolute" (1. 3. 13); but in which of the two available senses of "absolute" to be discussed presently, we can only guess. "Your scope is as mine own," he in-forms Angelo, "so to enforce or qualify the laws / As to your soul seems good" (1. 1. 65–67). But once again the information is distinctly uninformative, for "soul" is an equivoque, leaving the door open to either whim or choice, either pleasure or election; as where the Duke announces circumstantially that "we have with special soul / Elected him" (1. 1. 18–19). And later on, when Angelo asks for permission to use "the scope of justice" (5. 1. 234), the Duke obliges with irony: "Ay, with my heart; / And punish them unto your height of pleasure" (ll. 239–240).

Between election and pleasure there is a desperately far cry. No wonder the deputies are confused about the particulars of their deputation. "It concerns me," says Escalus,

> to look into the bottom of my place.
> A power I have, but of what strength and nature
> I am not yet instructed.   (1. 1. 78–81)

" 'Tis so with me," replies Angelo;

> let us withdraw together,
> And we may soon our satisfaction have
> Touching that point.   (1. 1. 82–84)

Presumably we are invited to expect that what follows will give satisfaction on the nature of power, either to the advocates of control per se or, for that matter, to those of conscience. "Assay the power you have," Lucio urges Isabella in a parallel exchange. "My power," she replies, "alas, I doubt" (1. 4. 76–77). The cogency of this doubt, one may well suspect, is the cogency of the play itself. For the denouement will not help us very much to avoid the impression that power is by nature unreasonable, and reason (in the moral sense, at any rate), not a power.

Punishment: War and Law

Claudio has asked whether government is essentially horsemanship. The closest the Duke comes to a direct answer is his characterization of legal institutions as "strict statutes and most biting laws, / The needful bits and curbs to headstrong steeds" (1. 3. 19–20). This does not, of course, quite force us to infer that law in the view of the Duke is the mere pretext of sovereign power; sovereign power may still, for all the Duke's *manège*, equally well be the tool of his justice. Yet the suspicious fact remains that the Duke *does* fancy himself a rider of "the body public"; and Viennese rumor seems to echo the suspicion.

Perhaps the most impressive support for the antiequestrian view of government in English juridical thought at the turn of the sixteenth century was the movement toward international law, *lex inter gentes*, which served much the same fulcral role in the argument for a universal law of reason as the hypothesis of a generally acknowledged civil law, *lex gentium*, in fostering the equity of the Roman praetors. In 1605 Alberico Gentili, Regius Professor of civil law at Oxford since 1587, was evolving a concept of political sovereignty as power absolute with respect to the common law, but duly limited with respect to the universal law of reason. It was the emergent if not the popular view; and its corollary was the regulation of war. A right war, the argument ran, was a legal process, the "tribunal of Mars," and a "just contest of public arms." Gentili's great treatise on the legitimation of war appeared in 1625, but Hooker had bestowed his magisterial prestige on the same position much earlier.[23]

The belief in an objective criterion for endorsing or disallowing aggression, it is clear, was a vital consequence of the theory of natural justice. What, then, are we to make of the second scene of Shakespeare's ambiguous drama of law and power? It is given over to a talk on the latest war gossip—dominated, appropriately enough, by the antic Lucio, the gay cynic:

> LUCIO. If the Duke with the other dukes come not to composition with the King of Hungary, why then all the dukes fall upon the King.
>
> FIRST GENT. Heaven grant us its peace, but not the King of Hungary's!
>
> SECOND GENT. Amen.
>
> LUCIO. Thou conclud'st like the sanctimonius pirate, that went to sea with the Ten Commandments, but scrap'd one out of the table.
>
> SECOND GENT. "Thou shalt not steal"?
>
> LUCIO. Ay, that he raz'd.
>
> FIRST GENT. Why, 'twas a commandment to command the captain and all the rest from their functions; they put forth to steal. There's not a soldier of us all, that, in the thanksgiving before meat, do relish the petition well that prays for peace. (1. 2. 1–17)

The pretext for the Duke's projected war is Hungarian intransigence and the resulting frustration of a longing for peace. But it is an open secret that the Viennese objective is larceny and the longing for peace a fraud. Can it be that the lawful claims of dukes are one and all a pirate's sanctimonies, and that the decisive difference between the triumphant Duke and the pirate Ragozine, dead of fever in the city jail, is success? "Justice is on our side," Machiavelli informed Lorenzo de' Medici in a notorious passage; "for a war is a just war to those who need it, and an army holy where one has no expectations without it."[24] The will of a sovereign power, whether in war or in the choice of penal arrangements, is accountable to no one but history. So at least imply the realist soldiers of Vienna.

If the gossipers have caught the true flavor of the dukes' *casus belli* (as of course we may still hope they do not), then the play raises the possibility that not only judicial but ducal sovereignty is at bottom a form of power—systematic perhaps, but not informed by reason. In both cases, not the general welfare, but the maintenance of order and control must then be the ultimate motive of action. Punishments in such a scheme of things must be suited, not to the gravity of crimes, or even exclusively to the requirements of deterring them, but to the satisfaction of a vindictive sovereign, at least as he embodies the laws that facilitate his effective reign.

As for the laws themselves, it is history's own witticism that the common law of the early seventeenth century, like a woman scorned, should have reserved its most hellish fury for those accused who declined to avail themselves of the right to plead, thereby making either conviction or acquittal technically impossible. The accused man who obstinately stood mute or appealed defiantly to God and conscience was condemned to be crushed to death against jagged stones by the weight, in effect, of the aggrieved law itself.[25] "Let no man imagine," Coke observes in his celebration of *peine forte et dure*, "that the common law, which is the absolute perfection of reason, could foster so unreasonable and unjust a means of encouragement to felons, that by their own contumacy against the common law they should suffer only one of the lowest punishments, *videlicet* imprisonment untill they would answer."[26] This from the man who, as we have seen, confessed that frequent punishment itself may be an incentive to felons.

Whether deterrence or vengeance is uppermost in the legalist mind of the early seventeenth century, its disdain for the concrete moral facts is notorious enough. Donne in his sermons will express the hope that the Virginia Colony may "redeeme many a wretch" from execution for minor offenses.[27] Donne is very far from thinking of the law of England as "the absolute perfection of reason"; reason has nothing to do with the matter. The harshness of a legal punishment cannot bind the conscience. It reflects the demands of public order rather than the gravity of a given crime.[28]

Punishment in this view, as in that of the Duke and his Deputy, is strictly regulatory and administrative; it is not concerned with its victims as particular moral agents. Even God's own penology works on this principle: "certainly God often punisheth a sinner more severely because others have taken occasion of sinning by his fact. . . . our interpretation of another's sin doth often give the measure to God's justice and mercy." As in law, so in providence: the individual is sacrificed to the general maintenance of a supreme will.

Indeed, equitable jurisprudence had long since felt the pressure of the divine analogy. In defending the justice of an eternal and hence purely vindictive damnation, Aquinas had seen fit, even in the human sphere, to set an arbitrary limit to the validity of therapeutic punishment: some degrees of guilt simply leave a soul unworthy of correction; vindictive punishment has a place in the cities of man and God, and its utility, if any, is solely deterrent.[29] There is a nice decorum in the circumstance that Claudio, the victim of the law in our play, is very well aware of this terrible analogy:

> Thus can the demigod authority
> Make us pay down for our offence by weight
> The words of heaven; on whom it will, it will;
> On whom it will not, so; yet still 'tis just.
>
> (I. 2. 124–127)

Claudio, we must remember, is the man who asks whether earthly government is equestrian, the will of the spurred rider. Clearly

Romans 9 : 14–21 has taught him to expect as much and no more
from the government of heaven:

> What shal we say then? Is there any vnrighteousnes with
> God? God forbyd. For he sayth to Moses, I wil have
> mercie on him, to whom I wil shewe mercie: and wil haue
> compassion, on whom I wil haue compassion. . . . But o
> man, who art thou which playdest against God? shal the
> worke say to the worke man, Why hast thou made me on
> this fasshon? Hath not the potter power ouer the claye:
> Even of the same lompe to make one vessel vnto honour,
> and another vnto dishonour?

It is not very hard to recognize in Claudio's vision of God as a model
of judicial caprice for the earthly judges who ape Him—in his vision
of God as a supreme will in a moral universe without other criteria
of value than wills—the very faith to which, as we have seen,
Hamlet eventually succumbs.[30] The stakes of equity's trial in *Measure
for Measure* are high. They include the integrity not only of a rational
ethics but of a theology with which a Christian humanist could live
in spiritual peace. Before we turn to the denouement and such
clarifications as it has to offer, it will be instructive to consider the
light shed on this matter of punishment by what actually happens to
Claudio and some other criminals in the jail of Vienna.

Punishment: Claudio and Barnardine

Claudio is a penitent, a man who eventually "professes to have
received no sinister measure from his judge, but most willingly
humbles himself to the determination of justice" (3. 2. 256–258).
He is precisely the sort of man for whom, by "Friar Lodowick's"
extension of equity (the correction of conscience), an extrinsic pain
is well-nigh superfluous, since the contemplation of his guilt is itself
a punishment. Crimes like Claudio's—the attacks of incontinence or
acrasia—involve only the eclipse of the evaluative sense, not its
nonexistence; and such criminals are by definition corrigible. Consequently, no traditional treatment of the problem of criminality could

claim to be exhaustive without going on to treat intemperance or *acolasia* as well, a moral affliction involving not compulsion but ethical color blindness and hence hopeless permanence.[31]

To study corrective punishment in the round, then, we must juxtapose the case of corrigible Claudio with the complementary case of incorrigible Barnardine, "a man that apprehends death no more dreadfully but as a drunken sleep . . . insensible of mortality, and desperately mortal" (4. 2. 149–153), an impenitent who "wants advice" but "will hear none" (ll. 154–155). How is one to punish, in the corrective sense, a criminality that is wholly disinterested, a caricature of innocence "as fast lock'd up in sleep as guiltless labour" (l. 69)? "Give him leave to escape and he would not" (ll. 156–157). The bewildered jailer (l. 71) exposes the nerve of the dilemma for the partisans of conscience when he asks, "Who can do good on him?" Punishment as a form of "doing good" would be totally without meaning in coping with *acolasia*.

The Duke, in his impersonation of Friar Lodowick, draws the inescapable moral, and the moral is a radical extension of the principle of equity:

> Unfit to live or die, O gravel heart!
> . . . A creature unprepar'd, unmeet for death;
> And to transport him in the mind he is
> Were damnable.   (4. 3. 68, 71–73)

Barnardine and Claudio must both be hidden from execution "in secret holds" (4. 3. 91); the punishment in question would profit neither, and an unprofitable punishment is "damnable." As the Friar prescribes for Pompey—another brand of Viennese *acolasia*—"correction and instruction must both work / Ere this rude beast will profit" (3. 2. 33–34). And Pompey, himself, as apprentice hangman, explains the paradoxical sine qua non of just execution to Barnardine with admirable though unintentional irony: "You must be so good, sir, to rise and be put to death" (4. 3. 28–29).

In short, the juxtaposition of Claudio and Barnardine is in effect both a total rejection of the Puritan or positivist view and a neat reduction to absurdity of the equitable justification for punishment.

The reduction is based on the requirements of equity itself. Extrinsic pain is not in itself an appropriate means of moral regeneration, and sometimes it even defeats its purpose by degenerating into a mere lawful vendetta. "What do you think of the trade, Pompey," Escalus asks the convicted bawd; "is it a lawful trade?" "If the law would allow it, sir," says Pompey (2. 1. 237–239). But law does allow hanging, he consoles himself later on: "I have been an unlawful bawd time out of mind; but yet I will be content to be a lawful hangman" (4. 2. 16–18). Significantly, both callings, we are told, aspire to the dignity of a "mystery" or ministry—that is, a public service (4. 2. 36–44). And of both these would-be "mysteries" the jailer remarks with contempt: "Go to, sir; you weigh equally. A feather will turn the scale" (4. 2. 31–32). The decisive feather in Pompey's case is law, and his newly professional view of capital punishment is a model of dramatic irony: "I do find your hangman is a more penitent trade than your bawd; he doth oftener ask forgiveness. . . . truly, sir [this to the hangman], for your kindness I owe you a good turn" (ll. 52–62). The point of the repartee does not lie very far beneath the surface. Punishment in accord with the dictates of charity purports, at least, to be a "kindness," a return of good for evil; it claims to do the unregenerate conscience "a good turn." But Pompey's words are studiedly ambiguous: Abhorson, a master in the guild of hangmen, may well have greater reason to ask forgiveness than gratitude for his "kindness."

Betrayal of Equity: Res Acta Probat

If *Measure for Measure* had confined itself to a symposium on what ought to be done with Claudio and Barnardine, we should, I think, be entitled to read it as a witty attack on the legalist frame of mind and a very trenchant criticism of the ethics of punishment. But the play interests us in the judges as well as in their judgments. And here we run into trouble. Instead of being chastened by his own experience of guilt or softened at least, as the Duke erroneously predicts, by the "fault's love," Angelo breaks his faith and confirms his sentence in an implacable directive: "swerve not from the smallest article of it, neither in time, matter, or other circumstance" (4. 2. 107–108). This is, right down to the inflexibility about circumstance, a total repudiation of equity. And it is important to see how it serves to measure the depth of betrayal to which nearly all the disputants descend.

Some years ago the interesting observation was made that the Duke's original motives for appointing Angelo deputy seem to correspond to key tactical steps in Machiavelli's strategy for co-ordinating absolute power with safe public relations: revival of severity, diversion of popular resentment, concealment of personal inconsistency, and testing of subordinates.[32]

As the Florentine himself informs us, the architect (Saint Louis) of the Parisian *parlement* saw that institution—a sort of supreme court—as a third party to absorb the rancor of the great and redress the grievances of the humble without the personal involvement of the Prince. Unpopular responsibilities, he concludes, should always be delegated, on the fundamental principle that public hatred is dangerous. An even more fundamental principle is to avoid the least shade of public contempt; for men are instinctively selfish and heed the threat of pain much more than the bond of love; affection is in any case not indispensable to the avoidance of hatred, and is never to be hotly sought. "I do not relish well / Their loud applause and Aves vehement," says the Duke; "nor do I think the man of safe discretion / That does affect it" (1. 1. 70–73). The appearance of indecision, like overexposure, is to be avoided because it suggests weakness. Even the Duke's final bravura display of magnanimity resembles another Machiavellian rule for strengthening popular confidence in slack seasons, when the Prince is urged to generate "con astuzia" some easily quelled opposition so as to add to his reputation in the quelling; and also to await the unique opportunity for a spectacular display of reward or punishment.[33]

Against the Prince himself there is, of course, no court of appeal—"non è iudizio a chi reclamare"[34]—none except his results. Results, however, are precisely "Friar Lodowick's" justification for the no-torious bed trick. The idea of blackmail had already occurred to Isabella (2. 4. 152–154); now the Duke refines on it as a pardonable expedient: "If the encounter acknowledge itself hereafter; it may compel him to her recompense; and here, by this is your brother saved, your honour untainted, the poor Mariana advantaged, and the corrupt deputy scaled. . . . the doubleness of the benefit defends the deceit from reproof" (3. 1. 261–269). In other words, the doubleness of the end justifies the duplicity of the means; and the duplicity can be further justified by an appeal to legality: "the justice of your [Mariana's] title to him doth flourish the deceit" (4. 1. 74–75). As Isabella sums up another of the Friar's dubious policies, " 'tis a physic / That's bitter to sweet end" (4. 6. 7–8).

Even on the level of convention, for a considerable segment of Shakespeare's audience the physic must have been bitter indeed. It is no doubt for these that Prospero, in *The Tempest*, is speaking when he warns:

> If thou dost break her virgin-knot before
> All sanctimonious ceremonies may
> With full and holy rite be minist'red,
> No sweet aspersion shall the heavens let fall
> To make this contract grow; but barren Hate,
> Sour-ey'd Disdain, and Discord shall bestrew
> The union of your bed with weeds so loathly
> That you shall hate it both.   (4. 1. 15–22)

The Duke himself, to avoid the "imputation" of his own Viennese Prosperos, is quick to wed Mariana to Angelo at his earliest opportunity (5. 1. 424–427). Not only contemporary mores, however, but the plan itself presupposes the moral risk of the bed trick; for to succeed, it apparently has to be a paradigm of retribution, returning evil for evil and guilt for guilt: "So disguise shall, by th' disguised, / Pay with falsehood false exacting" (3. 2. 294–295). Claudio's pardon indeed is to be the result of a precise barter of misdeeds, "purchas'd by such sin / For which the pardoner himself is in" (4. 2. 111–112). "Claudio, whom here you have warrant to execute, is no greater forfeit to the law than Angelo who hath sentenc'd him" (4. 2. 166–168). But significantly the equation is far from precise; legalist that he is, the Duke has typically allowed a formal "measure for measure" to obscure the asymmetry in the moral substance of the bed trick: the disparity between Claudio's and Julietta's "most mutual entertainment" (1. 2. 158, 2. 3. 27) and the unrequited lust that motivates both Angelo (2. 2. 165–168) and Mariana (3. 1. 248–252).

This last point seems to be crucial. The moral failure of the Duke's indirection, like that of Hamlet's, is a failure of sympathetic imagination resulting in a concomitant failure of justice and even of utility. In this connection it is instructive to compare the Duke's bed trick with Helena's in *All's Well That Ends Well*. Like "Friar Lodowick," Helena and her confederates induce in their victim the illusion of having achieved a "sinful fact" (3. 7. 47)—an illusion that admittedly "defiles the pitchy night" (4. 4. 24), both sustaining the culprit in his sin and, since the lubricious attempt occasioned is itself real enough, actually aggravating his guilt. But there is a considerable difference between the degree of guilt in the desires indulged by the two criminal attempts. Bertram, thanks to Helena's plan, supposes himself to have seduced his mistress by playing on her greed with an offer to "buy" her chastity (3. 7. 27, 5. 3. 190). Angelo, thanks to "Friar Lodowick," supposes himself to have extorted his mistress's consent by prevailing on her love for her brother. In the one case it is a question of exploiting corruption, in the other of corrupting innocence. The former attempt, compared with the latter, would seem to be almost venial.

Moreover, it is the former trick that genuinely exemplifies the pragmatic justification of means by ends to which both tricks lay claim: "All's well that ends well. Still the fine's the crown" (4. 4. 35). For the "end" or "fine" of Helena's physic of deceit is to bring about Bertram's confession and reconcilement, and in that aim it wholly succeeds (5. 3. 309, 316–317). In the Duke's case, the physic is bitter enough, but significantly the promise of sweetness—the double benefit—is not fulfilled; Angelo successively condemns Claudio and repudiates both Isabella and Mariana. If, as "Friar Lodowick" says, the plan is supposed to keep Isabella from dishonor (3. 1. 207), its failure is rather ominous. The Duke's calculations have gone wrong (5. 1. 399–401), the end this time has not justified the means after all, and he will at last be obliged to intervene directly.

Whereas Helena and her associates know their man so well that one of them can predict his behavior "as if she sat in's heart" (4. 2. 70), the Duke's understanding of Angelo is so faint that it leads both him and his deputies in the bed trick into a moral compromise that is as grave as it is fruitless.

Betrayal of Equity: Isabella

One of these deputies is Isabella, the erstwhile pleader against judicial rigor. Like her spiritual father, the role she is originally called on to sustain could not be poorer casting. The master of policy who as Duke makes matches by irresponsible fiat, yet in his cowl feels obliged to protect Barnardine from the impersonal mandate of law, is an incongruity equaled only by the aspirant to the regula of a strict sisterhood who as a sister of flesh and blood, feels herself obliged to plead extenuating circumstances (spurious ones at that) against the strict sense of the law. Lucio's "cucullus non facit monachum" (5. 1. 263) is true in more ways than one.

Isabella's native legalism is apparent from the outset. The first thing we hear from her is a request for the strictest possible monastic rule (1. 4. 3–5). Later we find that the very law whose justice we are waiting for her to impugn is "just, but severe" (2. 2. 41). "Your brother cannot live," Angelo informs her in their second interview. "Even so," she replies with rather unsisterly resignation; "heaven keep your honor" (2. 4. 33–34).

It is, then, no secret that the cause goes against the grain; even her objection to Angelo's equation of fornication and murder discloses an ambivalence, even a serene acceptance of just that vision of an arbitrary God which Claudio yields to in despair; for she all but allows that, in God's eyes at least, Claudio *is* a murderer. " 'Tis set down so in heaven" (2. 4. 50). And the choice of words in which she declares her refusal to save Claudio by forfeiting her honor (defensible in contemporary Christian terms as the refusal may be in itself) is tainted by the same icy formalism. All that she actually says is: "More than our brother is our chastity" (2. 4. 185), words that mean—not, as we might expect, the superiority of a sinless

heavenly life, her brother's as well as her own, to an earthly life of
sin for either—but instead the superiority of an abstract principle
(chastity) to a human being (Claudio). Isabella's most natural
appeal, then, is not to conscience but to law: "I had rather my brother
died by the law than my son should be unlawfully born" (3. 1. 194–
196). Isabella's legalism in this and other speeches does not consist
merely, as some critics have suggested, in discounting the spirit of
the law in favor of the letter.[35] There can hardly be a refuge in the
"spirit" of a law whose letter is the endorsement of a draconian
penalty. The recourse that we need, and that is denied us by the
legalism of Angelo and Isabella, is not the intent of the lawmaker
but the discretion of the judge. And the object of discretion that
has been so troublingly discounted in favor of the law, both letter
and spirit, is intrinsic value in its forensic role as equity. Indeed, so
loose is the hold of "lawful mercy" (2. 4. 112) on Isabella's allegiance that the spectacle of her brother's frailty in the face of death
provokes merciless denunciation, of Claudio and of mercy itself:

> Thy sin's not accidental but a trade;
> Mercy to thee would prove itself a bawd;
> 'Tis best that thou diest quickly.
>
> (3. 1. 149–151)

As with the Duke, the heart of Isabella's failure or incapacity to
exercise a higher justice is her failure or incapacity to make contact
with a mind other than her own.

As we have seen, Isabella's image of mercy, the mitigating principle, as a bawd is in effect a favorite of both the cynics and legalists
of Vienna. It is what inspires Lucio to give the slatternly Mistress
Overdone the nickname of "Madam Mitigation" (1. 2. 45–46). Of
course, in view of Isabella's inveterate legalism it is not after all so
very remarkable that she is easily brought to repudiate the figurative
Madam Mitigation. What is truly surprising is how easily she is
persuaded to play the lady herself and (in the grand tradition of go-
betweens) to go over all the details with a bona fide client (4. 1. 55–
56, 66–67).[36] "I have spirit," she assures "Friar Lodowick," "to
do anything that appears not foul in the truth of my spirit" (3. 1.

212–214). This is, of course, a noble assertion of moral autonomy. But it is important to see that Isabella's aversion to the jurisprudence of reason or conscience necessarily requires her to censor the truth of her spirit; for "Friar Lodowick" does not in fact put Isabella's conscience to sleep. Long after their initial talk she can still have misgivings: "To speak so indirectly I am loath. / I would say the truth" (4. 6. 1–2). The conscience is still awake despite the Duke; Isabella puts it to sleep *for* him, and with his own style of maxim: " 'tis a physic that's bitter to sweet end." Like her Machiavellian confessor, who always exploits a convenient substitute to do the dirty work—Angelo for himself, Ragozine's head (4. 3. 80) for Claudio's, his mercy deputies against his law deputies—Isabel in turn gets a Mariana to assume the dubious *cosa di carico* of the bed trick.

Ironically, her debut as frank antagonist of equity comes precisely at the moment when she is called on once again to "play with reason and discourse" (1. 2. 190), this time (the crowning touch) on behalf of Angelo. On the surface, her intercession looks like a new growth of charity. The news of Angelo's double-doublecross had revealed her at her worst, as a foiled conspirator—"O I will to him and pluck out his eyes" (4. 3. 124)—but now we find her defending the extortionist and murderer as eloquently as she had his victim. The rub is that her defense itself is the purest legalism. Let us examine the brief.

Isabella first speaks as a character witness; the Duke is urged to consider Angelo's saving grace, a Wildean ability to resist everything but temptation:

> I partly think
> A due sincerity govern'd his deeds,
> Till he did look on me.   (5. 1. 450–452)

As we proceed, it becomes clear that Isabella has embraced, not only the art of the legal quibble, but the legalist definition of justice as well. "My brother had but justice," she explains, "in that he did the thing for which he died" (ll. 453–454). Needless to say, the entire point of equitable jurisprudence on this score is that the nature of the guilt, and not the bare fact, is what justifies a particular punishment. But Isabella has never unequivocally called for equity, and her final plea for a verdict of not guilty is in effect a total conversion to an uncompromising positivism.

Angelo, she reminds us, only *thought* he was dishonoring her; since, unlike Claudio's liaison with Julietta, his attempt did not succeed, he is not in law a criminal:

> For Angelo,
> His act did not o'ertake his bad intent,
> And must be buried but as an intent
> That perish'd by the way. Thoughts are no subjects;
> Intents, but merely thoughts. (ll. 455–459)

Punishment in common law, as we have observed, does not aim at the correction of criminality; for the concept of correction (to the common lawyer) is a threat to freedom of conscience ("cogitationis poenam nemo meretur," as Coke says).[37] Punishment is public and external, a simple dynamics of action and reaction; but an abortive attempt, not being an action, can hardly warrant a legal reaction. This antiquated jurisprudence, which in its fear for the mind's privacy equates failure with inaction, is precisely what criminal equity was fighting to abolish in Shakespeare's England.[38] In Shakespeare's Vienna, however, the fight, if there is any, is half-hearted, and the leader has now clearly defected: Claudio in what ought to have been Isabella's previous plea was guilty, but not of a capital offense; Angelo in her current one is "innocent," but only on a point of law. And the Duke could just as well be speaking for the tradition of equity in his terse response to all this: "Your suit's unprofitable."[39]

Betrayal of Equity: The Duke's Amnesty

Isabella's brief, with its strange union of moral laxity and meticulous legalism, may stand as an emblem of what goes on throughout much of the play. For moral reason might have served as a kind of mean between these extremes of laxity and legalism. In its absence, or in the absence of intrinsic value itself, man is confronted, like Guyon without the Palmer, with a merciless Hobson's choice: anarchy or despotism, Pompey's trade or Abhorson's, Isabella's pliant legalism or Angelo's inflexible kind. If value is a mere name for a fiat of will or for a universal status quo, then man is at the "mercy" of that terrible God whose image, as we have seen, Claudio has glimpsed in his judge. And if reason is a mere name for the nauseous restraints imposed by flesh on the scope of appetite, then moral choice is a groping and ignoble mechanism such as Claudio sees in the nature of man:

> As surfeit is the father of much fast,
> So every scope by the immoderate use
> Turns to restraint. Our natures do pursue,
> Like rats that ravin down their proper bane,
> A thirsty evil; and when we drink, we die.
>
> (1. 2. 130–134)

Without a true mean, then, human nature is abandoned to an endless oscillation between extremes of self-indulgence and self-denial, scope and restraint. For lack of authentic mercy, we must settle for Angelo's venality,

>   a restraint
> [Though] all the world's vastidity you had,
> To a determin'd scope.   (3. 1. 68–70)

And for lack of justice (which in equity is the same thing) we must settle for Angelo's law. "Now good my lord, give me the scope of justice," he had asked the Duke. But Viennese justice is restraint and not scope. After his adventure with licence, Angelo has nothing to turn to but legalism. "When I, that censure him, do so offend," he had promised, "let mine own judgement pattern out my death" (2. 1. 29–30); now he keeps his promise: "I crave death more willingly than mercy" (5. 1. 481).[40]

Law in Vienna is the cenotaph of reason. And mercy is an amphibious thing captured faithfully enough by the Duke's parting attempts at definition—first a legal being whose native idiom is *lex talionis:*

> The very mercy of the law cries out
> Most audible, even from his proper tongue,
> 'An Angelo for Claudio, death for death!'
> Haste still pays haste, and leisure answers leisure;
> Like doth quit like, and *measure* still *for measure*.
>   (5. 1. 412–416)

And finally an indulgent creature who speaks the language of will: "Well, Angelo, your evil quits you well. . . . I find an apt remission in myself" (5. 1. 501, 503). It is clear that "apt remission" is a soubriquet of Madam Mitigation, and that the mercy for which Isabel was suing even at the outset was not, after all, Spenser's rule of equity

>   to measure out along,
>   According to the line of conscience,
>   When so it needs with rigor to dispense,

not that judicial bond by which it is always "better to reforme, then to cut off, the ill,"[41] but rather a burlesque of divine mercy as Claudio has portrayed it, resembling it not in doing good but only in a willful aloofness from the course of justice:[42]

>   how would you be,
>   If He, which is the top of judgement, should
>   But judge you as you are?   (2. 2. 75–77)

For while it is clear enough, as an earlier Shakespearean heroine puts it, that "in the course of justice none of us / Should see salvation,"[43] it is equally clear that the remission of sin as an act of salvation is not in the gift of a mortal judge, and that remission as a mortal judge may command it is far from a salvation. In the tradition of Christian equity, at any rate, refusal to correct offenders is simply refusal to be one's brother's keeper. To grant mercy in this sense is just such a hollow charade of authority as Isabella so triumphantly derides:

>   But man, proud man,
>   Dress'd in a little brief authority,

Most ignorant of what he's most assur'd,
His glassy essence, like an angry ape,
Plays such fantastic tricks before high heaven
As makes the angels weep; who, with our spleens,
Would all themselves laugh mortal.[44]

(2. 2. 117–123)

And it is this hollow mercy, aping the fiat of an Augustinian God, that Vincentio, with the aid of his bride-to-be, confers as a benefit on Mariana and her husband.

The Viennese law against fornication, one supposes, has been invented by the great comedian for its blatant absurdity. But as it turns out no one in the play's society sees the possibility of laughing law out of countenance but those few cynics or clowns who, like Lucio and Pompey, acknowledge no principles of moral choice that could replace it. This second and overarching absurdity—the persistent lack of a genuine corrective to legalism, autocracy, or moral anarchy—is bound to have a sobering effect on the onlooker in proportion as the imaginary community has for the time being supplanted his own. In effect he has become a minority of one in favor of a view he would take as self-evident but for the fact that a majority consisting of intelligent and eloquent men and women plainly disagree. Is it possible that the perception of moral value, the data of conscience, are simply habits of preference imposed by one's place and time? "What goodnesse is that, which but yesterday I saw in credit and esteeme, and that by the crossing of a River"—or by a visit to Vienna, shall we say—"is made a crime?"[45] Is the sense of absurdity itself a mere automatic response, and our recourse to it in such cases as Claudio's sentence or Angelo's pardon a kind of delusion? A Feste to the onlooker's Malvolio, the playwright forces us to insist on our reason a touch too shrilly: "I am not mad, Sir Topas. I say to you, this house is dark."

The darkness of Shakespeare's Vienna, as we have noted, seems to extend to the possibility of insight into other minds, a judicial function that turns out to be as much a failure as the rational criticism it ideally supplements. For it fails not only the callow judge being tested but the Olympian judge doing the testing, and the latter failure is if anything the more sordid, embodied as it is in the multiple corruptions of the ill-fated bed trick. Like Hamlet's Mousetrap the Duke's creation of a deputy was designed to help him test "what our seemers be" (1. 3. 54). Like Hamlet's, the test discloses, among other things, the limited vision of the tester.

Measure for Measure, it would seem, ends in a series of absurdities, as a comedy is well within its rights to do. It might be thought, perhaps, that the absurdities are rather tragic, but the description would mislead; for great tragedies, Shakespeare's included, are celebrations of justice and moral choice, whereas our play, though it loves these fine things after its fashion, is not even sure it knows what they look like. And in this embarrassing perplexity, it is rather like its one lyric. "Take, O, take those lips away," the disillusioned lover cries in the song at the moated grange—and yet adds with a shudder of ambivalence: "But my kisses bring again, bring again" (4. 1. 1, 5).

CHAPTER FOUR

King Lear *and the Meaning of Chaos*

THE RESULT for the audience of Hamlet's attempt to set right a time out of joint was twofold and ambivalent: a gloomy sense that the Prince's initial skepticism about the possibility of knowing other minds is, however intermittent and one-sided, only too likely to be right, and at the same time a consolatory sense that his submission to an ethic of will and revenge, however resolute and at the end even pious, is surely wrong. *Measure for Measure* seems to deny us even this latter consolation, putting us squarely in the midst of a moral chaos not very hospitable to convictions about "right reason" or "equity." Before considering how if at all *King Lear* manages to deal with these negations, it will be useful to return briefly to the parallel dilemma in *Troilus and Cressida*, a play whose relevance to Hamlet's notion of honor we have already considered.

In debating the advisability of returning Helen to the besieging Greeks, Hector and Troilus emerge as advocates of two conflicting views of moral choice. For Troilus, to deliberate at all is simply to ignore the only guide to responsibility on which the life of honor can rely—an absolute fidelity to previous decision. Once a commitment has been undertaken, or a precedent fixed, there is no excuse but cowardice for pausing to reflect on its intrinsic merits:

> Manhood and honour
> Should have [hare] hearts, would they but fat their thoughts
> With this cramm'd reason. Reason and respect
> Makes livers pale and lustihood deject.
>
> (2. 2. 47–50)

"What's aught but as 'tis valued?" he demands characteristically. Value (the value of human life included) is simply the reflection of a fluctuating market, not an appropriate object of rational estimate.

Hector meanwhile contends that this reduction of choice to a fanatic rigidity, of moral intelligence to blind logic, is not freedom but a disease of the will:

> the will dotes that is inclineable
> To what infectiously itself affects,
> Without some image of th' affected merit.
> (ll. 58–60)

> The reasons you allege do more conduce
> To the hot passion of distemp'red blood
> Than to make up a free determination
> 'Twixt right and wrong.   (ll. 168–171)

> Thus to persist
> In doing wrong extenuates not wrong,
> But makes it much more heavy.
> (ll. 186–188)

I think it would be fair to say that the issue between our two Elizabethan intellectuals ultimately resolves itself into a question of whether human choice has rational motives at all. Troilus is essentially arguing that there are no such data as moral facts to start with, that the intellectual faculty to which Hector appeals amounts to a talent for temporizing. What Troilus offers us by way of antidote is, in effect, an individualistic version of Angelo's legalism. The moral umpire for Troilus is one's own past, for, to be honorable, the will must never repeal its own legislation. In Hector's view, of course, all this is a mere euphemism for obstinacy; for there are indeed moral facts, and it is our duty to consider them:

> But value dwells not in particular will;
> It holds his estimate and dignity
> As well wherein 'tis precious of itself
> As in the prizer.   (ll. 53–56)

But in the bitter end the partisans of will prevail by default against those of intelligence. Hector eventually backs down by making a curious and sordid distinction between the "way of truth," which

he has been defending, and that of "resolution" (2. 2. 189–191),
and gaily proceeds to choose "resolution."

Now the standard rebuttal to such negation available to Elizabethan
conservatism is, of course, duly supplied by Shakespeare in Ulysses'
oration on degree in *Troilus and Cressida*, a speech that identifies the
good with the causal design of creation, the great principle of hierarchy. But this identification of good with order is, as I shall try to
show, clearly no answer to the kind of question our two Elizabethan
or Jacobean *esprits forts* are really posing. Let us briefly remind
ourselves of the position.

Ulysses' defense of the objectivity of natural law can be summed
up in two celebrated scholastic tags. One defines good as the motive
of appetite par excellence (*bonum proprie motivum appetitus*). The
good of a thing is what it desires by nature, its evil is nonconformity,
the perversion of natural desire. But what is "natural"? In the
celestial realm, where all movements are simple and regular, this
formula is charmingly straightforward; it is comparatively easy to
define the natural desire of the intelligences. But what of the world
beneath the moon, the world especially of human diversity, cultural
and historical? The orthodox criterion here is some kind of statistical
normality or consensus. "Choice being mutual act of all our souls,"
Nestor urges, "Makes merit her election" (1. 3. 348–349). But
for the age of Montaigne and the Donne of *Biathanatos*, normality
will not do. Fresh news of the anthropophagi has arrived by sea.
And a reading man need not depend on the gossip of maritime
topers: "By a law of Venice . . . a son shall redeem himself from
banishment by killing his father being also banished. And we read of
another state (and laws of civil commonwealths may not easily be
pronounced to be against nature) where when fathers came to be of
an unprofitable and useless age, the sons must beat them to death with
clubs: and of another where all persons above seventy years were
despatched."[1] In a world of vast personal and cultural variety, of
incessant change and perilous temptations, it is not at all clear that
the results of a universal referendum would be heartening to any
orthodoxy, whether Christian or cannibal.

But the orthodox Christian custodians of juridical equity, as we

have noted in connection with *Measure for Measure*, could not accept
the statistical definition if they would. Assume that right is merely
whatever happens as a general rule and wrong a departure from the
rule, and what becomes of all the departures from rule that turn out
in defiance of this equation to be right all the same? It is idle to ask:
right by what measure? for the very possibility of judging one thing
by another (as the presence of fire by that of smoke, or rightness by
a rule) may sometimes depend on the possibility of observing oc-
currences of both and finding them concomitant. In the case of rightness and its supposed rules or measures, the matching is not guaranteed by convention and is clearly imperfect. Experience tells us that
all ethical principles have exceptions, and it is the duty of the King's
Conscience to find them out.

The second definition Ulysses presupposes is the ancient tautology
that good is interchangeable with fullness of being (*bonum con-
vertitur cum ente*). To have full being is to have a fully determinate
nature or form; and the good of anything is simply its natural form,
its evil, a form that is unnatural to it (*debita forma, indebita forma*).
Manifestations that are familiarly held to be intrinsically evil, like
those of a distinctive pain or a diagnosable disease, on this definition
must be written off as either intrinsically good or, in some unspecified
sense,[2] lacking in a determinate nature. But the most embarrassing
difficulty of the definition is that to be good, on its terms, is not to
have any form at random, but to have one's own "natural" form. And
it sooner or later becomes uncomfortably plain that "natural" is
simply another way of saying "good."[3]

The point is that the Scholastic-Aristotelian formula of the good
as the natural, the byword of Anglican humanism, says precisely nothing. It is at best a mere shorthand for a morally neutral induction, at
worst a bare tautology. The induction is morally neutral because
what all things strive for is not necessarily good. The tautology is no
more than a tautology because to define "good" as "natural" is as
uninformative as to define "good" as "good." Against the likes of
a Troilus or an Edmund, Ulysses' philosophy of nature is useless, not
only because a voluntarist like Edmund can appeal to his own direct
observations of human nature and find only a wilderness of idiosyn-

crasy, but also because Ulysses, too, in identifying good with degree, makes distinctions of value merely de facto and extrinsic. This weakness is betrayed by his illustrative comparison of the sun's momentum to the uncontrolled royal prerogative or *non obstante*: "the commandment of a king. / Sans check to good and bad" (*Tro.* 1. 3. 93–94). The rub is in the last phrase. What if the "degree" and "place" Ulysses equates with dignity (l. 86) happen to be morally indifferent? That they amount to some sort of an order is not in itself a guarantee of value. Henry V disparages "ceremony," we may recall, precisely by reducing it to nothing but "place" and "degree" (*H5* 4. 1. 263). Degree, to be sure, can mean gradation in intrinsic rather than merely conventional value, and the danger of degree's being "vizarded" in this sense (*Tro.* 1. 3. 83), dire as it is, is simply that "right and wrong . . . should lose their names" (ll. 116–118)—that the distinction should cease to be honored. It is only if the distinction is purely nominal that right and wrong in a state of anarchy would lose not only their names but their natures as well. But Ulysses flirts with this dreary possibility when he says that in such a state "force should be right" (l. 116) and that then "everything includes itself in power, / Power into will, will into appetite" (ll. 119–120). Anarchy that robs us of order is terrible enough. Anarchy that exposes order too as absurd is beyond terror.

I should like to suggest that in *King Lear* Shakespeare calmly searches the chaos that Ulysses glanced at with a shudder, the chaos that Hamlet's world seems to reject, and to which the world of Vincentio and Isabella grinningly surrenders. The autonomy and irreducibility of moral qualities will be verified much in the spirit of Glaucon's *Gedankenexperiment* in the *Republic:* we shall in imagination abolish all mere insignia of justice, human dignity, and love; abolish the divine, the civil, and the psychological gendarmerie behind justice, the power and trappings of dignity, the mere self-interest in love; and then see whether the supposedly intrinsic values persist. Socrates' reply to Glaucon was an allegory of the just man writ large. Shakespeare's to Ulysses—more in keeping with the empirical spirit of his time, perhaps—is actually to perform Ulysses' implied experiment. The poetic laboratory is the world of Lear, the string untuned—a world that provides a wealth of specious evidence that love and loyalty lose their value with the vanishing of order: "Love cools, friendship falls off, brothers divide: in cities, mutinies; in countries, discord; in palaces, treason; and the bond crack'd 'twixt son and father" (1. 2. 116–118). Several of Lear's countrymen, moreover, will be only too eager to reduce conscience to the fear of retribution:

> 2. SERV. I'll never care what wickedness I do,
>   If this man come to good.
> 3. SERV.   If she live long,
>   And in the end meet the old course of death,
>   Women will all turn monsters.
>
> (3. 7. 99–102)
>
> ALBANY. If that the heavens do not their visible spirits
>   Send quickly down to tame these vile offences,
>   It will come,
>   Humanity must perforce prey on itself,
>   Like monsters of the deep.[4]   (4. 2. 46–50)

But before entering the world of *King Lear* ourselves, let us keep in mind the important fact that what a Pelagian Ulysses may have thought mere hypothetical chaos would be instantly recognizable to Protestant Spenser and Catholic Ronsard alike as none other than the fallen world in which we live:

> For that which all men then did vertue call
> Is now cald vice, and that which vice was hight
> Is now hight vertue, and so vs'd of all;
> Right now is wrong, and wrong that was is right,
> As all things else in time are changed quite. . . .
>
> Un même fait produit le blâme et la louange,
> Et ce qui est vertu semble à l'autre péché.[5]

King Lear begins with two royal acts that may be described as redistributions of wealth. The first is the partition of Britain, and what is principally dwelt on in this connection, for purposes of irony that will, I hope, become clearer as we proceed, is Lear's scrupulous impartiality in dividing the realm between two men who evidently do not share equally in his regard: "It appears not which of the Dukes he values most," Gloucester whispers to Kent for the audience's benefit.[6] With these words of praise ringing in our ears we pass to the principal symbolic business of the scene, Lear's celebrated impromptu catechism:

> Which of you shall we say doth love us most,
> That we our largest bounty may extend
> Where nature doth with merit challenge?
>
> (I. I. 52–54)

The love-auction, granted, is to be merely a ceremonial distribution of wealth, but for that very reason it is undilutedly symbolic, and in fact close to the heart of the poet's theme. Lear inaugurates a competition designed to prove the true merit and what he calls the nature of each of his daughters. But for the King, his daughters' essence mightily resembles an accident; verbal cash is to be the criterion of personal dignity. The meaning of the test strikes Regan immediately: "I am made," she begins, "of that self metal as my sister, / And prize me at her worth" (ll. 71–72). Then she offers in corroboration her own bid of pretended love.

Lear's invitation to eulogy, as the remainder of the scene is devoted to explaining, involves more than a crotchet of senile vanity. It is in fact rooted in the systematic confusion of conventional or utilitarian values and permanent ones. From the strictly economic point of view Lear is declaring a real estate auction in which land will be parceled out to the most lavish bid of affection. Love will be no longer an end in itself, but only a means to a material end, a kind of illegal tender: the price of land. Lear, in short, is a cousin to Wilde's cynic, an economic reductivist who knows the price of everything— and has no notion of value at all. But if love, like Troilus's or Hamlet's "honor," is exclusively a function of economic value, it is only too easily alienated. It is a currency or commodity, subject to the accidents of supply and demand.

As we have seen, not only love but human dignity as well is being debased in Lear's auction. When Cordelia refuses to try to outbid her sisters, her own exchange rate too, and not her value, proves to have been the real object of Lear's curiosity:

> Right noble Burgundy,
> When she was dear to us, we did hold her so;
> But now her price is fall'n.
>
> (1. 1. 198–200)

Lear is not punning on the two meanings of "dear," he is virtually equating them. Since market value depends on the vagaries of a collective will, *homo economicus* must reject Cordelia on essentially the same terms as Troilus, a fellow voluntarist, upholds the cause of Helen: "What's aught but as 'tis valued?"

Shakespeare takes elaborate verbal and dramatic pains to keep this issue at stage center by confronting Burgundy, a surrogate of Lear, with a trenchant antagonist. France plays the Hector of the scene to Burgundy's Troilus. For the former, Cordelia disinherited becomes a symbol of the crucial difference between the valuable and the merely valued: "most rich being poor, / Most choice forsaken, and most lov'd despis'd" (ll. 253–254) are not paradoxes or antinomies, but vital distinctions. Cordelia can be at once "unpriz'd" and "precious" for France precisely because the two things are not one. "Love's not love," as France urges, "When it is mingl'd with regards that stands / Aloof from th' entire point." Indeed, the vindication of the distinctions France is fighting to uphold is, I shall argue, quite literally the "entire point" of the play.[7]

The paradigm of right action for Lear, like that of value, is a primitive exchange in kind—good for good and evil for evil: its two cardinal manifestations are gratitude and revenge, and these are the only sanctions he has at his disposal to validate his claim to respect when respect, once denied him, is (on his market premises) no longer merited. The difficulty with gratitude is not, of course, that he should demand it in return for rearing his daughters. Nor is there a fallacy of some kind, as Professor Heilman oddly suggests, in Lear's appeal to the binding force of contract.[8] The false note is the narrowness with which Lear defines filial impiety as the failure to reciprocate a benefit, as if paternal love were a kind of payment on old age insurance; the King has simply taken the short step from seeing the protestation of love as money to seeing love as interest. The obverse of this ethic of barter is Lear's grotesque tribute to Regan's "kindness" on his behalf:

> I have another daughter,
> Who, I am sure, is kind and comfortable.
> When she shall hear this of thee, with her nails
> She'll flay thy wolvish visage.
>
> (1. 4. 327–330)

What "comforts" Lear in Regan's "kindness" is that her taloned loyalty comes with what he thinks the standard equipment.

We began our discussion of the Love Auction by noting that Lear intends it as a test of his daughters' "nature" (1. 1. 54). Even more disastrously than was the case with Hamlet and Duke Vincentio, this effort to see into others' minds turns out to be a failure. But here as in the other cases the test manages at the same time to disclose to *us* the rooted incapacity for such efforts of the tester himself. Though Lear will suppose himself to be radically altering Cordelia's circumstances by holding her henceforth "a stranger to my heart and me" (1. 1. 117), it is plain enough that this condition of estrangement is nothing new either to her sisters or to herself. Indeed, if Lear seems *almost* not to know the first thing about his daughters (he has, after all, reserved his most "opulent" gift for the best of them), it is also true that, old egoist that he is, "he hath ever but slenderly known himself" (1. 1. 296–297). In the prevailing Renaissance view, as we observed, selves are so hard to know that we know them little better when they are our own. Lear's is an acute case of this endemic illness.

The King's weaknesses, then, like those of Hamlet and the Duke, are of two kinds. He has no clear notion of the existence of intrinsic moral criteria, and he is unable to penetrate to selves, whether others' or his own. And once again the two difficulties admit of a unitary solution if they admit of any at all. The quest for a knowledge of the good and the quest for a knowledge of selves converge on the quest for Cordelia. Both enterprises, however, begin with the King's extended meditation—or mad revery—on justice.

The meditation begins as soon as the old King is forced to come to terms with the amoral cruelty, the "eyelessness" (3. 1. 8), of the physical universe into which he has been banished by his daughters. To be sure, he introduces his debate with the storm by exonerating his celestial tormentors on the strange grounds that he has never done them any favors and hence can expect no quarter:

> I tax not you, you elements, with unkindness;
> I never gave you kingdom, call'd you children;
> You owe me no subscription. Then let fall
> Your horrible pleasure!

Clearly the ethic of *do ut des* again. But the significant thing about this speech is that Lear abruptly changes his mind in mid-career. The submissiveness gives way to the conviction that not he but the elements and their high engenderers are the true slaves. Cruelty is despicable even where it is not a response to a benefit: the ethic of *do ut des* rejected. Let us note the transition:

> Here I stand your slave,
> A poor, infirm, weak, and despis'd old man;
> *But yet*—I call *you* servile ministers,
> That will with two pernicious daughters join
> Your high-engender'd battles 'gainst a head
> So old and white as this. Oh! Oh! 'tis foul!
> (3. 2. 19–24, italics added)

Lear verges on a blasphemous metaphor here, for the storm, with its high engenderers, is not his daughters' only servile minister. The other, and more obvious one, is Oswald, the man with a duty to vice, as Edgar describes him. The cosmic lackey and the human are colleagues after all, and Lear's search for intrinsic value begins with the terrible intimation of an amoral surd, neither good nor evil, an Oswald, in the heart of man and in the scheme of things. This absolute moral indifference is the nature Edmund worships. Though not strictly part of Lear's meditation, his ubiquitous presence continually reminds us of the view that Lear has yet to repudiate. Edmund has been accused of an atavistic theory, or even ideal, of human nature; but the truth seems to be that he follows his own *naturel*, as Montaigne calls it, without fathering it upon the race, and certainly without recommending it to anyone. For Edmund the law of nations—"the curiosity of nations," he calls it—is a social artifice superimposed on a nature that is not essentially lustful or predatory but essentially faceless. This nature, he realizes, expresses itself in Edgars as well as Edmunds; not that it "should" do either, but that it does. That the "should" has a meaning other than meddling in one's affairs—"curiosity"—he refuses to acknowledge. In the end his very caprice, like weather, betrays him into a kind of fair play. This nuance is finely dramatized in the sequence in which Edmund courageously refuses to avail himself of a chivalric technicality:

> EDMUND. What safe and nicely I might well delay
> By rule of knighthood, I disdain and spurn. . . .
> GONERIL.   This is [mere] practice, Gloucester.
> By th' law of war thou wast not bound to answer
> An unknown opposite.   (5. 3. 144–153)

A few lines further on, Goneril proudly confesses to Albany: "the laws are mine, not thine: who can arraign me for't?" (l. 158). Illegitimate Edmund thinks so little of law that he does not think to take charge of it in this way.

The most insistent doubt, then, that Lear raises in his meditation on justice concerns, not divine or elemental nature, but human. It is the very doubt Edmund rejoices in as a liberating truth. If, as Edmund assumes and Lear comes to suspect, man's dignity is a persona indeed, a mask over a void, then nakedness, physical and spiritual, will disclose the void; the dispossessed, madman or beggar, will reveal the essential cheapness beneath: "Allow not nature more than nature needs, / Man's life is cheap as beast's" (2. 4. 269–270). The well-known irony of the pantomime divestiture Lear performs in the course of the play is that man's nakedness, his animal and sensual being, is itself a kind of clothing. Old age and poverty, madness and absurdity are mere costumes for Lear's companions in the storm. And by implication Lear's own old age, madness, and poverty are no closer to the truth about the King than the masquerades of Edgar, Kent, and the Fool. These little seeming substances, fragments of an atomized society, as they huddle together in the hovel or stumble toward the farmhouse in the downpour, are brightly etched as the saints of a holy community united in concern for Lear. Humanity, in them at least, obstinately persists in being the wearer and not the garment. Clothing, not nakedness, symbolizes concupiscence in the play—the work of a tailor in which nature disclaims. Trousers are postlapsarian—the great-great-grandsons of the fig leaf.

Lear's own initial view is the reverse of this: nakedness does more than make men ridiculous, it cancels their humanity.[9] This is essentially the view that "Friar Lodowick" in *Measure for Measure* tries with some initial success to urge on Claudio. For as the "Friar" proceeds with his homily on man's wretchedness it is increasingly clear that the "thou" of his contemptuous apostrophe is not man's life, but man:

> Thou art not noble;
> For all the accommodations that thou bear'st
> Are nurs'd by baseness. Thou'rt by no means valiant;
> For thou dost fear the soft and tender fork
> Of a poor worm. Thy best of rest is sleep,
> And that thou oft provok'st; yet grossly fear'st
> Thy death, which is no more. Thou art not thyself;
> For thou exist'st on many a thousand grains
> That issue out of dust. Happy thou art not;
> For what thou hast not, still thou striv'st to get,
> And what thou hast, forget'st. Thou art not certain,
> For thy complexion shifts to strange effects
> After the moon.   (3. 1. 13–25)

The similarity of the "Friar's" language and intent to Lear's is striking but not surprising. What is at stake in both plays, after all, is the intelligibility of claims that are integral to that of the dignity of man. In the present play, however, the "bare fork'd animal" is none other than Edgar, so that the discourse on "lendings" (3. 4. 114) is undermined from the outset. Indeed, a little before Lear first sets eyes on Tom o' Bedlam, "loop'd and window'd raggedness" (3. 4. 31) has already begun to assert an increasingly strong claim of kinship and compassion on Lear; an intimation—less perhaps for his benefit than for ours—that even an unaccommodated man's life is not cheap.

The King's last official act on retiring was a ritual distribution of wealth based on a mistaken notion of merit. Standing before the hovel on the heath, Lear demands a redistribution in accord with common humanity and in the name of divine justice:

> Take physic, pomp;
> Expose thyself to feel what wretches feel,
> That thou mayst shake the superflux to them,
> And show the heavens more just.
>
> (3. 4. 33–36)

Up to this point the King has been clear enough about the conditions physically necessary to human life but has demonstrated only the flimsiest notion of the conditions morally sufficient to it—human rights, as we should say. Anything above the level of bare survival, from self-respect to conspicuous waste, from the basest beggar's poorest thing to a royal entourage, he has reckoned a form of excess, desirable but undeserved. Moreover, without such excess, he tells Regan (2. 4. 267–270), man's life is inherently as cheap as beast's. But according to the gospel of the soliloquy on the heath, superfluity must be abolished in favor of a just sufficiency to which every life is entitled. Lear has not quite been converted to a conviction of the elementary dignity of human life, but his intuition of its inherent rights belies the Plinian rhetoric about unaccommodated man.[10]

This incipient affirmation is apt to be misunderstood. There is, as I shall try to argue in detail at a later stage, no sign of optimism in *King Lear*, least of all about men's capacity for moral perception and decency. The assumed ground of the human claim to respect and care seems, instead, to be quite simply the human capacity for joy and suffering. Indeed, at least at one point, awareness by itself acquires inherent rights for the agonists of the play. In Gloucester's famous lines (4. 1. 38–39), the anguish and dismemberment of man at the hands of the gods are assumed to be a cosmic atrocity; but so, if to a lesser degree, are the anguish and dismemberment of flies at the hands of wanton boys. Isabella, in *Measure for Measure*, seconds "Friar Lodowick's" belittlement of human life by attempting to argue that whatever the size of the victim, dying is not very painful:

> The sense of death is most in apprehension;
> And the poor beetle that we tread upon
> In corporal sufferance finds a pang as great
> As when a giant dies.   (3. 1. 78–81)

The intended argument is typical of a legalist not very proficient in the exercise of the sympathetic imagination, but the language is strangely, perhaps ironically, subversive of the intent: that the beetle's pang is as great as the giant's is rather less likely on the face of it to mean that the giant's pang is insectival than that the beetle's is gigantic. Gloucester's lines on boys and flies and, I would argue, the play of which they are a part dismiss Isabella's conclusion, in effect, by taking her statement at its word.

Lear's obsessive concern throughout his quest, however, is not so much with social as with criminal justice. The obsession has reached the surface before, but emerges with particular clarity in the phantasy trial over which he presides in his madness, and in which his colleagues of the King's Bench are none other than the naked maskers —old soldier, mad beggar, and fool. Both categories of judicial function are invoked:

> Thou robed man of justice, take thy place;
> And thou, his yoke-fellow of equity,
> Bench by his side.   (3. 6. 38–40)

Indeed, one might suppose that, unlike the pattern in *Measure for Measure*, the appeal to equity gradually supersedes or transforms the demand for justice. In an earlier scene we had the following:

> Hide thee, thou bloody hand;
> Thou perjur'd, and thou simular of virtue
> That art incestuous!   (3. 2. 53–55)

The "bloody hand" then was that of the criminal. At the trial convened by Lear, it is that of the penal officer: "Thou rascal beadle, hold thy bloody hand! / Why dost thou lash that whore? Strip thy own back!" (4. 6. 164–165).

The point here, however, is in fact not an unqualified challenge to the legalistic model of retributive justice. Such a challenge will come, but not yet, and not spontaneously or unequivocally from Lear himself. The rebuke to the beadle is not only a reflection on the unseemliness of sin flaying sin (and even in that case it would not be a categorical attack on the flaying); it is also part of a despairing sarcasm in the face of powerlessness to enforce the bloody retribution for which Lear yearns and raves as for a lost manhood. In that context the speech reflects very much the same moral orientation as his impotent threat:

> I will have such revenges on you both
> That all the world shall—I will do such things,—
> What they are, yet I know not; but they shall be
> The terrors of the earth. (2. 4. 282–285)

The demand for a stop to weeping, to be sure, is couched as a travesty of the hard saying that he alone who is without sin may cast the first stone. But the travesty rather stresses than otherwise the underlying tone of demoralization, for the Gospel text was never construed as an argument for universal amnesty: "None does offend, none, I say, none; I'll able 'em" (4. 6. 172). Indeed, interpreted ironically, Lear seems in act 4, scene 6 to share with Angelo and Othello the kind of mentality by whose lights fornicators and adulterers deserve to be visited with death (4. 6. 113). Offenders like these are being bitterly granted a royal dispensation, in short, largely because in the King's view they have it already: "To't, luxury, pell-mell! for I lack soldiers" (4. 6. 119). If Lear had his soldiers, mercy would be in somewhat shorter supply. Even his compassionate

disgression on the human predicament—"thou must be patient, we
came crying hither"—fails to quench the thirst for blood that wells
up to cut it short:

> It were a delicate stratagem, to shoe
> A troop of horse with felt. I'll put 't in proof;
> And when I have stol'n upon these son-in-laws,
> Then, kill, kill, kill, kill, kill, kill!
>
> (ll. 188–191)

The old King's progress, then, what there is of it, is far from steady.
We are at best being shown a dim corner yet to be fully illuminated.

The pattern, then, is of intuitions that, however compelling to
the audience, are neutralized for the hero by chaos—by the confusion
of the storm within and without. In reproaching the elements, for
example, Lear discovers in himself inherent rights of which it seems
he cannot, after all, have been divested along with the trappings of
power; much as Kent has already pointed out to Lear the latter's
possession of an inalienable "authority" (1. 4. 32). But at the same
time the storm has brought home to Lear the possibility that brute
nature, "servile" to human malice, pays no deference to such things
as rights; a view by which men like Edmund, at least, believe
themselves justified in concluding that no such things as rights
exist. Again, before the hovel in the rain, the inherent rights Lear
has discovered in himself assume for him the status of a general
human birthright—but a moment later, inside the hovel, he seems
to find in unaccommodated man a want of any such dignity as
might form the ground of such a birthright. Or, finally, Lear calls
for a halt to penal cruelty, but in part because he lacks the power
to use it himself (4. 6. 119, 187–191). Lear's intuitions come paired
with negations.

On the other hand, the nay in each case is at cross purposes with
the yea, and the yea left unrefuted. Universal unwillingness to respect
rights or other moral facts does not imply their nonexistence. Men's
desolation does not imply their worthlessness. Lear's contradictory
motives for demanding a stop to the flogging do not impugn the
justice of the demand, or the insight, however limited, embodied in

one of the motives. These fallacies are merely the stock in trade of a sophist like Edmund. To be sure, Lear's ability to identify fallacies is hardly enhanced by the chaos of his mind and circumstances. But the fact remains that without the chaos there could have been no intuitions—no proof that value is independent of de facto rank or order and can survive their disruption. This last point hardly justifies chaos as a benign event in the life of the King, but it quite justifies the playwright's use of chaos to affirm something about the unaccommodated man and about unaccommodated life. In the latter case, what is affirmed amid chaos seems to be most hauntingly, if enigmatically, expressed by the word *miracle*.

Indeed, miracle is the mode of proof characteristically demanded by the people of the play. Cordelia's impurity of heart, France says in the first scene, is "a faith that reason without miracle / Should never plant in me" (1. 1. 225–226). "Nothing almost sees miracles / But misery," Kent says in an important soliloquy (2. 2. 172–173). And Edgar calls Gloucester's life, misery and all, a miracle in one of the two central scenes of the play.[11] It will be useful to examine that scene in some detail.

"Why I do trifle thus with his despair," Edgar explains, "is done to cure it" (4. 6. 33–34). The nature of the despair to be cured is subtly exhibited to us by Gloucester's way of justifying suicide:

> This world I do renounce, and in your sights
> Shake patiently my great affliction off,
> If I could bear it longer, and not fall
> To quarrel with your great opposeless wills,
> My snuff and loathed part of nature should
> Burn itself out.   (4. 6. 35–40)

It is arguable that "quarreling" with divine will here means opposing it and refers to suicide. But this reading seems unlikely. If it were allowed, the notion in "bearing it longer" would become a tautologous echo of the notion in "not falling to quarrel," and Gloucester would in the same breath be pointlessly denying and affirming that divine will is "opposeless" (l. 38). More important, it happens that Gloucester is so far from thinking suicides impious that he sees his own as involving an unexceptionably pious virtue, that of "patience" (l. 36).[12]

This last point, I think, is the key to the passage and the scene. In committing suicide Gloucester will in his own estimate be surrendering to the divine will and at the same time avoiding the impiety of blaspheming against Providence, a sin of "quarreling" he knows from past experience (4. 1. 38–39) to be unavoidable if he permits himself to live on. This reading, if allowed, enables us to take the measure of Gloucester's despair and to understand the terms of Edgar's "cure." Death, voluntary or otherwise, seems to Gloucester an end divinely ordained for the unaccommodated life. A life stripped of its commodities is merely "snuff," the "loathed part of nature" (l. 39). The moral with which Edgar's "cure" will permit him to edify Gloucester is that true "patience" resists the suicidal impulse (l. 80), and especially that life refined by ordeal to its essence is not "snuff" but "miracle."

It is the sort of moral we might expect from a man capable of thinking maturity or "ripeness" (5. 2. 11) the ultimate value of life rather than satisfaction or "sweetness," and of thinking the intrinsic "sweetness" of life intense enough by itself to make even hourly death pangs endurable (5. 3. 184–186); a man thus determined to preserve himself "whiles I may scape" (2. 3. 5–6) even at the cost of being "the worst and most dejected thing of Fortune" (4. 1. 3), and of relinquishing even the sorry assurance of having hit rock bottom (l. 27). A man, in short, for whom to lose hope, if it is only luck one is hoping for, is not necessarily to despair, since luck is not "all."

For his own part, then, Edgar can utter the sentence "Thy life's a miracle" with full conviction. But the obstinate fact remains that he has persuaded Gloucester of its truth only by dint of hoaxing and equivocation. A true conclusion, to be sure, can validly be drawn from false premises, but the whole point was to prove what Gloucester, to say the least, does not know to be true. What then becomes of the proof? And why use lies as premises at all if not to call the conclusion in doubt?[13] Before attempting a specific answer to these questions, it has to be observed that they presuppose a model of moral

Edg. ll to Cord.

causation far simpler than is warranted by the play itself. We have already had a cautionary example of a daughter's stubborn insistence on telling her father the truth in language he is doomed to misunderstand. If telling the truth without regard to decorum of language and hearer only ends by conveying a lie, then it is at least possible that telling a lie, at least of a certain sort, may be a means of conveying truth—for some hearers and some orders of truth perhaps a unique means.

One celebrated case in point is mimetic art, in which a misrepresentation of singular fact—what Aristotle calls the poetic lie—becomes a special means of expressing a philosophical truth. That Edgar in his fashioning of a "cure" for Gloucester is operating as a mimetic artist seems to be attested by the technical resources of the imaginary landscape with which he sets the stage for his hoax. It is a tissue, in fact, of painterly and histrionic subterfuges: foreshortening, gradual decrease of size with distance, a continuous outward trajectory for the eye (to mimic the psychology of visual perception), an imitation of empathic fear, and a kinesthetic imitation of dizziness (again to create psychological verisimilitude). All these harmoniously arrayed in a diorama or stage setting of life seen in perspective.

The answer, then, to our question about the contamination of conclusions by premises is that, for its intended audience, Edgar's announcement that "thy life's a miracle" does not stand to the lie that corroborates it as a conclusion to its premises, but rather as an intuition to its imaginative prerequisite. The lie that Gloucester's life has been spared by a miracle is a way, perhaps the only way, to let him experience what it is like to be spared one's life, even such life as remains to Gloucester; to let him see that life without prepossession, as something newly given. It is only by assuming a giving that one can confront the world as if it were a gift. The miracle of the giving is a poetic lie. The miracle of the gift, for Edgar at least, is the truth it has been created to subserve.

The lie, in other words, is a heuristic myth designed to make Gloucester's experience of the value of life intelligible to him. Unlike the dying Lear's, Gloucester's loss (by his own admission, 4. 1. 23–26) is not substantial enough to outweigh the claim of life; his current woes are of the kind that "by wrong imaginations lose / The knowledge of themselves" (4. 6. 290–291). By grace of Edgar's hoax, two wrong imaginations cancel out each other, and what remains—fitfully, to be sure—is truth. The divinity Edgar is talking about is immanent, and Gloucester has reached it by introspection; he has seen it feelingly. But he will now be able to articulate what he has felt in terms of the language of piety that is second nature to him, in terms of "ever-gentle gods" (4. 6. 221) and "the bounty and the benison of heaven" (l. 229). It is clear that Edgar has delicately honored the sensibility of the man he is trying to teach.

It is not at all clear, on the other hand, that he is also abusing Gloucester's superstition; for there is no reason to suppose, with some critics, that Gloucester is, by the presumed standard, superstitious. In a nondeterministic form his belief in stellar influence was too widespread among savants of Shakespeare's day to identify Gloucester as a mere gull; and Edmund's caricature of that belief as a simplistic determinism (1. 2. 128–145) must be taken from whom it comes. Gloucester, to be sure, is capable of accepting the story of a monstrous demon "upon the crown o' th' cliff" (4. 6. 67), but that story does not differ in substance from Horatio's warning to Hamlet:

> What if it tempt you toward the flood, my lord,
> Or to the dreadful summit of the cliff
> That beetles o'er its base into the sea,
> And there assume some other, horrible form,
> Which might deprive your sovereignty of reason
> And draw you into madness? (1. 4. 69–74)

This latter speech, at least, is clearly not intended to make the skeptical Horatio out a gull. If it is harder to explain in this way Gloucester's readiness to accept the suggestion that he is climbing rather than walking on a level, it must be borne in mind that Gloucester is presented to us as an old man freshly released from extreme torture. That he should be exhausted or disoriented, and willing to dismiss the testimony of his senses, bears little resemblance to a stroke of satire at his expense.

To be sure, Gloucester's therapy is either incomplete or impermanent, and he will suffer at least two relapses into despair (4. 6. 286–291 and 5. 2. 8). But it seems possible to conclude that in act 4, scene 6 a son, by resourceful use of a maieutic art, the art, in his phrase, "of known and feeling sorrows" (4. 6. 226),[14] has enabled his father to recognize in his own forlorn being something worth cherishing, a criterion of the justice Lear has been groping for with mingled success. In this recognition lies the rejoinder to the negations of Lear's discourse on "lendings" (3. 4. 105–114), and to "Friar Lodowick's" oblique homiletic assault on the dignity of man in *Measure for Measure*. In the process Gloucester has been able to learn something, however readily forgotten, about a self that happens to be his own. It remains for another child to help a father, however briefly, to achieve an intuition of a self other than his own, and to recognize in it the thing above all worth cherishing.

A number of critics have taught us how consistently Cordelia recalls, for the poet, the life of Christ. She is, we are reminded, the daughter "who redeems nature from the general curse / That twain have brought her to." Cordelia's redemptive imitation of Christ seems to be twofold. First, she has resisted strong pressure to blur the distinction between God and Caesar, dignity and price, inward and outward worth. Once again on rejoining us, she scrupulously reaffirms the distinction: "He that helps him take all my outward worth" (4. 4. 10). Cordelia's inward worth, by implication, is inalienable in precisely the sense of the Sermon on the Mount: "Be not careful for your life, what ye shal eat, or what ye shal dryncke; nor yet for your body, what ye shal put on. Is not the life more worth than meat and the body more of value than rayment?" (Matt. 6 : 25).

Second, she embraces a way of life that universalizes the loyalties of blood and bond. This adherence to an expanded, even a supererogatory view of kinship and duty is what alienates Cordelia from Lear at the outset; mankind is not ready to understand it, as the Gospel foretells with tragic lucidity: "And the brother shal betray the brother to death, and the father the sonne, and the children shal arise against their fathers and mothers, and shal cause them to die" (Matt. 10 : 21).

That this prophecy is actually coming to pass in Lear's timeless Albion is one meaning of Cordelia's allusion to Luke: "O dear father, / It is thy business that I go about" (4. 4. 23–24). The child Jesus in the temple, we remember (Luke 2 : 48–51), tries to explain to His parents why He had seemingly abandoned them; the fact is that His commitment both includes and transcends them, but they cannot grasp this. Cordelia, of course, has similar trouble explaining to her own parent a similar apparent defection.

It is, I think, very important to see that the way of life Cordelia lives, and whose validity she blithely treats as axiomatic, might well strain the credulity of the least pharisaical among us. "Mine enemy's dog," she exclaims, "Though he had bit me, should have stood that night / Against my fire" (4. 7. 36–38). Under the spell of the play we tend to give this hard saying an easy assent, but a moment's thought about welcoming a hostile dog to the comforts of the hearth tends to rouse an echo, in one form or another, of the Fool's earlier bit of pragmatism: "He's mad that trusts in the tameness of the wolf" (3. 6. 8). For the flaws Lear manifests in the play are designedly the reverse of extraordinary. In kind if not in degree they are the inveterate faults of Everyman, consisting principally in the fact that he is not Cordelia; faults whose belated reformation we are usually, and mercifully, spared.[15] Those, on the contrary, who, like Gloucester, have through martyrdom become fools to the world are very much at home with Cordelia's axiom: "If wolves had at thy gate howl'd that stern time, / Thou shouldst have said, 'Good porter, turn the key!' " (3. 7. 63–64). It is the hardest of hard sayings all over again: "For if ye love them which love you, what reward shal ye haue? Do not the Publicans euen the same?" (Matt. 5 : 46–48). With this absolute commitment to charity—a commitment in which Lear's "barbarous Scythian" and cannibal (1. 1. 118–122) would seem to have a share—goes a categorical renunciation of revenge as an ethical motive:

> LEAR. If you have poison for me, I will drink it.
> I know you do not love me; for your sisters

> Have, as I do remember, done me wrong;
> You have some cause, they have not.
>
> CORDELIA.   No cause, no cause.
>
> (4. 7. 72–75)

For Cordelia, there can be no possible sense in exacting retribution—
not only in her dealings with her father, but as we have seen, in all
her transactions with the world. Hers is the voice heard in *Hamlet*
only ironically, in some of the unheeded ramblings of Ophelia, and
in the Prince's fraternal but unfocused pity for the remains of the
venal dead or the frailties of the living; it is a voice reduced in
Measure for Measure to an even more enfeebled undertone. Now, as
a firm refusal to pay back evil for evil, that voice has come into its
own. Lear had knelt to his wicked daughter in a lurid burlesque of
contrition.[16] Henceforth both Cordelia and Lear will kneel to each
other in benediction and forgiveness. The wheel of fire has come
full circle.

Lear's recognition of Cordelia's true identity coincides with a
mature apprehension of his own worth as man: "*as I am a man,* I
think this lady / To be my child Cordelia" (4. 7. 69–70, italics
added). But it is of considerable importance that this flowering of the
King's awareness does not bring a remission of his torment. Throughout the great climactic scene of reconciliation, Lear remains bound
upon his wheel of fire, and symbolically this is as it must be, for the
King's reinterpretation of a personal anguish is to be the measure of
his new if transitory ripeness.[17]

The earlier Lear had stated his case as an individual grievance:
"I am more sinn'd against than sinning." But now the King can
make it comprehensible to himself only by seeing it under the aspect
of a universal grief: "I should even die with pity, / To see another
thus" (4. 7. 53–54). The scandal and mystery of pain is not that he,
but that any man should suffer. The King who had cried out against
superfluity on behalf of all the naked wretches of the world had, to
be sure, begun to generalize from his own suffering to that of others;
but he had not yet broken the iron circle of his own awareness.
Lear's manic insistence (3. 4. 72–77) that nothing could have so
wholly degraded Tom-a-Bedlam (or, by implication, any man's

nature) but what Lear himself has suffered reflected the inherent limitations of the normal human capacity for pity.

Lear's vision of the good in the course of this great scene is in effect a rejoinder to the unabashed voluntarism of Troilus, the covert voluntarism of Ulysses, Hamlet's amoral doctrines of honor and divine will, and the legalism of Angelo and Isabella. Good is after all not to be reduced to will or to its expression in de facto order or government. It is an irreducible datum of human experience, like a color or a taste. Good is as visible as green, as John Donne says. And this simple cognition—the love of Cordelia or the dignity of man—is our warranty for the meaningfulness of intrinsic value, and for its endurance in any conceivable chaos or creation, no matter what its lawlessness or its laws or the decrees of its Maker. A modern writer has put a similar defiance of Ulysses' vizarding of degree very succinctly:

> Suppose you take a particular patch of colour, which is yellow. We can, I think, say with certainty that any patch exactly like that one would be yellow, even if it existed in a Universe in which causal laws were quite different from what they are in this one. We can say that any such patch *must* be yellow, quite unconditionally, and whatever the causal laws. . . . To say of "beauty" or "goodness" that they are "intrinsic" is only, therefore, to say that this thing which is obviously true of "yellowness" and "blueness" and "redness" is true of them.[18]

This idea is not entirely alien to the scholastic tradition. Aquinas finds it necessary, in his discussion of the epistemology of morals, to posit an "evaluative power" (*vis aestimativa*), an interior sense that supplies the intuitive data of right reason. But he is constrained at last to identify these data with natural law, and hence with the fiat of the Creator, the de facto expression of His ordained power.

For "God has free will in respect of things other than Himself, which He wills without necessity"; and among these "others" is numbered, not only creation, but the causal and hierarchical order of creation: "to will an end is not for Him the cause of willing those things which exist to that end; but rather He wills that those things which exist to an end shall be ordered to that end." "Providence governs things according to a particular reason; and yet this reason is taken from the supposition of a divine act of will." What is reassuring about the doctrine of Providence, then, is not that the cosmic order, moral and physical, is other than arbitrary, but that God's external acts of will are, as Aquinas declares, "conditionally necessary"; once having decreed a cosmic order, God cannot revoke it. The system, in short, can be relied on; though from time to time, as with God's occasional endorsements of patriarchal murder, theft, or fornication, that system clearly emerges as grounded on pure imperative, not on any property—good or right or value—inhering in itself or what it orders: "Nor is it in human affairs alone that anything God commands is *eo ipso* what ought to be, but in the things of nature, too, anything He does is in a sense natural."

Already by the beginning of the sixteenth century this arbitrary kind of sanction was coming to be regarded by a few as rather questionable, for it had led Aquinas on occasion to speak of the moral life as if it were simply a means to salvation, and not an end in itself; the paradigm of evil is the neutral but proscribed apple in the garden. Aquinas had indeed attempted to show that the mortality of the soul would leave benevolence without meaning. "If death were real, a man would be bound to commit any crime whatsoever rather than incur it," says the *Doctor Communis* in his treatise on the Creed.[19] It is a sentence on which the great Paduan doctor Pomponazzi sprinkles his most pitiless acerbities, though perhaps with less than entire justice. Pomponazzi's concept of an immanent sanction is paralleled in Suarez and Erasmus, and later still in moral philosophy of the early seventeenth century. Grotius, for example, is moved to assure us, though somewhat gingerly, that "even were it granted (which, without the deepest scandal, granted it may not be) that there is no God, or no divine care for man's doings, these moral principles would keep their place."[20]

Of course, to affirm the autonomy of the moral life as Grotius or, in my view, *King Lear* affirms it is not at all to reject either afterlife or divinity. At the same time it would certainly make it a rather

frivolous enterprise to reduce the *imitatio Christi* Cordelia accepts
unconditionally to so many intimations of heavenly reward. Shakespeare himself has come very near to supplying us with a fitting
epigraph for his play in France's first act couplet:

> Gods, gods! 'tis strange that from their cold'st neglect
> My love should kindle to inflam'd respect.
>
> (I. I. 257–258)

It seems to follow from what has been said that the chaos and
suffering that prevail in Lear's world furnish the occasion neither for
an acquittal nor for an arraignment of Providence, but rather for
the examination of quite another issue. The possibility that the play
does involve such acquittal or arraignment, however, ought not to be
summarily dismissed, and we may begin to assess it by considering
a classic argument for what seems, on the face of it, the less likely
alternative: that what we have to do with ultimately is a kind of
theodicy.

Bradley faces up candidly to the unlikelihood by drawing our
attention to the satanic abruptness of the final calamity. Cordelia's
murder, Lear's death are, he points out, "a bolt from a clear sky,"
"a sudden blow out of the darkness which seems so far from inevitable, and which strikes down our reviving hopes for the victims
of so much cruelty." This is an unnatural "sad ending," especially
when one considers the play's resemblance to the late comedies. Yet
for Bradley the ending is the crowning of the poet's argument, for
the great theme of the play is the justification of human suffering.
Shakespearean tragedy "provokes feelings which imply that this
world is not the whole truth, and therefore not the truth"—the
feeling, for example, "that what happens to such a being as Cordelia
does not matter; all that matters is what she is." So far so good; but
the critic goes further. In the course of his moral reeducation Lear
suffers far beyond his guilt, Bradley willingly grants. "Well, but
Lear owes the whole of this [moral reeducation] to those sufferings
which made us doubt whether life were not simply evil."[21]

It is very doubtful, however, that theodicy has ever been much
advanced by a recourse to the maxim that the end justifies the means.

Whether one is Christian or Hegelian, praise to the end need not inspire thanks to the means (in this case, divine pedagogy) which nature deigned to employ. Nor, as a matter of fact, does it seem at all surprising that Regan, no less, gives this pedagogy her strongest endorsement:

> O, sir, to wilful men,
> The injuries that they themselves procure
> Must be their schoolmasters.
>
> (2. 4. 305–307)

Regan's "must" is question-begging, like Bradley's. Men "must" choose means, but God does not require them; for Him they are either ends in themselves or perfectly arbitrary intermediate steps.[22] Moreover, it should not be overlooked that the pedagogy in question is far from a resounding success. Lear concludes his meditation on the theme of judicial forbearance without showing much profit: "Then kill, kill, kill, kill, kill, kill!" (4. 6. 191).[23] And he contrives to take momentary comfort for his final bereavement in recalling a meaningless act of revenge (5. 3. 274–277). The old Lear survives. If Shakespeare is justifying the means by appeal to the end, he has oddly undermined his position. What he seems to be doing instead is to shame Job's comforters. To acquiesce in the apologetics of the *auto da fé*, or to congratulate the purified victim, still bound to his refining wheel of fire, on the blissful convalescence awaiting him elsewhere, would be worse than heartless in any case. But in this case it is groundless to begin with.

The alternative possibility, painstakingly set forth by W. R. Elton, is that the play's first audience would have been inclined to see a disturbing arraignment of Providence in the catastrophe of *King Lear*, an arraignment embodying certain "ideas about Providence" in which Elton detects "a Calvinist tinge": "the *Deus absconditus;* the gods as somehow not consonant with human happiness; human reason as corrupted and dark; man's position in relation to cosmic forces as one of helpless despair; and mankind a 'worm.' While such conceptions are, of course, not necessarily all in total accord with the intention of Calvin, they represent, at least in effect, feelings which the Calvinist premises could have produced."[24]

Two objections to this list occur at the outset. First, it is hard to see how Calvin or anyone else can coherently have entertained all these notions at once. If the nature of divinity is hidden (in a *Deus absconditus*), then the truth about divine consonance with human happiness, or (what comes to the same thing) about man's ultimate relation to cosmic forces, will be hidden as well. Further, the historical credentials of these ideas are not in order; to present them as not *necessarily* all in total accord with Calvin's intention is to allow the *possibility* that all of them are, and this allowance will not do.

For Calvin's belief in a hidden God is not unqualified; a few crucial truths about God's counsels have been revealed—for example, that only the reprobate are capable of despair; that they alone are deprived of God's help; that only some of them are aware of this desperate position; and that, far from being "somehow not consonant with human happiness," God is Himself the supreme human happiness, powerful enough to overwhelm the total unworthiness of the elect; as for the others, the dissonance with happiness is not God's but their own, a bad fruit of the collective breach of faith in which all men participate. Whatever "feelings" may be generated by the ordeal of awaiting the random distribution of a mercy to which one has no claim (and despair is no new discovery of Calvin), Calvin's "premises" effectively rule out both divine hostility and the categorical desperateness of man's position.[25]

Only three of Elton's items, then—divine inscrutability, the total depravity of man, the limitations of his reason—are recognizably Calvinist; of these, as I shall try to show, only one can legitimately be inferred from what happens in *King Lear*. The point that most immediately concerns us, however, is that none of the three unequivocally confirms any theological conclusion at all; no negative conclusion, certainly, for all are perfectly consistent with the tenets of the traditional belief in divine Providence, a belief on which Rome and the Reformers were more nearly in agreement than

Elton's account would lead one to suppose. A brief review of this belief, and a glance at its antecedents, will, I hope, make this point sufficiently clear.

It was the Reformation, in fact, as W. K. Ferguson long ago observed, that "brought a complete return to the divinely motivated conception of history that had prevailed in ecclesiastical tradition from Augustine and Orosius through the Middle Ages." But that conception is not accurately represented by the popular fundamentalism, for example, of John Carpenter's view that the function of Providence is "to rewarde vertues with honours, or to defende the oppressed from theyr foes in this life, or to give victorie in battaile, or to punish horrible sinnes with horrible plagues." The central tradition, on the contrary, is as ready as Sidney to recognize that "the Historie beeing captiued to the trueth of a foolish world, is many times a terror from well-doing, and an encouragement to vnbrideled wickednes." Nor is William Baldwin discrediting the role of Providence as traditionally conceived when he exhorts his readers:

> Although you shall finde . . . that sum haue for their vertue been enuied and murdered, yet cease not you to be vertuous, but do your offices to the vttermost; punish sinne boldly, both in your selues and other, so shall God (whose lieutenauntes you are) eyther so mayntayne you, that no malice shall prevayle, or if it do, it shal be for your good, and to your eternall glory both here and in heauen, which I beseech God you may covet and attayne.[26]

The earthly good here promised obviously coexists with the triumph of evil.

But a mature view of Providence, one that could be confidently received as adequate to historical experience, would always be obliged to acknowledge the spectacle of malice prevailing and virtue undone, and hence to avoid the error of reducing Providence to a self-enclosed system of earthly reward and punishment. Calvin is merely responding to this old imperative when he insists that the key to the riddle of God's providential workings in history lies beyond the sphere of those workings.[27]

Since the end of Providence is beyond earthly life, Calvin argues, the punitive theory of affliction is grossly oversimplified.[28] Affliction, to be sure, is always occasioned by Original Sin; but it is a fallacy to conclude that final judgment is being pronounced on some actual sin as well. The divine purpose is as likely to be monitory: "He must indeed be a blind and depraved judge who thinks that where there is affliction there must be sin. It is not true that the most wicked are dragged for punishment first. God chooses to punish a few out of a multitude, so that through them he may condemn the rest and fill them with the terror of his vengeance."[29]

The fundamentalist view, in short, is an offense against charity and a reflex of pride: "The point Christ makes is that those who suffer hardship at the hands of others are not the worst of men; and his purpose is to condemn our depraved judgment which turns us habitually against those who are afflicted by some calamity, and to root out that self-indulgence with which everybody treats his own self. God exercises his judgments freely, in his own way and order."[30] Any dogmatic attempt to disclose the providential function of a particular human success or reverse, since all such attempts are founded on insufficient data, must clearly be tentative and open to question.

It is hard indeed to see how this outlook differs from that of Aquinas, for whom Providence is "a system of ordering things toward an end" (*Summa Theologica* 1. 22. 1), and "the end of this world's governance must be something outside the world" (ibid., 1. 103. 2). Elton nonetheless considers that Calvin's exposition of God's concealment marks a radical change dividing the thought of the Reformation from that of the central medieval tradition: "This change involved the breakdown of the traditional analogy between Creator and creature, in the reawakened consciousness of fallen man's rational incapacity. Beyond human reason, *totaliter aliter*, the transcendent, rather than immanent, Deity inscrutably hid himself."[31]

But these generalizations leave much to be desired. No Christian theologian could well deny the immanence of God, and Calvin's homage to it is indistinguishable from the Thomist *oportet quod Deus sit in omnibus rebus et intime* (*STh* 1. 8. 1): "And he [God] himself says through the prophet that he is not confined to any particular region but is diffused through all things."[32] The Calvinist universe, likewise, is fully as eloquent of God as the Thomist. Though man is too corrupt to take spiritual advantage of it, the natural evidence is clear enough to deprive the infidel of every excuse.[33] The Thomist doctrine of *analogia entis* promises but little more.[34]

Moreover, neither Calvin's disesteem nor Aquinas's admiration for the capacity of human reason is to be taken without important reservations. It is Calvin, on occasion, who extols the inventiveness and penetration of human reason.[35] And it is Aquinas, on occasion, who sees in faith divine compensation for a human understanding that is weak in judgment, mingled with images of sense, and chronically disabled by dilemmas of conflicting authority.

It required no revolutionary shift in perspective to force religious thought to recognize what it had always understood and insisted on— that a finite mind is hard put to it to encompass an infinite. Indeed, for Aquinas the necessary finitude of creation is in itself an insuperable bar to any naively punitive theory of evil in human experience, Fall or no Fall: outside God there is simply not enough substance to go around, not because of divine ill will, but because it is logically absurd that divine self-sufficiency should be duplicated. Providence is in part, therefore, simply the allocation of a scarce commodity— a kind of divine thrift.[36] The same discrepancy between creature and Creator that makes evil unavoidable also makes the Creator's way of sublimating evil impossible for the creature to grasp in detail.

That a hidden God should somehow be reconciled with a benign if inscrutable Providence, then, is no innovation of Calvin; indeed, the commonplaces we have been examining are simply the most durable parts of that academic and Stoic theodicy of which Plotinus's treatise on Providence is the typical document. Since on this view Providence must assimilate to itself the natural struggle for existence, those who aspire to be as innocent as doves enjoy no divine dispensation from the duty to be as wise as serpents.[37] Divine Providence can hardly consist in paying human improvidence to ignore divine provisions.

But for Plotinus as for his Christian successors the necessity of affirming a special Providence is not so easily avoided; it would be idle to blame all suffering on unwariness, and it would be a blasphemy against divine Providence itself to justify the agony of a part by pleading the interest of the whole.[38] The ultimate principle of order in the world, after all, is not matter and its exigencies; it is reason or *logos*, which is the beginning of all.[39]

The dual Neoplatonic solution to this problem is, for better or worse, the common Western solution too: eschatology (in Plotinus's case, the theory of transmigration), supplemented with the metaphysical depreciation of evils; granted, the visible scheme on its own terms is imperfect, but it is not the whole scheme or an intrinsically important part of it:

> For in real life, too [as in the theatre], it is not the soul within but the shadow outside a man that moans and repines and performs everything he performs, men having pitched their stages in many places on the stage of the earth at large. . . . Toys are taken seriously by those who do not know how to be serious—by those who are themselves toys. And should some playmate of these incur such things, let him understand that he has taken a fall in a children's game, and put his toy away. . . . One must not take weeping and lamentation as pointing to the existence of evils, because even over what is not evil children shed tears and fall to grieving.[40]

But the crucial point is that even the grief of toys has an ultimate justification, one that is inexplicable merely because it lies beyond the scheme.

In the same spirit Boethius's Philosophia, after showing by examples how the uses of adversity might be at once in accord with human ideas of justice and yet impossible to ascertain in practice, warns her disciple that "it is not granted to man to grasp all the sleights of God's working or to unfold them in speech." It is this common and traditional view of Providence that Hooker is summoning up when he quotes Boethius in support of his exposition of the *lex aeterna:* "Seeing therefore that according to this law He worketh, 'of whom, through whom, and for whom, are all things'; although there seem unto us confusion and disorder in the affairs of this present world: . . . 'let no man doubt but that everything is well done, because the world is ruled by so good a guide' as transgresseth not His own law: than which nothing can be more absolute, perfect, and just.''[41]

According to immemorial notions shared by both Rome and Reform, God's dealings with men in the natural domain are (*a*) consistently lawful, no matter (*b*) how arbitrary the basis of the law they and the human conscience obey, and how unconfined by law the distribution of mercy in the supernatural domain. On the latter point I have already argued that the catastrophe of *King Lear*, far from confirming theological voluntarism, is essential to denying its implications for the grounds of ethical judgment, and a little later I shall have to return to the matter for a last look.

At the moment it is the former point that concerns me; for the tradition we have been reviewing clearly leaves no scope for refutation by calamity. It is designed, on the contrary, to put belief in Providence beyond the logical reach of even the cruelest *force majeure* by dint of a thorough apriorism; reason is what carries the brief for divine Providence, and faith is the chief witness. Experience, beyond hinting inconclusively, is powerless to bring evidence. There is thus little to recommend Elton's view that "an implicit direction of the tragedy" is "annihilation of faith in poetic justice" (p. 334), and that "the devastating fifth act shatters"—or indeed is capable of shattering—"the foundations of faith itself" (p. 337). Poetic justice is not an article of faith. As for divine justice, foundations cannot be shattered in absentia. The substance of things unseen is by definition untouched by what a playwright can show, and a metaphysical argument can be dislodged only by a counterargument, not by a set of dramatic circumstances, however devastating.

What is true of circumstances in general would seem to be equally true of the circumstance that a particular character has been led by his experiences to repudiate Providence. But it will repay us, I think, to inquire whether at the end of the play Lear does indeed, as Elton holds, meet this and other "criteria of the Renaissance skeptic": "(1)

he considers God's providence faulty; (2) he denies the immortality of the soul; (3) he holds man not different from a beast; (4) he denies creation *ex nihilo*, deriding the traditional tenet that God created the world out of nothing, and he ridicules it by applying it to a natural context, concluding *ex nihilo nihil fit;* and (5) he attributes to nature what belongs to God" (p. 54).

Elton's supporting arguments on each of these heads are not entirely convincing. On the first: "he [Lear] questions—rather, he denounces—God's providence in allowing lower creatures to live, while Cordelia's existence is cut short by the horror of a senseless hanging" (p. 54). "If we assume that the Shakespearean spectator analogically transformed the characters and situation in *Lear* into Christian terms, we are left with the spectacle of a Christian tragic hero who ends as a skeptic blaspheming his Deity" (p. 337). But Lear ends in a transport not of blasphemy but of joy; he has detected signs of life in his daughter—"a chance which does redeem all sorrows / That ever I have felt" (5. 3. 266–267)—and dies at peace with the scheme of things: "Look there, look there."[42]

Nor (on the second head) need the joy itself be seen as an ironic invitation to religious doubt merely because it is a delusion or because it is ultimately prompted by ignorance of an alternative to the physical survival of Cordelia. For Elton's requested assumption cannot be lightly granted, as he himself has made very clear to us elsewhere: "For the most part, the play is at least ostensibly pagan in its premises—Shakespeare seems deliberately striving for fidelity to heathen life and experience as the Renaissance could have understood them" (p. 254). Lear's disconsolateness, we are told, is precisely the "attitude of the Pagan mourner" as described by John Jewel (p. 55). We are therefore entitled to ask how a Renaissance audience can have read Christian impiety into pagan ignorance, unless the latter was the result of neglecting what even a pagan (with his wits intact, at least) could not help but know. The standard to which Lear holds Providence, in any case, is quite irrelevant. That Providence fails to measure up to it is not enough to vindicate Lear's earlier reproaches. That he is made to think it measures up is as suggestive of mercy as of mockery.

Moreover (on the third head), is it quite true that in the end Lear "holds man not different from a beast?" Here is Elton's analysis:

> Lear in his last lines, over the body of Cordelia, demands "Why should a dog, a horse, a rat, have life, / And thou no breath at all?" (5. 3. 306–307), the culmination of the beast imagery of the play.
>
> Indeed, Lear's descending animal order in this speech is significant, for that is the order in the drama; to appreciate *King Lear*, less a twentieth-century naturalistic view than a more exalted medieval and early Renaissance view of man's hierarchical place and potential is requisite. For, disordering the great chain of being, the play's lines seem to reverse the great self-flattering tradition from Aquinas to Hooker: man *is* no more than this. (P. 192)

But surely Lear's question here, far from reducing man to beast, turns on the sharpness of the contrast. Cordelia, unlike the beasts, has apparently received far less than her due, a disparity increased by the fact that her due is far greater than theirs.

The textual basis for Lear's alleged anticreationism (the fourth head) is equally dubious: " 'Nothing will come of nothing,' he shouts (1. 1. 92) at Cordelia; while in a more reflective mood he replies to his Fool's 'Can you make no use of nothing' (1. 4. 143–146)" (p. 179). These statements are doubtless objectionable, but one thing they are innocent of is metaphysics. Lear is simply giving us the obverse of his code of moral barter; if all good turns have a price, no good turn is free. The heterodoxy of denying that anything comes of nothing depends, in any case, on the size of the universe of discourse. As a generalization about nature the denial is impeccably Christian. Why should Lear go beyond the capacities of nature to make a point about those of Cordelia? Moreover, creation is a revealed truth, not a rational thesis (cf. Aquinas *STh* 1. 46. 2); how can Lear reject what he has not been offered?

Elton argues that Lear satisfies the fifth criterion of "the Renaissance skeptic" by asking a question that could occur only to a naturalist and a heretic:

In his question, then, Lear seems, in effect, to be withdrawing an area from the Department of Theology and requesting a grant for a scientific research project: "Then let them anatomize Regan, see what breeds about her heart. Is there any cause in nature that makes these hard hearts?" (P. 223)

This appeal to second causes rather than to first, to nature rather than to God, was a mark of the new materialist doubt. But, to aggravate the problem, Lear turns paradoxically to natural causation for the solution to a question traditionally within the divine realm. "Hard hearts" were caused, as every devout Elizabethan knew, by falling from grace, by reprobation and sin. (P. 220)

It should at least be mentioned that Lear's outburst seems very like an innocuous hyperbole not unknown among distraught and indignant heroes of Jacobean drama:

> Tell me thy thoughts; for I will know the least
> That dwells within thee, or will rip thy heart
> To know it.[43]

Even on its face, the reduction of mind to matter need not be taken literally.

But Lear can, I think, be fully exonerated both of materialism and of a heretical theory of obduracy. For his question, if anything, would seem to avoid the blasphemy of making God and not nature the *ultimate* cause of the hardening of hearts. Aquinas draws the relevant distinction very clearly:

> Blinding and hardening [jointly] signify two things, of which one is the movement of man's mind clinging to evil and turning away from the light of God, and in this respect God is not the cause of blinding and hardening, as he is not the cause of sin. The other is the withdrawal of grace whose sequel is that the mind is not divinely illuminated so as to see aright and the heart of a man not softened so as to

live aright, and in this respect God is the cause of blinding and hardening.

Since blinding and hardening, as arising from the withdrawal of grace, are kinds of punishment, man is not made worse by them; but having become so by his own fault he incurs these as he does the other punishments.[44]

There is, then, a clear sense in which Lear's view is theologically impeccable. Original Sin, according to Article 9, "is the fault and corruption of the nature of every man . . . whereby man is very far gone from his original righteousness and of his own nature inclined to evil, so that the flesh lusteth always contrary to the spirit." It is in this respect that the cause of hardheartedness is not God but rather flesh and will. The lust of the flesh in itself, according to Article 9, "deserveth God's wrath and damnation. . . . concupiscence and lust hath of itself the nature of sin." If there is materialism in the acknowledgment that man is flesh, or naturalism in the acknowledgment that the corruption of nature is prior to the withdrawal of grace, then these paragons of orthodoxy must join Lear in the dock.

Of the stipulated items, then, the only one that is both applicable to Lear and reprehensible even in a pagan is the first—his impugning of the divine beneficence, first during the storm and then for a brief period just before his final delusion. And here it is very curious that Elton for once attempts to spare the old King a full blast of the *odium theologicum* on the grounds that Lear's "developing distrust of 'ethnic' deities could be construed as a fortunate change toward a theologically more enlightened position" (p. 212).

The position might perhaps appear more enlightened were it not for the traditional theory that ethnic deities represent, not the primitive state of religion, but the corrupt survival of a primitive monotheism. "When they knew God," says Saint Paul, "they glorified him not as God, neither were thankful; but became vain in their imaginations, and their foolish heart was darkened. Professing themselves to be wise, they became fools, and changed the glory of the incorruptible God into an image made like to corruptible man, and to

birds, and four-footed beasts, and creeping things" (Rom. 1 : 21–
23). Such, too, was the Stoic theory preserved for Renaissance an-
thropology in the essays of Plutarch, among others: "As sun and
moon and heaven and earth and sea are shared by all men but
among different men go by different names, so to the one Reason that
orders these things and the one Providence that guides, its auxiliary
powers being assigned to the tendance of all men, different forms of
homage and address have been established among different men."[45]
Salutati's argument agrees on the main point: "as it is one and the
same deity that [the poets] call Luna when it is in heaven, Diana
in the woods, Proserpine in the netherworld, so all that multiplicity
of gods has been diversely named [by the poets] on the assumption
that all have a single essence, and according to the variety of the
latter's powers and operations."[46] Where it is accepted literally,
however, as Donne says, the pantheon is simply a last vestige of the
original faith of Adam:

> the Heathen made them severall gods
> Of all Gods benefits, and all his Rods. . . .
>   by changing that whole precious Gold
> To such small Copper coynes, they lost the old,
> And lost their only God.

On such a view, to deny Providence in the context of paganism
would be to progress, but in the wrong direction—to compound the
deterioration in man's knowledge of God's attributes by deleting
not only the note of unity but also that of benevolence. And on this
latter point a rational pagan is not generally supposed to be in-
vincibly ignorant. Chaucer's Palemon, to be sure, seems to be ignorant
enough, but he is not rational:

> Thanne seyde he, 'O crueel goddes that governe
> This world with byndyng of youre word eterne,
> And written in the table of atthamaunt
> Youre parlement and youre eterne graunt,
> What is mankynde moore unto you holde

> Than is the sheep that rouketh in the folde?
> For slayn is man right as another beest,
> And dwelleth eek in prison and arreest,
> And hath siknesse and greet adversitee,
> And ofte tymes giltelees, pardee.

Arcite's reasoning, on the other hand, illustrates the availability of the truth about Providence to the ethnic mind:

> Allas, why pleynen folk so in commune
> On purveiaunce of God, or of Fortune,
> That yeveth hem ful ofte in many a gyse
> Wel bettre than they kan hemself devyse? . . .
> Infinite harmes been in this mateere.
> We witen nat what thing we preyen heere.

Even Palemon, in the end, sticks at positive assertion, and this precisely because such positiveness would be intolerable in a hero, just as the reproaches hurled at the Olympians by Dante's Capaneo, far from being hailed as a first step toward his deliverance from paganism, earn him a fiery berth among the blasphemers in the seventh circle.

This attitude is not confined to the Middle Ages. Fracastoro, in *De morbo Gallico* (1536), contrives an earthly retribution little less disagreeable than Capaneo's for a heathen shepherd of Hispaniola who finds the sun's performance disappointing: "Why do we call you father and god of the universe and set up altars consecrated to you, unlettered hinds that we are, and worship you with slaughtered ox and thickening incense, if you care not for us and my chieftain's herds touch you not? Or am I rather to suppose that you and your heavenly brethren burn with envy?" And the chieftain himself is similarly scourged for having declared, among other things, "that the gods dwell in heaven and this lower realm does not belong to them."

Heathen denial of Providence, then, is not excused by heathen assumptions, and it is notable that as late as 1669 an editor of Petronius is unable to justify his author's most notorious remark ("primus in orbe deos fecit timor") simply by pointing out that Petronius is discrediting the gods, not God. Nothing short of a full acquittal will do: "But that the charge of Epicureanism may fall as by a single blow, and lest the reader be imposed on in the least by this frivolous opinion, here are the words of our Satirist in favor of the Providence of the gods."[47] I have remarked that Lear's final delusion is as suggestive of mercy as of mockery, and I think I may now add that it would be a mercy extended to him not only as a sufferer but as a tragic sufferer. For a Lear who died accusing Providence would have run the risk of demeaning not Providence but Lear, and would in any case leave Providence itself untouched.

Providence would be untouched because, as I have tried to show, the traditional case for it rests not on experience but on reason alone. If Lear does indeed entertain "undissembled skeptical views" that are "shown not to be a priori or innate but to develop through actual experience" (p. 57), then they are *eo ipso* out of court. For an exercise of pure reason, on the other hand, Lear's qualifications at the end of the play are not reassuring; indeed, there could hardly be a less likely vehicle for an assault on "the foundations" of belief in Providence, or a more likely candidate—if the end did not belie Elton's description of it—for the apology with which Mantuan's Fortunatus excuses his own incoherent challenge to that belief: "Sorrow and other passions often unhinge the mind. From a sick spirit comes a sick speech" (*Eclogue* 3. 43–44).

Much of what Elton says about the dark theological suspicions latent in the plot itself comes once more, it seems to me, of not realizing that the orthodox argument for Providence is not only compatible with the assumption of divine inscrutability but proceeds on it. By corrupting the natural order in the wake of his Fall, man is himself responsible in a high degree for erasing the clearer signs of God's informing presence in human affairs, a presence that now must partly consist in redeeming the visible order from its own corruption by fitting it into an order that is beyond corruption—and invisible. It will not do, therefore, to say that "in at least one sense there (V.iii) 'ripeness' is shown not to be all, when the young and most unripe Cordelia is carried onstage dead in her father's arms" (p.

107). A devout playgoer is not debarred from replying, with Hamlet, that to die betimes (or while unripe in the worldly sense) is nothing, and that to die when one is ready (or ripe in the providential sense) is all. An apostate playgoer, to be sure, is not debarred from saying the opposite, but this license hardly amounts to an endorsement.

In the same way, it will not do to infer from the absence of miracles in the world of the play the corresponding "gracelessness" (p. 107) of that world. Only the Papists claimed a wider field for God's miraculous interventions than biblical history; and Calvin's sarcasm at their expense is well known: "But compared with us, they have a strange power: even to this day they confirm their faith by continual miracles!"[48] Indeed, an heir of Augustine might well maintain, like Donne, that if "*Miracle* is against the whole *Order* of nature, I see not how there is left in God a power of Miracles. . . . For, Saint *Augustine* says truly, that is Naturall to each thing which God doth, from whom proceeds all Fashion, Number and Order in Nature."[49]

Nor, on the other hand, need Edgar's affirmation that Gloucester's life is a miracle have been taken as categorically false merely because it is false in the sense in which Gloucester understands it. For it is scarcely accurate to describe Edgar's contrivances at Dover in Elton's terms, as "a benevolent and admitted 'trifling' (4. 6. 33) played, in the audience's full view, upon a suicidal and blind old man" (p. 93). This is to damn by partial quotation. Edgar's "admitted" aim in trifling is to "cure" Gloucester of his urge to suicide. One does not "cure" states of mind that are sane, or save lives that are no longer worth saving. We are not being invited to infer that Edgar

> hates him,
> That would upon the rack of this tough world
> Stretch him out longer.   (5. 3. 313–315)

The implication is clear that Gloucester's suicidal disposition is itself a sort of blindness, and hence that Gloucester is already the victim of trifling—his own. As a cure for suicidal trifling, Edgar's countermeasure is classic homeopathy, and presupposes that the worth of Gloucester's life, if not its miraculousness, is self-evident.

Both these claims may seem hardly credible to us, but it is worth remembering that there is an impressive secular tradition behind the first and an impressive theological tradition behind both, and that these traditions cannot fail to have been familiar to the playwright and his audience. The *Nicomachean Ethics*, to be sure, recognizes that there may be a difference of opinion "whether we choose to live for the sake of pleasure, or to have pleasure that we may live," but the consistent Aristotelian view is that life is good of its essence precisely because "if no other good should attend it, it is still desirable in itself." For "life is good by nature," and especially (for Aristotle) the life of man. Milton's Belial is simply rehearsing a Stoic-Peripatetic axiom, as well as paying grudging tribute to his Creator, when he asks

> who would loose,
> Though full of pain, this intellectual being,
> Those thoughts that wander through Eternity,
> To perish rather, swallow'd up and lost
> In the wide womb of uncreated night,
> Devoid of sense and motion?[50]

Our hypothetical Augustinian can go further; for if miracle is not essentially distinct from nature, then by the same token all that is natural, including life, has some title to be thought miraculous. "There are as many miracles," says Calvin, ". . . as there are kinds of things in the universe, indeed, as there are things either great or small."[51] The specific grounds for this view are clearly set forth in Aquinas. For though creatures are all subject to the order of nature, the fact that they were created at all and the fact that they are preserved lie outside the causal chain that comprises the natural order. In this sense, to be a creature at all or to be preserved in being is both a miracle and a manifestation of grace.[52] In Edgar's statement, then, that "the gods, who make them honors / Of men's impossibilities, have preserv'd thee," Gloucester may be understanding a lie and his son at the same time telling the truth as he understands it.

It would not follow, however, that Edgar as theist may not be mistaken all the same, and indeed this has been my point from the outset: Providence, being ordinarily concealed from us, is ascertainable not by observation or intuition, but only by rational argument. Without this last, Edgar's bare avowal carries no more weight than the suicidal negations he is trying to cure. Elton concludes from what he calls "the sequential irony" of the play "that ripeness may *not* be all and that the gods may *not* be just," but he does so without appearing to recognize that the logical concomitant of a possibility is the opposite possibility. Both inferences from the play—Bradley's "may" and Elton's "may not"—are compatible, and both equally doomed to innocuousness by the play's refusal to confront the real terms of the case for Providence.

This case, in short, is not at issue in *King Lear*, not the occasion for its dramatic appeal to our direct experience. But there is another great principle that by definition can be established only by such an appeal: the immanence of value. It is the appeal France makes as he celebrates his betrothal, that Lear makes as he recognizes his daughter, that Edgar makes as he extols ripeness and endurance. For Elton is not wholly faithful, I think, to the epistemological heritage of the Renaissance when he asserts, on behalf of the play, that "in a world where neither truth nor prudence suffices, neither honesty nor expediency, neither Cordelia nor the Fool (5. 3. 305), feeling must suffice for knowledge" (p. 96); or that Edgar figures in the play as "the fool of feeling," a role to which, in Elton's view, Edgar puts an end when "he admits that endurance and ripeness are *not* all and that, indeed, suicide or death might be preferable to the drawn-out calamity of so long life (5. 3. 184–186)" (p. 107).

Elton sums up the speech he is referring to—"O our lives' sweetness, / That we the pain of death would hourly die / Rather than die at once!"—as asserting "that painful clinging to life may itself be irrational, keeping us from cutting short our suffering" (p. 99). But the paraphrase is a serious distortion. Edgar states quite explicitly the reason for our willingness to endure the pain of death-in-life. It is the countervailing sweetness of life itself, a value whose authenticity he clearly takes for granted. To dismiss this reason in turn as groundless and hence irrational is to blur a distinction meticulously observed in Renaissance thought. "For," as Hooker says of moral principles,

> to make nothing evident of itself unto man's understanding were to take away all possibility of knowing anything. And herein that of Theophrastus is true, "They that seek a reason of all things do utterly overthrow Reason." In every kind of knowledge some such grounds there are, as that being proposed the mind doth presently embrace them as free from all possibility of error, clear and manifest without proof.

Hooker and Theophrastus are merely paying homage to Aristotle's remark that "it is a want of education not to know which things require proof and which not. For it is simply not possible that there should be a proof of everything. One would proceed to infinity, so that there would be no proof even so."[53] Perceptions of value too (when their object is immediate experience) are ultimate in this sense. They are "irrational" only because they are the very ground of rationality. And they are, as Aristotle tells us in the *Ethics*, unique in being acts at once of sensation and understanding. So, too, in *King Lear* valuing is an art in which the higher and lower faculties become one—"the art of known and feeling sorrows" that makes one "pregnant to good pity" (4. 6. 226, 227), and that enlightens the man "that will not see / Because he does not feel" (4. 1. 71–72) by enabling him to "see . . . feelingly" (4. 6. 152). In the world of the play, then, moral feeling need not "*suffice* for knowledge." It *is* knowledge.

This, I submit, is the point of contact between the theological neutrality of the play and its theme. For if, as Elton rightly states, "the voluntarist tradition of Calvin and Ockham affirms [of the moral law] that its rules exist, not through reason and knowledge, but simply because God has willed them" (p. 32), what better way of affirming the opposite view, the Erasmian faith that "the measure of the binding force in a law is not taken from the author alone but from the substance as well,"[54] than by vindicating such a measure without consideration, and indeed in possible defiance, of God's will?

In *King Lear*, then, the assumption that the divine purpose of suffering cannot be known is just that; a heuristic premise and not a conclusion.

Maynard Mack has suggested that in the world of Lear "the capacity to grow and ripen—in relation and love—is in some mysterious way bound up with the capacity to lose, and to suffer, and to endure."[55] The critic concludes his study with the observation that "it is a greater thing to suffer than to lack the feelings and virtues that make it possible to suffer."[56] This seems to mean (*a*) that in *King Lear* the capacity to love is inseparable from the capacity to suffer grief—for suffering of other kinds is surely not denied to the morally insensible in the play; (*b*) that we should vastly prefer grief to moral insensibility were these our only alternatives, as in *King Lear* they appear to be. These sentiments do indeed seem to be the burden of the play at its close. But they do not seem to justify the interpretations Mack places on them. It is doubtful, for one thing, that they are intended to suggest a "victory" over grief on Lear's part.[57] Love can hardly be said to "vanquish" the suffering of which it is supposed to be the necessary condition. On such a view it is not love but the lack of it that is proof against grief. More important, the question to which Mack fits these answers—that of "the meaning of our human fate"[58]—is too ambiguous to bring out their bearing.

In his *obiter dicta* Mack seems to admit four distinct glosses on this ambiguous question: "what becomes of us," "what we are," what we "may be," and "what we become."[59] The first of these he disavows, and rightly; not all and perhaps not most of us will endure a loss so untimely and inconsolable as Lear's. But the others should be rejected on the same grounds; not all and perhaps not most of us are such pure cases of Lear's initial weaknesses or are capable of achieving, much less do achieve, his final "grandeur."[60] Defined in these ways, "the meaning of our human fate" as the play presents it is diverse, atypical, and inconclusive; *de te fabula* stops short, at the very least, of the likes of Goneril and Regan. What we are made to recognize about Lear's grief is rather that it is, as Mack says, "greater" than the lack of certain "feelings and virtues"; that though Lear "has made his choice, and there will be no reward,"[61] nevertheless "the choice of relatedness must be recognized as its own reward."[62]

The question that can be answered by showing how far grief surpasses moral imbecility is, I would suggest, the question whether pleasure (or the absence of suffering) is the essential ground of human preference. The answer supplied by the play, nihilist Edmund to the contrary notwithstanding, is no. It is, to be sure, shallow to welcome suffering, especially on others' behalf, as a source of edification. But compassion, even when it entails suffering and can be of no avail, is a good. The inability to suffer compassionately is an evil no pleasure can countervail. Moral discourse, in short, does not shrink in the heat of experience to the mere "curiosity of nations," to a ceremonial expression of caprice or appetite or brute command— an expression of what pleases us or what we please.

Somehow, the end of the play does not leave our mouths full of the taste of ashes; there is something grandly if mysteriously affirmative about it—a peculiar kind of affirmation, to be sure, in response to a peculiar kind of negation. What we have been allowed to take part in is a victory, not of good over evil, but of the tragic vision over the absurd; a tribute, not to the power of goodness, but to its reality. The scheme of things may, for all the play tells us, tolerate pointless calamity and malignity, in an alternation with their opposites as arbitrary as Edmund's cult of the amoral. But the arbitrariness does not extend to the moral alternatives themselves; we are not spectators to the strife of Dum and Dee over their rattle, and we need not, like Hamlet and Troilus and Angelo, compensate for the presumed lack of a standard by making idols of law or constancy or our febrile guesses as to the will of God. Even if it is true that the universe and its contents are less good than evil, it is by the same token false that they are neither. Even if the universe conspires against a man or, stumbling, grinds him under its heel, the victim is a victim and not a worm. The criteria by which actions are rightly chosen and suffering rightly deplored are not fictions; and if not fictitious, then there is, after all, something "serious in mortality."

The oddity of *King Lear*, then, is that the play achieves its affirmation by dint of a hypothetical rejection of hope, at least for the individual. For the intrinsic value of justice and love cannot be vindicated by appeal to their success, or to any other extrinsic standard, but rather by showing us these virtues flickering on the verge of extinction, in surroundings that are ostentatiously indifferent to them. But to show us the intrinsic value of these virtues is ultimately to show us the minds of those who have achieved them— the minds especially of Lear and Cordelia. And to show us these, not in the narrow clinical sense affected by a Hamlet or a Vincentio, is to give the lie to the notion that estrangement is implicit in the human condition, and to do so as much by our own example as by that of the old King's fleeting epiphany.

The controlling condition of Shakespeare's great experiment is gratuitous and inordinate suffering, the torment of doom, or an "image of that horror." In the midst of this horror, there is a great love, and knowledge, and much praise. But to the torment itself, the only decent response is compassion, not cursing and not hosannah; compassion, bewilderment, and mourning.

CHAPTER FIVE

Love and Responsibility in Othello

King Lear is designed to counter skepticism about moral criteria and knowledge of other minds by offering a measure of the disputed kinds of insight not so much to the heroes as to the audience. *Othello* does the same, but here the means to our illumination are the villains, especially that villain of the piece who is also its hero. As we witness the degradation of Othello's faculty for compassionate insight and equity we are guided by degrees toward a new kind of compassionate insight of our own, and hence a new kind of equity; in the process we come to appreciate these faculties as a source of knowledge by being shown the peculiar and terrible ignorance that attends their absence. Part of the new equity we are taught to exercise consists in recognizing that, paradoxically, malicious intent extenuates rather than aggravates malicious action as grounds for blame. But intent, as I am using the term, is an event in mind; we must first ask what Othello's ordeal has to tell us about his mind. We shall find, as elsewhere, that Shakespeare's trees are to be known by their fruits.

In the present chapter I shall argue that the Moor gives a special reason for being disappointed in the pitiable showing he makes against his tempter: he fails eventually to meet the requirements of a test for conjugal love that he himself in effect lays down at the outset. These requirements, moreover, would carry both moral and imaginative weight with the play's first audience; for they agree in substance with the prevailing ideal of Christian marriage as well as with the surviving canons of courtly love. We shall begin by considering one by one the virtues Othello either lays claim to or pointedly commends.

Magnanimity

To be sure, the mere fact that he claims any form of superiority might seem to discredit him from the outset as a romantic lover in the traditional sense; as in his cool assurance that

> my demerits
> May speak unbonneted to as proud a fortune
> As this that I have reach'd.   (1. 2. 22–24)

The proper attitude even of an accepted suitor, one would think, should have a little humility in it. But this impression, as it happens, is false; from a much earlier stage in the Western refinement of *eros*, the expected show of humility was never allowed to suggest that the lover's attentions were degrading to his lady. On the contrary, a perfectly decorous "greatness and nobility of soul" inspires one of Andreas's knights to remark: "So much trust do I put in the achievements of my honor and in the scales of your gentility that though the largesse I seek be delayed, I cannot think that my service will long be cheated of its deserts."[1] In Christian marriage, of course, the Pauline precept that husbands are to love their wives "even as Christ also loved the church," construed in the light of the formula that "the husband is the head of the wife even as Christ is the head of the church" (Eph. 5 : 25, 23) could be taken to rule out humility altogether. Both streams of opinion join in endorsing Raphael's counsel to Adam that in love as elsewhere "oft times nothing profits more / Than self-esteem grounded on just and right."

Othello may seem to be carrying this principle far beyond "just and right" when he goes on to include among things that "shall manifest me rightly," not only his "parts" and his "title," but his "perfect soul" (1. 2. 31–32). But one is hard put to it to read Pelagianism into a character who not long after mentions casually how "to Heaven / I do confess the vices of my blood" (1. 3. 122–123). It is more satisfactory to suppose that what Othello is claiming perfection for here is only figuratively his soul, by much the same metonymy of mind for volition as enables the Duke in *Measure for Measure* to perform an act of choice "with special soul" (1. 1. 18). It is Othello's intentions toward Desdemona that he is vindicating as "perfect."

The fact remains that Othello conducts himself at first with precisely that "magnanimity" which Aristotle defines, in a celebrated passage,[2] as a high and warranted regard for one's own value, and which the Renaissance found some difficulty in reconciling with Christian humility. Such a reconciliation, however, on aristocratic and humanist assumptions, was not only possible but de rigueur. That man's self-regard could be relatively high and yet warranted is something only the theologians of "total depravity" would have been prepared to question. For the central tradition, human dignity is grounded in a resemblance to God that the Fall did not wholly undo, and a capacity for grace attested to by no less than the Atonement. The sin of spiritual pride, in that tradition, is "love of one's own excellence" not in any circumstances, but only "insofar as it results in an inordinate claim to superiority." When such love is not inordinate it is, Aquinas tells us, at once our instinct and our duty. And it is also, according to a commonplace of both scriptural and pagan morality, the indispensable measure of our love for others.[3] If one does not love oneself, one does not love. On these terms, a knight of Magnificence—one impelled to Christian valor by "prais-desire" and an aspiration to the hand of Gloriana—might well agree with Aristotle that if the self is properly defined, an active love for it is the crown of its nobility.[4]

Moreover, a loving suitor is bound to exhibit self-esteem of a more vulgar but no less respectable kind. For as Guazzo concludes on behalf of an impressive body of sixteenth-century opinion: "We will maintaine then for most true, touching generation, that as a man of men, and of beastes a beast, so of the good for the most part, is ingendered the good."[5] A suitor whose lineage may not "speak un-bonneted" to that of his intended, on this assumption, can have no lofty or loving concern for her welfare. When Othello says that "I fetch my life and being / From men of royal siege" (1. 2. 21–22), he is once more contending that his suit and success have been no affront to Desdemona, this time because he brings to their union a life and being of independent source and dignity:

> for know, Iago,
> But that I love the gentle Desdemona,
> I would not my unhoused free condition
> Put into circumscription and confine
> For the sea's worth.   (1. 2. 24–28)

Like the assertion of "demerits," that of independent noblesse implies that the lover has been and will remain an independent moral agent: "For it is a great deal lesse dispraise for him that is not borne a gentleman to faile in the actes of vertue, then for a gentleman. If he swerve from the steps of his ancestors, hee staineth the name of his familie. And doth not onely not get, but looseth that is alreadie gotten."[6] By his active life, the gentleman has confirmed his lineage; by his lineage, the suitor has, in part, deserved his bride; by continuing such a life, the general will keep faith with both lineage and bride.

Othello assures us, then, that his fundamental reasons for thinking well of himself are not accidental but essential, and hence quite distinct from the fact that he has won over Desdemona; and, at least by the traditional criterion, he could hardly be said to love Desdemona at all were he mistaken. But it turns out, as with other assurances of his we shall examine, that he is mistaken all the same; that the flimsiness of Othello's self-esteem strengthens him in his conviction of Desdemona's infidelity, just as his surrender to that conviction marks the end of what passes for his self-esteem.

An important element in the strength of his jealousy is Othello's surprising readiness to entertain the minority thesis, originated by Brabantio, that Desdemona's attraction to a Moor was unnatural to begin with, and hence, as Iago hastens to conclude, bound to fail. The implication is all the clearer as no one ever acknowledges the symmetrical possibility that Othello's attraction to Desdemona was equally unnatural, though this would be strictly entailed were miscegenation the real object of abhorrence and not presumed racial inferiority—not, in Brabantio's words, "the sooty bosom / Of such a thing as thou" (1. 2. 70–71). "If she had been bless'd," Iago elaborates, "she would never have lov'd the Moor" (2. 1. 257–258). It is the unnatural want of disgust in Desdemona, not the unnatural affection on both sides, that Iago appeals to as axiomatic proof that Desdemona must sooner or later deceive her husband: "Foh! one may smell in such, a will most rank, / Foul disproportions, thoughts unnatural" (3. 3. 232–233). And the likelihood founded on this premise—"haply, for I am black . . . she's gone" (ll. 263, 267)— is readily accepted by a man for whom illustrious descent was, by his own account, an important claim to the hand of his bride. It is helpful to remember that the same vulnerability meets the same fate in Othello's prototype:

> "You must know, then, that no otherwise does your Lady grieve at the sight of your Leader of Squadron in disgrace than for the pleasure she takes with him whenever he visits your house, for she has long since come to be galled by this blackness of yours." These words pierced the heart of the Moor even to its roots; but in order that he might know further (howbeit he took for true all that the Ancient had said because of the suspicion already born in his mind.)[7]

The gradual effect of Iago's news is, similarly, a surprising about-face. We begin to detect an unfamiliar note of self-abasement: "Not from mine own weak merits will I draw / The smallest fear or doubt of her revolt" (3. 3. 187–188). We are permitted to gather, from a desperate return to self-assertion, to what lengths Othello is willing to go in protesting his "greatness"; his "forked plague," we must know, is "the plague of great ones; / Prerogativ'd are they less than the base" (ll. 273–274). And we discover that a dominant theme in Othello's grief is a loss of face conceived so trivially as to bespeak a shocking meanness of spirit:

> OTH. Cuckold me!
> IAGO. O 'tis foul in her.
> OTH. With mine officer!

IAGO. That's fouler—

(4. 1. 211–215)

as if a liaison with a Duke would have been less of a betrayal than one with a lieutenant. There is perhaps a hint of this falling off in the confession with which the fatal interview begins, that the source of Othello's "life and being," independent as it may be of Desdemona, is not after all the source of his moral integrity; for "when I love thee not, / Chaos is come again" (3. 3. 91–92). But here at least it is Othello's love for his bride that makes a cosmos, and not, as we are made to see at last, hers for him—"the fountain from the which my current runs / Or else dries up" (4. 2. 59–60). Magnanimity, in the traditional sense of a justified self-esteem, is not maintained on another's sufferance.

The esteem of one's lady (to use the play's terms) may well be a jewel of the soul; but it cannot, as we have seen, replace the magnanimity that is the soul's immediate jewel. A fortiori, one can hardly refer one's magnanimity to a jewel so far from immediate as the esteem of people in general. Yet that, of course, is precisely what Iago argues, and what raises Othello's suspicion to a frenzy of vindictiveness. In the prevailing Renaissance view Iago's assumption that "Good name in man and woman, dear my Lord, / Is the *immediate* jewel of their souls" (3. 3. 155–156, italics added), if it is not simply hyperbolic, is simply mistaken. And the mistake, as Montaigne informs us, is elementary:

> There is both name, and the thing: the name, is a voice which noteth, and signifieth the thing: the name, is neither part of thing nor of substance: it is a stranger-piece joyned to the thing, and from it God who in and by himself is all fulnesse, and the type of all perfection, cannot inwardly be augmented or encreased; yet may his name be encreased and augmented, by the blessing and praise, which we give unto his exteriour workes.

The confusion becomes dangerous when it tempts us to erect name or repute into a justification, and ultimately into a criterion, of virtue:

"Vertue is a vaine and frivolous thing, if she draw her commendation from glory. In vaine should we attempt to make her keepe her rancke apart and so should we disjoyne her from fortune: for, what is more casuall then reputation? . . . It is chance that applieth glory unto us, according to her temeritie. I have often seene it to goe before desert; yea, and many times to out-goe merit by very much." Erasmus insists at length on the same distinction in his colloquy "On Things and Words":

> BEATUS. But if man is a reasoning animal, how remote is it from reason, in the goods (nay rather the conveniencies) of the body, and in outward things that Fortune at once gives and takes away as she pleases, to prefer the thing before the name; in the true goods of the mind, to set greater store by the name than the thing?
> BONIFACIUS. Marry, if you heed it well, it is but a backward judgment.[8]

So far Iago's remark to Cassio that reputation is a gift of fortune "oft got without merit, and lost without deserving" (2. 3. 269–270) is an unexceptionable truism. Iago's sophism in pursuing the argument is to draw the categorical inference that "reputation is an idle and false imposition," and to disregard the possibility that good name, when it does coincide with virtue, has at least the value of a practical resource. But Cassio's assumption that reputation is "the immortal part of myself" (ll. 263–264)—the soul's immediate jewel, in Iago's metaphor—is the more serious confusion; for "each honourable person chuseth rather to lose his honour, then to forgoe his conscience."[9] In conflicts between these two, as we have seen, it is the ill fortune of both Hamlet and Troilus to be capable of extolling the former by equating the latter with cowardice; Iago is rather more discreet. He pays the distinction a left-handed compliment when he exploits the double meaning of the word *honour*: "Her honour is an essence that's not seen; / They have it very oft that have it not" (4. 1. 16–17). The honor they have is a mere name for the honor they lack. A readiness to extend this confusion from oneself to others—to personify the name at the expense of the owner—

makes it easy for the slanderer to get at the owner by working on the name:

> Am I that name, Iago?   (4. 2. 118)

> Her name, that was as fresh
> As Dian's visage, is now begrim'd and black
> As mine own face.   (3. 3. 386–388)

Othello will belatedly recognize the distinction by admitting the possibility, and hollowness, of letting "honour outlive honesty" (5. 2. 245). His failure to see the distinction earlier has given Iago a weapon in the campaign to have Desdemona's honesty outlive her honor.

This failure, as I have suggested, is simply the obverse of a defect in the ground of Othello's self-esteem. The defect is symbolized with cruel precision by the image of derisive monstrosity that dominates the story of the Moor's fall. At the close of act 1, Iago promises a "monstrous birth" to be delivered by "hell and night" (3. 409–410). The storm that begins act 2 assumes the form of an impudent sea monster that "seems to cast water on the burning Bear" (1. 14). In act 3 Iago echoes Othello "as if there were some monster in his thought /Too hideous to be shown" (3. 107–108). The monstrous birth that Iago eventually reveals is an incubus of ridicule—"the green-ey'd monster which doth mock / The meat it feeds on" (ll. 166–167); an incubus that fuses at last with its victim:

> OTH. Dost thou mock me?
> IAGO.   I mock you not, by heaven.
>   Would you would bear your fortune like a man!
> OTH. A horned man's a monster and a beast.
>   (4. 1. 61–63)

The dread of a ridicule imagined by the sufferer as entailing his own monstrosity is the nightmare of a man whose self-esteem is wholly vicarious; it is this nightmare of being unmasked as "the fixed figure for the time of scorn / To point his slow and moving finger at" (4. 2. 54–55) that Iago makes it his essential business to conjure up:

> Do but encave yourself,
> And mark the fleers, the gibes, and notable scorns
> That dwell in every region of his face.
>
> (4. 1. 82–84)

Vocation and Self-Control

Magnanimity is not the only virtue that, from the earliest tradition of the "order of courtly knighthood," has been taken to qualify a lover as noble and his love as sincere. Among the others claimed by Othello are two that are quintessentially courtly: a sense of military calling and a capacity for self-control. Othello combines the two in an oath to his Venetian masters that will prove to have been searingly ironic:

> And Heaven defend your good souls, that you think
> I will your serious and great business scant
> When she is with me. No, when light-wing'd toys
> Of feather'd Cupid seel with wanton dullness
> My speculative and offic'd instruments
> That my disports corrupt and taint my business,
> Let housewives make a skillet of my helm
> And all indign and base adversities
> Make head against my estimation!
>
> (1. 3. 267–275)

The background of the General's disciplined commitment to his profession, we learn at the outset, is immemorial custom grown to be second nature:

> For since these arms of mine had seven years' pith
> Till now, some nine moons wasted, they have us'd
> Their dearest action in the tented field.
>
> (1. 3. 83–85)
>
> I do agnize
> A natural and prompt alacrity
> I find in hardness.   (ll. 232–234)

In an age of ardent if nostalgic chivalry, Othello's devotion to calling
has the most intimate bearing on his claim to be worthy of his bride.
"The chiefe profession of the Courtier should bee in armes," for only
in arms will he have an opportunity to display "that courage of
spirite which we seeke to have in our Courtier."[10] It is at least as true
for the courtly ethos of the sixteenth century as for that of the twelfth
that, in the words of Andreas, "love diminishes if the Lady considers
her lover timorous in battle."[11] Something of the flavor of such
an ethos may perhaps be guessed from the circumstance that for
the aristocratic Montaigne the expressions "honneste homme" and
"homme de guerre" are in some contexts virtually synonymous.
"Soldiership," a modern critic well observes, "is almost the condition
of nobility, and so the Shakespearean hero is usually a soldier."[12]

Disciplined valor presupposes self-control. Othello not only keenly
appreciates this connection: "Let's teach ourselves that honourable
stop, / Not to outsport discretion" (2. 3. 2–3); the menacing grace
of his forbearance in confronting Brabantio reflects a kind of crafts-
man's pleasure, a "prompt alacrity," in living by the principle:

> Keep up your bright swords, for the dew will rust them;
> Good signior, you shall more command with years
> Than with your weapons.   (1. 2. 59–61)
>
> Were it my cue to fight, I should have known it
> Without a prompter.   (ll. 83–84)

And once again, self-control is an amatory virtue. The compleat lover
of courtly tradition, as has not always been adequately recognized, is
required to be "moderatus moribusque compositus";[13] inevitably so,
for all virtues may be thought of as rooted in the moral equilibrium
of this one virtue, which

> free from all disquieting, is like the Captaine that without
> resistance overcommeth and raigneth. . . . on every side
> framed of a certaine agreement with himself, that filleth
> him with such a cleare calmenesse, that hee is never out of
> patience; and becommeth wholly and most obedient to
> reason, and readie to turne unto her all his motions, and

follow her where she lust to leade him, without any resistance.[14]

Othello sets the highest value on these commitments. The "ad-
versities" that should properly attend their abandonment, he says,
ought to be "indign and base," and to "make head against my
estimation." But a forfeit of "estimation" is precisely what Othello
will prove unable to avoid. Indeed, his farewell to the life of valor
is explicitly a farewell to virtue and pride as well:

> Farewell the plumed troops and the big wars
> That make ambition virtue! O, farewell!
> Farewell the neighing steed and the shrill trump,
> The spirit-stirring drum, th' ear-piercing fife,
> The royal banner, and all quality,
> Pride, pomp and circumstance of glorious war!
>
> (3. 3. 349–354)

What is perhaps more surprising is the discrediting of Othello's
pretension to self-control, under circumstances that form an ideal
test of that pretension. For it should be borne in mind that the
quality at issue, according to the usual definition, is the habit of being
swayed only by one's best judgment; but the obligation under which
Othello finds himself when confronted by Iago's testimony is to
exercise self-control in precisely this sense—to resist every impulse
to be satisfied by less than the exacting standard of evidence he
stipulates at the outset: "I'll see before I doubt" (3. 3. 190); "Give
me the ocular proof" (l. 360). In the absence of the faith to acquit
Desdemona out of hand, there remains the duty not to condemn her
to death unfairly.

"Ocular proof," to be sure, is useless if pressed beyond its immediate application, as is nowhere clearer than in Othello's high
regard for the "honesty" of Iago,

> Of whom his eyes had seen the proof
> At Rhodes, at Cyprus, and on other grounds
> Christen'd and heathen.   (1. 1. 28–30)

But the quality of which Othello had seen the proof is Iago's competence as ancient and nothing more, and for this purpose the evidence is no doubt reliable; Cassio corroborates it by implication when he assures Desdemona, regarding Iago, that she "may relish him more in the soldier than in the scholar" (2. 1. 166–167). Othello's mistake about Iago's character is a failure, not of ocular proof, but of conjecture, and failures in conjecturing character are partly due to inexperience—"little of this great world can I speak / More than pertains to feats of broils and battle" (1. 3. 86–87)— but chiefly to the unavailability of ocular proof whenever what is in question is a state of the soul:

> OTH.   I'll know thy thoughts.
> IAGO. You cannot, if my heart were in your hand.
>   (3. 3. 162–163)

Here one is reduced to indirect evidence of the kind that the opportunistic lawyer can interpret to suit his case:

> Stay you, good gentlemen. Look you pale, mistress?
> Do you perceive the gastness of her eye?
> Nay, if you stare, we shall hear more anon.
> Behold her well; I pray you, look upon her.
> Do you see, gentlemen? Nay, guiltiness will speak,
> Though tongues were out of use.
>   (5. 1. 105–110)

The experience of disillusion with an appraisal of character, however, is, if anything, a vindication of ocular proof properly applied: "Fathers, from hence trust not your daughters' minds / By what you see them act" (1. 1. 171–172). It is precisely because there is ocular proof of untrustworthiness that Brabantio has occasion to vouch for the fact that there is no such proof of its opposite. In the same way, "knavery's plain face is never seen till us'd" (2. 1. 321), but when used it can be seen plainly enough. The verdict of Desdemona's impromptu trial for elopement in the first scene establishes clearly that, where the issue is not a mental state or process but an external act, it is possible to satisfy oneself, as Brabantio does, by consulting ocular proof:

> Straight satisfy yourself,
> If she be in her chamber or your house,
> Let loose on me the justice of the state
> For thus deluding you.   (1. 1. 138–141)

By the standard of feasibility and equity the play itself endorses, Othello has both a right and a duty to demand ocular proof. Under the stress, however, of emotions we shall have to consider at a later stage in our argument, he is induced to attempt various compromises. Iago contrives to avoid the rigorous terms altogether by a blatantly sophistic inference:

> It were a tedious difficulty, I think,
> To bring them to that prospect. . . .
> It is impossible you should see this—
>   (3. 3. 397–398, 402)

—reasoning in which Othello acquiesces even though Iago himself toys with repudiating it—"What / If I had said I had seen him do you wrong?" (4. 1. 23)—and though folklore teems with "wittoles" who "make conscience to mistrust any il, though they see another and their wife in bed togither."[15] This relaxation of guard on Othello's part seems clearly meant to be interpreted as derelict.

But it is possible to find adequate evidence short of catching the offender in the act. Othello may reasonably demand, as he does, that Iago

> so prove it
> That the probation bear no hinge or loop
> To hang a doubt on,   (3. 3. 364–366)

and his witness makes appropriate assurances. The kind of thing Iago delivers instead (l. 206) is a repetition of Brabantio's old argument that "she has deceiv'd her father, and may thee" (1. 3. 294). And here the point is not that "strong circumstances" cannot be conceived "which lead directly to the door of truth" (3. 3. 406–407), but that imperfect analogy—between filial disobedience and wifely infidelity, for example—is not such a circumstance. Iago's argument for Desdemona's chronic mendacity, like Brabantio's for Othello's witchcraft, turns out not to be, as promised, "probable, and palpable to thinking" (1. 2. 76). The Duke sets the latter brief aside, not because it is too circumstantial, but because it is not circumstantial enough:

> To vouch this is no proof,
> Without more wider and more overt test
> Than these thin habits and poor likelihoods
> Of modern seeming do prefer against him.
>   (1. 3. 106–109)

The play, unlike *Hamlet*, is far from leaving its hero adrift in a universe grudging of criteria for distinguishing an "overt test" from a "poor likelihood." "Poor likelihoods" puffed up, indeed, are what Othello rejects in advance in an oath, like others to which he is addicted, that will rebound bitterly against him:

> Exchange me for a goat
> When I shall turn the business of my soul
> To such exsufflicate and blown surmises,
> Matching thy inference.   (3. 3. 180–183)

Moreover, we have already been given a painstaking and hopeful demonstration of how conflicting reports can be made to yield a common truth:

> DUKE. There is no composition in these news
>   That gives them credit. . . .
> 2 SEN. But though they jump not on a just account,—
>   As in these cases, where the aim reports,
>   'Tis oft with difference—yet do they all confirm
>   A Turkish fleet, and bearing up to Cyprus.
> DUKE. Nay, it is possible enough to judgement.

I do not so secure me in the error
But the main article I do approve
In fearful sense.   (1. 3. 1–12)

And a demonstration, besides, of how irreconcilable reports can be
sifted in the light of careful observation:

SAILOR. The Turkish preparation makes for Rhodes. . . .
DUKE. How say you by this change?
1 Sen.   This cannot be,
     By no assay of reason; 'tis a pageant,
     To keep us in false gaze. . . .
     We must not think the Turk is so unskilful
     To leave that latest which concerns him first,
     Neglecting an attempt of ease and gain
     To wake and wage a danger profitless. . . .
MESSENGER. The Ottomites, reverend and gracious,
     Steering with due course towards the isle of Rhodes,
     Have there injointed them with an after fleet.
1 SEN. Ay, so I thought. . . .
MESS. . . . and now they do restem
     Their backward course, bearing with frank appearance
     Their purposes toward Cyprus. . . .
DUKE. 'Tis certain, then, for Cyprus.
                                   (ll. 14–43)

This vindication of the senators' "assay of reason" is triumphant
and emphatic: the most egregious of Othello's compromises with
his original standard of evidence is to let himself be distracted from
the duty to seek a source of information independent of his single
witness. On this point even the primitive code that bears Othello out
on the propriety of putting adulteresses to death is duly meticulous:
"At the mouth of two witnesses, or three witnesses, shall he that is
worthy of death be put to death; but at the mouth of one witness he
shall not be put to death" (Deut. 17 : 6).
We have been prepared for this unhappy tendency to distraction

under pressure by an earlier scene of interrogation, the aftermath of Cassio's nocturnal brawl (2. 3. 204–249). Here Othello's express purpose is to find out

> who set it on;
> And he that is approv'd in this offence,
> Though he had twinn'd with me, both at a birth,
> Shall lose me.   (ll. 210–213)

Othello ends by abandoning the search for the *agent provocateur* and punishing one of the provoked parties instead.

The salient point here is not that the punishment finally meted out is petulant or despotic; we are reminded again and again, in fact, that Cassio's "action" has been staged by Iago in order to "offend the isle" (ll. 62–63), "whose qualification shall come into no true taste again but by the displanting of Cassio" (2. 1. 281–283); that Montano

> is of great fame in Cyprus,
> And great affinity, and that in wholesome wisdom
> He [Othello] might not but refuse you;
>   (3. 1. 48–50)

that Othello plans to keep Cassio at no more than "a politic distance" (3. 2. 13); in short, that Cassio has been dismissed "more in policy than in malice" (2. 3. 274). Nor does Othello's evaluation of Iago's testimony mark him out as a respecter of persons; his ability to resist the charms of his ancient has been tested in the matter of preferment, and in the present case he gently chides Iago for having been moved to flirt with perjury, if not as to the facts, at least as to the gravity of Cassio's misbehavior:

> I know, Iago,
> Thy honesty and love doth mince this matter,
> Making it light to Cassio. (2. 3. 246–248)

The glaring weakness in Othello's disposition of the case is that, though Iago lacks his usual advantage of being able to resort to lies, a simple rhetorical trick is enough to divert Othello from the purport of his original question "who began't" (l. 217), and from the part of Iago's testimony that is responsive to that question. For in the course of Iago's narrative it does transpire "how this foul rout began, who set it on" (l. 210); but the wanted man by Othello's definition— the man who insulted Cassio (l. 245) and whom Iago pursued "lest by his clamour, as it so fell out, / The town might fall in fright" (ll. 231–232)—receives unobtrusive mention four times, by periphrasis ("a fellow," "this gentleman," "the crying fellow," "him that fled"); and Cassio, who has thereby been plainly exonerated of the specified "offense," is prominently named six times, once in full (l. 222), in connection with a violence for which Iago insists on apologizing volubly, to Othello's mild but firm disapproval. The violence and (in consequence) the apology are of course beside the original point; but the repetition and the volubility are too much for Othello's patience. As he warns us at the outset:

> Now, by heaven,
> My blood begins my safer guides to rule;
> And passion, having my best judgement collied,
> Assays to lead the way.   (ll. 204–207)

Like Hotspur, Othello "apprehends a world of figures here, / But not the form of what he should attend." He is, throughout our acquaintance with him, a prisoner of his imagination, a man for whom "to be once in doubt / Is once to be resolv'd" (3. 3. 179–180), for whom no protestations can prevail against "the strong conception / That I do groan withal" (5. 2. 55–56), and the mere vivacity of a thought is enough to give it the semblance of a thing.

This last, indeed, appears to be the moral of a remarkable transition in the series of recurring cognitive terms that threads the scene of Othello's temptation: "satisfaction of my *thought*" (3. 3. 97, italics added here and following), "thy *thought*, Iago" (l. 98), "*think*, my lord" (ll. 105–106), "monster in his *thought*" (l. 107), "show me thy *thought*" (l. 116), "I *think* that he is honest" (l. 125), "I *think* so too" (l. 126), "as to thy *thinkings*" (l. 131), "utter my *thoughts*" (l. 136), "*thinkst* him wrong'd" (l. 143), "stranger to thy *thoughts*"

(l. 144), "let you *know* my *thoughts*" (l. 154), "I'll *know* thy *thoughts*" (l. 162), "long live you to *think* so" (l. 226), "let me *know* more" (l. 239), "sees and *knows* more" (l. 243), "*knows* all qualities" (l. 259), "*know't* a little" (l. 337), "let him not *know* it" (l. 343), "so I had nothing *known*" (l. 347). "Thinking" thus achieves the status of "knowing" by dint of sheer insistence; later on, we are not surprised to hear the grotesque parody of ontological proof in the mad reasoning that heralds Othello's fit: "Nature would not invest herself in such shadowing passion without some instruction" (4. 1. 39). For so clear and distinct a shadow, there cannot help but be the corresponding substance.

There is, we are told, nothing in Othello's career to prepare one for this debacle:

> Can he be angry? I have seen the cannon
> When it hath blown his ranks into the air,
> And, like the devil, from his very arm
> Puff'd his own brother. And is he angry?
>
> (3. 4. 134–137)

But the reaction of a professional to stresses under which he has been reared from boyhood is perhaps not the ideal test of his resistance to stress, just as Aristotle denies that an old salt can be called brave merely because of his practiced ease in the thick of the storm. Those who have judged Othello by his military performance have been, in Lodovico's words, "deceiv'd in him" (4. 1. 293)—deceived because the form taken by Othello's loss of control reveals the spuriousness of that control. To Lodovico it is a question of virtue:

> Is this the noble Moor whom our full Senate
> Call all in all sufficient? Is this the nature
> Whom passion could not shake? whose solid virtue
> The shot of accident nor dart of chance
> Could neither graze nor pierce?
>
> (ll. 275–279)

If, in other words, a solid virtue is never pierced, then a pierced virtue was never solid. To the audience, which knows the prurient revery of "noses, ears, and lips" (4. 1. 43) to which Othello has succumbed, and with which he himself has embroidered Iago's suggestions, it is a question of love. For as Iago mockingly reminds us, it is a commonplace that even "base men being in love have then a nobility in their natures more than is native to them" (2. 1. 216–218).

Constancy

The dependence of virtues on self-control is not the only reason the latter is deemed necessary by Renaissance theory to any love worthy of the name. Another and more essential one underlies the disclaimer in Othello's petition for Desdemona's company in Cyprus, though the speech has not always been very fairly dealt with:

> Vouch with me, Heaven, I therefore beg it not
> To please the palate of my appetite,
> Nor to comply with heat, the young affects
> In my defunct and proper satisfaction,
> But to be free and bounteous to her mind.
> (1. 3. 262–266)

According to one critic, "Othello foolishly thinks that he is not as other men and is underrating the physical commitments of marriage and the emotional complications following therefrom."[16] This view hardly sorts very well with the warm candor of Othello's later invitation to his bride:

> Come, my dear love,
> The purchase made, the fruits are to ensue;
> That profit's yet to come 'tween me and you.
> (2. 3. 8–10)

More important, the text in question clearly points another way; Othello is not in fact denying that he is, even as other men, subject to sensual appetite. Nor is he denying that such appetite is part of his reason for wishing Desdemona's company. Indeed, he is not explaining why he wishes her company at all, but rather why he has ventured to "beg" (l. 262) this indulgence of the Duke, who may well object to the conversion of a military expedition into a honeymoon.

Whatever subsidiary motives Othello may have, the only one he thinks urgent enough to warrant a petition and sway the Duke is love, which Othello is rightly careful to avoid reducing to "appetite," referring it instead to what he calls the freedom and bounty of the mind. For as the poet reminds us elsewhere, the necessary concomitant of an authentic love is constancy; love "is an ever-fixed mark / That looks on tempests and is never shaken." As such, its vital energy can hardly arise from a kind of desire that is by nature inconstant:

> Sweet love, renew thy force; be it not said
> Thy edge should blunter be than appetite,
> Which but today by feeding is allay'd,
> Tomorrow sharpen'd in his former might.

"Alas, their love may be call'd appetite," says Duke Orsino in disparagement of women, "No motion of the liver, but the palate, / That suffer surfeit, cloyment, and revolt." From this point of view, Troilus's anxiety about his finite capacity for love, conceived as a libidinal *haute cuisine*—"when that the wat'ry palates taste indeed / Love's thrice repured nectar"—is inauspiciously akin to his brother's definition of love as "hot deeds," the third generation after hot blood and thoughts; a pedigree in which Pandarus himself can see the desecration: "Is this the generation of love—hot blood, hot thoughts, and hot deeds? Why, they are vipers. Is love a generation of vipers?" Blood, as even the febrile Troilus is half aware, cannot be the seat of an affect "outliving beauties outward, with a mind / That doth renew swifter than blood decays."[17]

Love is thus irreducible to appetite, not because it excludes it, but because, as a union of the lovers in all their dimensions, it includes much more. And here Desdemona's parallel appeal may serve as an apt gloss on the real tenor of Othello's petition: "My heart's subdu'd / Even to the very [that is, the true] quality of my lord" (1. 3. 251–252). "A friend," as Guazzo declares, "loveth not so well his friend, a brother his brother, or a childe his father, as a wife doth her husbande: who not only confirmeth her selfe to his will, but wholly transformeth her selfe into him."[18] But the true quality or calling of Desdemona's lord, in its highest expression, is valor; and it is to Othello's valor that Desdemona counts her heart especially "subdu'd":

> to his honours and his valiant parts
> Did I my soul and fortunes consecrate.
> So that, dear lords, if I were left behind,
> A moth of peace, and he to go to the war,
> The rites for which I love him are bereft me,
> And I a heavy interim shall support
> By his dear absence.   (ll. 254–260)

Desdemona must try to be a soldier, at least by her presence at the field, if she is to perform "the rites" of union in which her love consists. It is this sharing of a life that Desdemona means when she tells the Duke that she "did love the Moor to live with him," and not merely, as one critic has it, the sharing of a bed—an interpretation wholly out of keeping with the occasion of the speech and with its plain sense.[19]

Desdemona's claim points in the same direction as Othello's; lovers' hearts are readily subdued to each other's qualities because their mutual fitness is essential and permanent rather than random and of the moment. As a standard idealizing view it is perhaps traceable to the notion of spiritual affinity by which Neoplatonism seeks to account for the universal attraction of physical beauty; even sexual attraction, when it is not merely perverse, presupposes an innate psychic harmony with its object.[20] From a generalized kinship it is a short step to a kinship binding individual pairs of lovers:

> For Love is a celestiall harmonie,
> Of likely harts compos'd of starres concent,
> Which ioyne together in sweet sympathie,
> To worke ech others ioy and true content,
> Which they haue harbourd since their first descent
> Out of their heauenly bowres, where they did see
> And know ech other here belou'd to bee.

Then wrong it were that any other twaine
Should in loues gentle band combyned bee,
But those whom heaven did at first ordaine,
And made out of one mould the more t'agree.[21]

When Othello denies that appetite is the sufficient condition of his desire to be with his wife, he is saying that the ground of that desire is permanent; that it is not witchcraft but rather, as the First Senator generously guesses, "such fair question / As soul to soul affordeth" (1. 3. 113).

Indeed, the Christian humanist interpretation of sexual love, a doctrine inherited and extended by Reformation theologians, is that, in Erasmus's words, "the more fervent one's charity toward one's wife, the more delightful is that conjugal coming together. And no men more fervently love their wives than those who love them as Christ loves the Church, for those who love them for pleasure's sake do not love them at all."[22] This view represents an advance on a Scholastic tradition that, while it concedes the goodness of sensual love, looks on it as wholly unrelated to spiritual.

In his treatise on ecstasy, Aquinas draws a typical distinction between "love of concupiscence" and "love of amity": "In the love of concupiscence the lover is somehow carried out of himself, insofar namely as, not content to enjoy the good he has, he seeks to enjoy something outside himself. But because he seeks to have that exterior good for himself, he does not transcend self absolutely; such emotion is ultimately self-confined. But in the love of amity a man's emotion goes absolutely beyond self, because he wishes well to his friend, as it were taking trouble and counsel for the sake of love." Aquinas's dichotomy answers more or less exactly to the *amare* and *bene velle* of the Roman poets; and the Renaissance idealization of love may be thought of as simply repudiating the dichotomy by amalgamation, a result perhaps enshrined in modern idioms like *vouloir du bien* and *voler bene*.

For according to the humanist and especially the Neoplatonic teaching, the "love of concupiscence" is simply the last enhancement of an experience rooted in the "love of amity": "Once the souls are

united in spiritual love, the bodies long to enjoy the union possible
to them, so that no separation may remain and the union may be
wholly perfect, particularly since with the correspondence of bodily
union, love is intensified and achieves greater completeness." By the
same token, however, the essential character of love is not the appetite
it dignifies but an overriding concern for the welfare of another person accepted as one's spiritual match. By this definition, an affection
withdrawn vindictively must have been something else:

> Love is not love
> That alters when it alteration finds,
> Or bends with the remover to remove.[23]

Hence the danger and irony of Othello's vow "Perdition catch my
soul / But [that is, unless] I do love thee" (3. 3. 90–91). For by the
test of the tradition expressed in sonnet 116, Othello is already a
candidate for "perdition." He is shortly to promise that his love is
the sort that alters when it alteration finds: "And on the proof, there
is no more but this,— / Away at once with love or jealousy" (ll. 191–
192). And soon after he will be as good (or bad) as his word:

> Look here, Iago;
> All my fond love thus do I blow to heaven.
> 'Tis gone. (ll. 444–446)

By this declaration Othello fulfills in advance the thinly veiled warning in the story of his mother's handkerchief:

> if she lost it,
> Or made a gift of it, my father's eye
> Should hold her loathed and his spirits should hunt
> After new fancies. She, dying, gave it me
> And bid me, when my fate would have me wiv'd,
> To give it her. I did so; and take heed on't;
> Make it a darling like your precious eye.
> To lose't or give't away were such perdition
> As nothing else could match. (3. 4. 60–68)

Given the Moor's oath of renunciation, his threat of "perdition" has a double edge. The love he protested with such vehemence is belied by his own inconstancy. From this point of view, there is a certain fitness in the parallel Desdemona implicitly draws between Othello and the maid Barbary's "false love" (4. 3. 55), who "prov'd mad / And did forsake her" (ll. 27–28).

It is significant that Desdemona herself thinks of Othello's desertion as an acid test of her own constancy: "his unkindness may defeat my life, / But never taint my love" (4. 2. 160–161). Ironically, it is Othello's victim who keeps faith in this exacting sense:

> My love doth so approve him
> That even his stubbornness, his checks, his frowns
> . . . have grace and favour in them.
>   (4. 3. 19–21)

> DES. A guiltless death I die.
> EMIL. O, who hath done this deed?
> DES. Nobody; I myself. Farewell!
> Commend me to my kind lord.
>   (5. 2. 122–125)

Trust and Knowledge

Part of the faith essential to love, in Othello's case a part even more crucial than his own constancy, is faith in the constancy of the beloved. It is a faith Othello proclaims at the outset in the form of a wager—"my life upon her faith" (1. 3. 295)—and, during his ordeal, in the form of a counterfeit certainty: "If she be false, O, then heaven mocks itself! / I'll not believe't" (3. 3. 278–279). Perhaps to enforce an invidious comparison, genuine certainty on this score takes parallel forms, and more daring ones at that:

> I durst, my lord, to wager she is honest,
> Lay down my soul at stake.   (4. 2. 12–13)

> Moor, she was chaste; she lov'd thee, cruel Moor;
> So come my soul to bliss, as I speak true.
>   (5. 2. 249–250)

As we have had occasion to notice, Othello is addicted to ironic vows, and the present one is no exception. He will lose his life, and much more, when he is no longer willing to wager it, thus tragically confirming the validity for human love of the divine paradox: "Whosoever shall seek to save his life shall lose it; and whosoever shall lose his life shall preserve it."

In the common Renaissance idealization, the faith that is taken to be essential to love between man and woman is not so much the substance of things hoped for as the evidence of things unseen. Inhering as it does in "waking soules, / Which watch not one another out of feare," it is a wager on a certainty, and rests on intuition. This is the point of Desdemona's remark that she "saw Othello's visage in his mind" (1. 3. 253), and not that "she, by implication, assents to her father's description" of Othello's ugliness.[24] Desdemona is simply pronouncing Brabantio's description irrelevant, whether true or false. If she is assenting to anything, it is to the commonplace that "vertues seat is deep within the mynd, / And not in outward shows but inward thoughts defynd";[25] if she is implying anything, it is that love does not require outward shows to see the visage in the mind. There is, then, no hint whatever, in her own speech or in the exchange as a whole, that the marriage "is, to some extent, unnatural in its uniting people of different social and ethnic background."[26] On the contrary, no union could be more natural; for, as the Duke assures Brabantio: "If virtue no delighted beauty lack, / Your son-in-law is far more fair than black" (ll. 290–291).

It is not enough, then, that there be a natural bond or affinity between a man and woman; the knowledge of that bond must be the motive of any attraction that fully deserves the name of love. And here the Renaissance had its choice of authorities. Even on the sensual level, as Ovid testifies, what is unperceived is undesired. And in general, no one wholly loves what he does not know, according to Augustine.[27] For the central current of Western thought, will, including the will expressed in love, is understanding in action; and the resulting priority of understanding to will is, as in Aquinas, a basic assumption. Ficino substantially agrees,[28] and succeeding Neoplatonists tend to follow suit.[29] True love (as opposed to infatuation) is thus commonly taken to be a cognitive emotion, and even a practical writer like the author of *Civile Conversation* manages to bow to the axiom, though the cognition he intends is to be had from a source less hieratic than intuition:

> I presuppose that to converse kindly with ones wife it is necessary first that hee bee well framed to love her; but for that a man cannot perfectly love that which he thoroughly knoweth not, it is needfull first to learne to knowe (as we have done) the good qualities and conditions of ones wife.[30]

According to the popular Neoplatonist tradition, the lover apprehends the higher spiritual possibilities of the loved through what Plotinus had called an act of nondiscursive understanding. On this view a lover's trust in his lady, like Calvin's "fiduciary faith," is the safest kind of bet. And it is of the essence of his love.

If Desdemona has seen Othello's visage in his mind, there are ominous indications that, despite Othello's resolve "to be free and bounteous to her mind," what he has seen in Desdemona's visage is only her visage. " 'Tis not to make me jealous," he says,

> To say my wife is fair, feeds well, loves company,
> Is free of speech, sings, plays, and dances well;
> Where virtue is, these are more virtuous.
> (3. 3. 183–186)

But the question of virtue itself is left open. And it would seem from a later passage that for Othello Desdemona's appearance and accomplishments are not so much what she has as what she is:

> OTH. Hang her! I do but say what she is. So delicate with her needle! an admirable musician! O! she will sing the the savageness out of a bear. Of so high and plenteous wit and invention!
> IAGO. She's the worse for all this.

OTH. O, a thousand thousand times. And then, of so
gentle a condition!
IAGO. Ay, too gentle.
OTH. Nay, that's certain.   (4. 1. 198–205)

Desdemona's "gentle condition" is part of her exterior, and hence
incapable of protecting Othello from the "certainty" that there is
nothing within. It is not the "condition" that Caxton's *Boke of
Good Manners* speaks of when it counsels "men . . . that purpose
to marye . . . to advyse and beholde the condicyoun of her that thay
desire to haue to wyf."[31] If Desdemona's music and needlework are
"what she is," we are not to wonder that the shaken Othello is
reduced to asking her "Why, what art thou?" and that he fails to
recognize the answer: "Your wife, my lord; your true / And loyal
wife" (4. 2. 34–35). Like the story of Lear, Othello's shows us a
failure to love another mind rooted in a failure to know it. It is this
kind of ignorance that Othello is conceding when he defers to Iago's
superior knowledge:

> Why did I marry? This honest creature doubtless
> Sees and knows more, much more, than he unfolds. . . .
> This fellow's of exceeding honesty,
> And knows all qualities, with a learn'd spirit,
> Of human dealings.
>   (3. 3. 242–243, 258–260)

Othello is not only incapable of mustering up a faith in Desdemona
commensurate with his mighty wager; if we are to judge by his
response to Iago's initial hints, he is equally incapable of so much
as a strong prejudice in her favor. For those hints are broad enough
to leave Othello no room for doubt about what Iago is trying to
convey:

> I heard thee say even now, thou lik'st not that,
> When Cassio left my wife. What didst not like?
> And when I told thee he was of my counsel
> In my whole course of wooing, thou criedst, "Indeed!"

And didst contract and purse thy brow together,
As if thou then hadst shut up in thy brain
Some horrible conceit.   (ll. 109–115)

Indeed, Othello's plea that Iago should reveal his meaning to his
friend "if thou but think'st him wrong'd" (l. 143) is virtually an
announcement that the pleader already has his wish. The ancient's
first hints, in short, are as transparent as those of the *alfiero* in Cinthio's account:

> "Perchance Desdemona has reason to see him willingly."
> "And why?" quoth the Moor. "I am not fain," the ancient
> replied, "to put a hand betwixt husband and wife: but if
> you will give over winking you will see it for yourself."
> Nor for all the Moor's importunity would the ancient
> proceed further; although such words left in the Moor's
> mind so piercing a thorn that he gave himself with much
> travail to thinking what such words could mean and grew
> passing melancholy thereby.[32]

Othello will eventually (ll. 180–182) affect to dismiss Iago's "inference," on grounds the latter himself has provided by speaking of
his information as a "guess" (l. 145) and a "scattering and unsure
observance" (l. 151). But the Moor's initial reaction is neither a
dismissal nor a rebuke. Instead, he pretends incomprehension and
begs Iago to put the innuendo into words. Even after Othello is
finally granted his disingenuous request (ll. 193–213) his first definite
response is to declare himself eternally obliged ("I am bound to thee
forever," l. 213).

Far from being ready to bet his life on Desdemona's faith, Othello
puts up scarcely a crumb of resistance to the opposite suggestion. He
reacts not out of trust but out of impatience to end the misery of doubt
by having himself talked into the beginnings of conviction—only to
find in those beginnings a far deeper misery (l. 171). One might
perhaps argue, in Chaucer's words, that "alwey the nye slye / Maketh
the ferre leeve to be looth"—that Desdemona is absent, Iago a
plausibly diffident and reluctant witness, and that Othello is thereby

maneuvered into a false alternative: not Iago's representations against Desdemona's, but Iago's information about Desdemona against his own. But Othello himself gives the lie to this hypothesis:

> By the world,
> I think my wife be honest and think she is not;
> I think that thou art just and think thou art not.
>
> (ll. 383–385)

Othello clearly sees that Iago's veracity is itself an issue; his subsequent assumption of that veracity results from a conscious choice between faith in Desdemona and faith in Iago. If there are any prepossessions operating here, they are not in Desdemona's favor.

Othello has shown himself more than ready to arraign Desdemona on the strength of an innuendo. For a diametrical contrast to such want of faith, one need only consider Desdemona's parallel moment of reckoning. Confronted with clear evidence of Othello's "unkindness," she refuses to condemn him for it:

> Beshrew me much, Emilia,
> I was, unhandsome warrior as I am,
> Arraigning his unkindness with my soul;
> But now I find I had suborn'd the witness,
> And he's indicted falsely.
>
> (3. 4. 150–154)

One need not conclude that Desdemona's excess of faith is, like Othello's want of it, the mark of infatuation and ignorance. We are given no reason to question Othello's "honours and his valiant parts," and these indeed are the "rites" for which she loves him. On the other hand, though Desdemona's love may be grounded in a truth, it is certainly unwise as the world sees wisdom. And in this sense it is she and not Othello who loves not wisely but too well. But then, it is part of Othello's undoing to embrace wisdom as the world sees wisdom, as in his reply to a cynicism of Iago's: "O, thou art wise; 'tis certain" (4. 1. 74); or in his bitter critique of what he takes to be a flaw in his wife's veneer of fidelity: "Are you wise?" (l. 245).

Temptation and Jealousy

I have been arguing that Othello has been put to a test that is
substantially of his own choosing, and one that, according to the most
exacting and respectful definition available to him, is a test of love.
By that definition love is a kind of virtue, and includes others. If
the virtues Othello proves to lack are indeed the makings of the love
that is a "marriage of true minds" as well as an appetite, he has
failed the test—failed in magnanimity, devotion to calling, self-
control, constancy, and trust.

This result is not new, and above all, not surprising. Iago, we
remember, defines his art as essentially temptation—the sort of thing
devils do when they "will the blackest sins put on [i.e., incite]"
(2. 3. 357). But "temptation" in the strict theological sense, like its
etymon, means not inciting a man but putting him to the test:
tentare est proprie experimentum sumere de aliquo. For "some men,"
as Aquinas explains, "are more inclined to one vice than to another.
And therefore the devil makes trial, probing the inner condition of
a man in order to test for that vice to which the man is more inclined."[33] Hence, when Dante is rendering the relevant petition in
the Pater Noster (*ne nos inducas in tentationem*), he pregnantly
uses the Italian cognate of *experimentare*, which Du Cange cites as
a medical term. Tempting is the diagnostic or reconnoitering phase
of "putting on." A man is tripped up by exploiting the very tremor
in his moral gait that helps the devil do the tripping.[34]

Moreover, vindictive jealousy itself is notoriously a besetting vice
of the wrong kind of love, and more truly a matter of expectation
than of response. "Canne you tell mee," asks the teacher in *Civile
Conversation*, "wherof commeth that common distrust that menne
have in their wives?" "Perchaunce of the fragilitie and weaknesse of
the flesh, which is attributed to most women," ventures the pupil;
but he is of course mistaken: "Nay rather of the weaknesse of love,
which ought to be attributed to most men."[35] In a later Jacobean
play, the tragicomedy *Philaster*, we find an instructively clinical study
of the theme. The Prince of Sicily expresses to his lady at the outset

a noble contempt for gratuitous distrust: "To suspect / Were base, where I deserve no ill" (1. 2. 93–94). It is also evidently to his credit that, in spite of her apparently sincere urging, he proudly refuses to surrender the royal succession to her (1. 2. 57–63). Later on, the same young man, now betrothed to the lady, succumbs to a libel on her honor after very perfunctory resistance: " 'Tis false! by heaven, 'tis false! It cannot be! / Can it?" (3. 1. 94–95). And the other side of perverse distrust in the lady is perverse trust in the libeler: "he that tells me this is honourable, / As far from lies as she is far from truth" (ll. 140–141). The desperation that ensues is aggravated by a mood of facile skepticism foreshadowed in the remark of a minor character: "Every man in this age has not a soul of crystal, for all men to read their actions through: men's hearts and faces are so far asunder that they hold no intelligence" (1. 1. 259–262). Ironically the credulous hero suffers increasing frustration on this score, as when he attempts to force a confession from his supposed rival:

> Tell me thy thoughts; for I will know the least
> That dwells within thee, or will rip thy heart
> To know it. I will see thy thoughts as plain
> As I do now thy face.   (3. 1. 228–231)

And the motive of his bullying, as an earlier gambit makes clear, is a recognizably pathetic and itchy masochism:

> I bade her do it; I charg'd her, by all charms
> Of love between us, by the hope of peace
> We should enjoy, to yield thee all delights
> Naked as to her bed. I took her oath
> Thou shouldst enjoy her. Tell me, gentle boy,
> Is she not parallelless? Is not her breath
> Sweet as Arabian winds when fruits are ripe?
> Are not her breasts two liquid ivory balls?
> Is she not all a lasting mine of joy?
>   (3. 1. 198–206)

This transport of homemade pornography is entirely gratuitous.

Before the jealousy has run its course, the Prince's pride in his title goes the way of his trust: "Now you may take that little right I have / To this poor kingdom" (3. 2. 105–106); he declares all women "a mere confusion and so dead a chaos / That love cannot distinguish" (ll. 125–126); and not long after prepares, in the name of justice and with an executioner's punctilio, to put the lady to the sword as a disgrace to her sex:

> Then guide my feeble hand,
> You that have power to do it, for I must
> Perform a piece of justice! If your youth
> Have any way offended Heaven, let prayers
> Short and effectual reconcile you to it.
> (4. 3. 72–76)

To the innocent bystander the jealousy has presented itself as a visitation of nemesis:

> O what god,
> Angry with men, hath sent this strange disease
> Into the noblest minds? (3. 2. 146–148)

To the sufferer himself it seems a pollution:

> O where shall I
> Go bathe this body? Nature too unkind,
> That made no medicine for a troubl'd mind![36]
> (3. 1. 243–245)

The case of Shakespeare's own Posthumus, though psychologically cruder, would support similar conclusions. Jealousy, in short, is a state of degradation midway between a vice and a disease, and perhaps a shade more akin to the former. "Of all the vices in the mind," as Spenser apostrophizes it, "thou vilest art." His paradigm of the jealous man is a "foredamned spright," reprobate and ridden by self-hatred:

> And he himselfe himselfe loath'd so forlorne,
> So shamefully forloren of womankind;
> That as a Snake, still lurked in his wounded mind.

Such emotions, to say the least, do not bespeak a firm nobility of mind. They never did. In the earliest literature of courtly love a man capable of being moved to despair or hatred by a woman to whom he attributes despicable conduct is "judged unworthy of being cured at all and is lower down than carrion." For Cinthio, the Moor's ruling passion is "beastly" and has no mitigating effect; when he is killed at last, he is simply getting what he deserves.[37]

The abject lovelessness of the spirit capable of jealousy is well illustrated by the Moor's fellow sufferers in the play. Jealousy, in one case, is the obsession of the abused concubine painfully aware of her replaceable function as "hobby horse":

> BIAN. This is some token from a newer friend;
>   To the felt absence now I feel a cause.
>   Is't come to this? Well, well.
> CAS.   Go to, woman!
>   Throw your vile guesses in the devils' teeth,
>   From whence you have them. You are jealous now
>   That this is from some mistress, some remembrance.
>   (3. 4. 181–186)

> BIAN. This is some minx's token, and I must take out
> the work? There; give it your hobby-horse. (4. 1. 158–159)

The "love" she is so eager to solemnize, we find, is based on the frank assumption that her company is discreditable to her partner:

> BIAN. Leave you! Wherefore?
> CAS. I do attend here on the General;
>   And think it no addition, nor my wish,
>   To have him see me woman'd.
> BIAN.   Why, I pray you?
> CAS. Not that I love you not.
> BIAN.   But that you do not love me.
>   (3. 4. 192–196)

What she sees of that partner is as unlovely as what he sees of her:

> CAS. What do you mean by this haunting of me?

BIAN. Let the devil and his dam 'haunt' you!

(4. 1. 151–153)

The only binding pledge of that love she has received is a delusion: "She is persuaded I will marry her, out of her own love and flattery, not out of my promise" (ll. 131–133). In sum, the companionship she cannot do without, and that consists in being continually reminded of her status as a human "fitchew" and "monkey," is a demeaning addiction, a "dotage." "It is a creature," Iago says of her with his usual pitilessness, "That dotes on Cassio, as 'tis the strumpet's plague / To beguile many and be beguil'd by one" (4. 1. 96–98).

Jealousy is also the obsession of the mawkish prodigal whose ideal of love admits of an "unlawful solicitation" (4. 2. 202) in which one's patrimony is wasted in attempts at bribing affection. The affection behind both jealousy and bribe, we find, is living in the hope that a sum of jewels large enough to have "half . . . corrupted a votarist" (ll. 189–190) will succeed in wholly corrupting, if not a votarist, at least a nature "full of most bless'd condition" (2. 1. 254–255). Not love, then, or ordinary lust, but the kind of morbid impulse that drives Angelo, in *Measure for Measure*, to question his feeling for Isabella:

> Having waste ground enough
> Shall we desire to raze the sanctuary
> And pitch our evils there? (2. 2. 170–172)

The conscience that allows this impulse ends by entertaining the thought of a murder, provided it is shown "such a necessity in his death that you shall think yourself bound to put it on him" (*Oth.* 4. 2. 246–248), and finally makes the attempt on the assumption that "satisfying reasons" for murder are perfectly compatible with having "no great devotion to the deed"; for " 'tis but a man gone. Forth, my sword; he dies" (5. 1. 8–10). The lover whose passion is fit food for jealousy is the "sick fool . . . whom love hath turn'd almost the wrong side out" (2. 3. 53–55), and whose love at bottom is no more than a "carnal sting" and a "lust of the blood" (1. 3. 335, 339).

The play itself, then, is quite explicit on two points. First, whatever the provocation, jealousy is essentially self-generating:

> DES. Alas the day! I never gave him cause.
> EMIL. But jealous souls will not be answer'd so.
> They are not ever jealous for the cause,
> But jealous for they're jealous. It is a monster
> Begot upon itself, born on itself.
> (3. 4. 158–162)

It is the disease of "credulous fools" (4. 1. 46) who are "fools" long before they express themselves in credulity, the disease that actively "shapes faults that are not" (3. 3. 148). Jealousy is also the reflex of a spiritual corruption incompatible with love. Such corruption, to be sure, can go with valor and genius:

> As where's that palace whereinto foul things
> Sometimes intrude not? Who has that breast so pure
> But some uncleanly apprehensions
> Keep leets and law-days and in sessions sit
> With meditations lawful?
> (3. 3. 137–141)

But the fact remains that to prove oneself "true of mind and made of no such baseness / As jealous creatures are" (3. 4. 27–28), it is necessary first not to be a jealous creature.

Self-Pity

The seed of jealousy, then, is lack of love; and the play has prepared us for this realization by offering us an early glimpse of the emotion Othello mistakes for love. The occasion is Othello's sketch of his life (1. 3. 128–169), a life typified in his account as much by "most disastrous chances," by the memory of "some distressful stroke /

That my youth suffer'd," as by "moving accidents" and "hair-breadth scapes."

But it is the strokes and not the scapes, as it turns out, that Othello regards as decisive; for what he loved in Desdemona, he tells us, was not that she was Desdemona but that her response to the story of those strokes answered a need: "And I lov'd her that she did pity them." Othello is bound to Desdemona by gratitude; and gratitude, unlike love (love as the Renaissance conceived it, at any rate), is strictly a quid pro quo. Remove the benefit and the bond is dissolved, to be replaced, perhaps—if what was removed was needed intensely enough—by some darker emotion. In Othello's case, the benefit apparently withdrawn is pity. And the intensity of Othello's need for it would seem to arise from that very condition of being "unhoused" and "free" in which we have seen him (1. 2. 26) take such ostentatious pride. For when Iago describes him as "an erring barbarian" (1. 3. 362), the dramatic portent in "erring" should not distract us from its radical meaning. To the Venetians, as more than one critic has remarked, Othello is "the Moor," a stateless officer of the state whose race is a badge of alienation. He is an "extravagant and wheeling stranger" (1. 1. 137). His life is only too literally a wandering, a "pilgrimage" (1. 3. 153) or a "journey" (5. 2. 267), and he will greet his death as the "butt / And very sea mark of my utmost sail" (ll. 267–268). As an outlander and a "barbarian," he is scornfully but defensively conscious that he has not "those soft parts of conversation / That chamberers have" (3. 3. 264–265). The vernacular itself is allied with his own inexperience against him, and therefore "little shall I grace my cause / In speaking for myself" (1. 3. 88–89). With such a history, it must surely come as both a destiny and a minor betrayal that Desdemona, in a moment of tact-lessness that plays into Iago's hands, tells her husband how, during their courtship, she "spoke of you dispraisingly" (3. 3. 72).

Othello's interest in marriage with Desdemona, then, is quite selfish and is confined to the "comfort" that dominates his speeches to her on landing in Cyprus (2. 1. 185–209). The false note in those speeches is not "an excessive delight in the pleasures of marriage"[38] but an exclusive delight in them, one that the speaker himself comes near to detecting:

> O my sweet,
> I prattle out of fashion and I dote
> In mine own comforts   (2. 1. 207–209)

There is no love in a dotage that reduces the "valiant Moor" (1. 3. 47) to a prattler. Dotage is a wasting infatuation, like the "voluntary dotage" (4. 1. 27) of which Desdemona will be accused, or the "plague" of the "creature that dotes on Cassio." A complete love must dedicate itself to its object, and not merely the object to itself; it must complement *amare* with *bene velle*.

And hence it is at least suggestive that the playwright has ignored one of the few lengthy exchanges in his presumed source, in which the cause of the Moor's apology for taking Desdemona with him to Cyprus is not military but amorous; for "his happiness waned none the less whenever he bethought him of the distance and hardship of the voyage."[39] Desdemona's own enjoyment must go unregarded by the Shakespearean Othello because her value to him, however high, is that of a possession to be enjoyed, like the "entire and perfect chrysolite" for which he would not have "sold" her (5. 2. 145–146). To sell, one must own; and as Othello's degradation proceeds, the note of trespass, of outraged ownership, becomes more strident:

> O curse of marriage,
> That we can call these delicate creatures ours,
> And not their appetites! I had rather be a toad
> And live upon the vapour of a dungeon
> Than keep a corner in the thing I love
> For others' uses.   (3. 3. 268–273)

It goes without saying that the "thing" Othello loves is "kept" for his own "uses"; he will surely not "keep it as a cistern for foul toads / To knot and gender in" (4. 2. 61–62).

There is, to be sure, nothing wrong in itself with putting the highest earthly value on one's wife; and if this is what is meant by

"uxoriousness," then it is quite mistaken, from the Renaissance point
of view, to say that "the root of Othello's desolation lies in his
uxoriousness."[40] The husband, as Guazzo tells us, "must account of
his wife as his onely treasure on earth, and the most precious Jewell
he hath." But when Guazzo and his contemporaries write in this vein,
the jewel they are commending is not so much a personal possession
as a mutual commitment, a commitment that justifies the highest
zeal: "to beare this honour bravely, there is nothing that maketh
them [i.e., man and wife] better in breath, then to exercise themselves in faythfull and fervent love, which once beginning to fayle,
either on the one syde or the other, this honoure forthwith falleth
to the ground." When the priest in Thomas Becon's catechism asks:
"Must the love of a married man toward his wife excel his love
toward all other persons?" the prompt and orthodox reply of the
catechumen is "Yea, verily"—an idealizing strain in the Christian
view of marriage that will be festively summarized much later by
Jeremy Taylor.[41]

Othello's difficulty, unfortunately, is not an excessive desire to
give comfort to his wife but rather an excessive desire for wifely
comfort, and one irony of this excess, according to the Erasmian
view we considered earlier, is that the latter comfort cannot endure
without the former. In this connection it would be of obvious interest
to arrive at a satisfactory interpretation of the lines in which Othello
confesses his fears for his own "comfort":

> If it were now to die,
> 'Twere now to be most happy; for, I fear,
> My soul hath her content so absolute
> That not another comfort like to this
> Succeeds in unknown fate. (2. 1. 191–195)

The principal stumbling block in this crucial passage appears to
be the meaning of "unknown fate." Depending on the inclusiveness
of this expression, two paraphrases suggest themselves: My immediate death would mark the summit (*a*) of my mortal happiness,
which will not be equaled in this life ("unknown fate"), or (*b*) of
my happiness in general, which will not be equaled in this life or

the next ("unknown fate"). On the latter view Othello "ascribes to [Desdemona] a place in his life that properly belongs to God" and is therefore blaspheming.[42] But Desdemona's reply indicates quite clearly that she understands "unknown fate" to include only this life:

> The heavens forbid
> But that our loves and comforts should increase
> Even as our days do grow!   (ll. 195–197)

If Othello were disparaging, not only the future happiness possible to this life, but the happiness possible to the next life as well, Desdemona's haste in praying for the former without a word of concern for the latter would bespeak an incredible lapse either in her piety or in her attention. The truth of Othello's ironic premonition, moreover, would lose its bite were he fearing a general decline in joy whatever the source (whether man or God) rather than a particular decline in the joy of his rapport with Desdemona.[43] Far from deifying her, he conspicuously lacks the confidence she does not hesitate to express in the capacity of their marriage ("loves and comforts") for growth.

Such misgivings in the face of intense elation are as old at least as Horace's warning to the ardent Lydia and are usually based on the reasoning of Friar Lawrence:

> These violent delights have violent ends,
> And in their triumph die, like fire and powder,
> Which as they kiss consume: the sweetest honey
> Is loathsome in his own deliciousness,
> And in the taste confounds the appetite:
> Therefore love moderately; long love doth so;
> Too swift arrives as tardy as too slow.

If the substance of love is simply physical, its own intensity will burn it out. But love in the fullest sense, in Donne's phrase, "doth every day admit new growth," and Juliet, for her part, though she thinks her contract "too rash, too unadvis'd, too sudden," does not share the Friar's unflattering fears for her love: "This bud of love, by

summer's ripening breath, / May prove a beauteous flower when
next we meet."[44]

Othello's fear for himself is unflattering for the same reason as
the Friar's for his charges, and it is not surprising that it corresponds
exactly to Iago's calculations about Desdemona: "It was a violent
commencement in her, and thou shalt see an answerable sequestration" (1. 3. 349–351). The operative word here is "violent"; "mark
me," he resumes later, "with what violence she first lov'd the Moor"
(2. 1. 224–225). But there is, on the more optimistic view, no reason
at all why "violence," or, in Othello's terms, the soul's absolute
content, should suffer an abatement or a "sequestration." It is worth
pointing out that amorous "violence" has no such ominous ring for
Desdemona:

> That I did love the Moor to live with him,
> My downright violence and storm of fortunes
> May trumpet to the world. (1. 3. 249–251)

Othello's attachment to Desdemona, then, combines with a need
for pity a concentration on personal "content" that, with nothing
deeper to sustain it, is all too likely to end by fading. And Desdemona's attachment to him, on his theory of it—"she lov'd me for
the dangers I had pass'd" (1. 3. 167)—is equally likely to end in
discontent. For pity is a very unpromising ground of attraction.
The same "dangers" that have made Othello worthy of it may, for
all he knows, make him unattractive as well, especially to a Venetian
woman whose "country disposition" (3. 3. 201) is a mystery to him.
His forebears have been kings; but he has also been "taken by the
insolent foe / And sold to slavery" (1. 3. 137–138), a fact about
Desdemona's partner in elopement that has not been lost on Brabantio: "if such actions may have passage free, / Bondslaves and pagans
shall our statesmen be" (1. 2. 98–99). In status, then, Othello will
receive from his marriage very much more than he gives, and Iago
may be depended on to recognize this fact: "If it prove lawful
prize, he's made forever" (1. 2. 51).

Moreover, "dangers pass'd" do not keep a man young, and
Othello grudgingly concedes that he is "declin'd into the vale of

years" (3. 3. 265–266), just as earlier in the play he seems to
suggest that "the young affects" are "defunct" in him (1. 3. 264–
265).[45] If pity is indeed the substance of Desdemona's love for
Othello it is not impossible to suppose, as Iago does, that "she must
change for youth" (l. 355–356). If Desdemona is attracted by neither
esteem nor appetite, it would seem that in the end she is attracted
by nothing at all, and that the inevitable result will be frustration and
the end of pity: "her delicate tenderness will find itself abus'd, begin
to heave the gorge, disrelish and abhor the Moor" (2. 1. 234–236).

But Othello's theory of Desdemona's love is, of course, quite
false, as we can see from his own account:

> 'Twas pitiful, 'twas wondrous pitiful,
> She wish'd she had not heard it; yet she wish'd
> That Heaven had made her such a man.
> (1. 3. 161–163)

It is not the pitiful trials that inspire her wishes, but the man who
proved equal to them, a man to whose "quality" she would willingly
be "subdu'd." Nor need we follow Iago in writing off Othello's
odyssey as "bragging and . . . fantastical lies" (2. 1. 225–226) and
Desdemona's wonder, by implication, as childish. Hakluyt and Drake
would have agreed with her evaluation, as (at the outset) Brabantio
himself had done:

> Her father lov'd me; oft invited me;
> Still question'd me the story of my life
> From year to year, the battles, sieges, fortunes,
> That I have pass'd.   (1. 3. 128–131)

Othello's failure to appreciate Desdemona's love is perhaps quite as
decisive as his failure to love; for it is a commonplace of Christian
lore that such an appreciation can be redemptive. As one medieval
writer has it: "the love of a person's good qualities has this mighty
power, that it always forces its own requital by the person beloved,
provided only that it appear outwardly by some clear sign."[46] The
sign, in Othello's case, is there, but it is in a language he is unable
to read.

This spiritual illiteracy is an affliction that has become familiar enough to us from the plays we have already considered, in which self-transcendence is similarly elusive. Even more than the behavioral testing involved in Hamlet's Mousetrap, Duke Vincentio's deputation of Angelo, and Lear's Love Auction, Othello's obsession with flimsy conjecture, eavesdropping, and the significance of a missing handker-chief speaks pathetically to us of a lifelong, if unwitting, solitary confinement. But again as in the other cases, the play as a whole judges Othello more searchingly and with a finer compassion than Othello ever thinks to judge his enemies, real and imagined. From the possibility of that judgment, as we shall see, Shakespeare has drawn a tragic affirmation complementary in meaning to that of *King Lear.*

CHAPTER SIX

Justice and Responsibility in Othello

THE PSYCHOLOGY of wrongdoing has a certain fascination for the principals of the plays we have considered. Hamlet, for example, reflects that often "reason panders will" (3. 4. 88), and a "vicious mole of nature" (1. 5. 24) or a "habit" (l. 29), which is second nature, can end by "breaking down the pales and forts of reason" (l. 28); there is, he suggests, something unfair in blaming the owner of the "vicious mole" for the behavior that results; "nature cannot choose his origin" (l. 26). Claudio speculates on his way to prison that

> our natures do pursue,
> Like rats that ravin down their proper bane,
> A thirsty evil; and when we drink we die.
>
> (1. 2. 132–134)

And once arrived at the prison we encounter an inmate hopelessly, if comically, beyond the reach of appeals to conscience; "careless, reckless, and fearless" (4. 2. 150), he piques and frustrates the curiosity of those who would understand him. Lear, once more, is puzzled not only by "the cause of thunder" (3. 4. 160) but by the "cause in nature," if any, "that makes these hard hearts" (3. 6. 81–82). In *Othello* we are invited to descend into the private hell that is the subject of these speculations, less to assign it a "cause in nature" than to assure ourselves that the view from hell, plausible as a glib Edmund or Iago may sometimes make it appear, is as false as we hope and think it to be. The theme of *Othello*, in effect, is the Importance of Not Being Iago—or Othello, for that matter; and the play helps us begin to think about that importance by focusing, subtly and even insidiously, on certain paradoxes in the assessment of guilt.

We have found that Othello's compulsive belief in his own betrayal is presented by the playwright as rooted in an inveterate habit of mind. But this raises a question of responsibility that can hardly be ignored without ignoring the characterization of the central figure. For it is hard to see how a man can be to blame for a compulsive act, or for habits contracted under circumstances not very likely to have been of his own choosing; is it possible that Othello, as the play characterizes him, is not to blame for his act of belief?

One plausible approach to this question is simply to consider how questions of the kind are approached in the tradition of moral analysis to which Shakespeare and his contemporaries were heirs; and for an exemplary statement of this approach, craftily shorn of its ambiguities, we could hardly do better than to study Iago's exhortation to Roderigo, who has begged to be excused from trying to shake off his dotage "because it is not in my virtue"—that is, not in his power or disposition—"to amend it." It is this sense of the word that Iago retorts on with "Virtue! a fig! 'tis in ourselves that we are thus or thus"; far from being a limitation on choice, character or habit is itself subject to choice, or to revision.

Iago proceeds to amplify by combining two illustrative metaphors, the garden and the scales:

> Our bodies are our gardens, to the which our wills are gardeners; so that if we will plant nettles or sow lettuce, set hyssop and weed up thyme, supply it with one gender of herbs or distract it with many, either to have it sterile with idleness or manured with industry, why, the power and corrigible authority of this lies in our wills. If the balance of our lives had not one scale of reason to poise another of sensuality, the blood and baseness of our natures would conduct us to most preposterous conclusions; but we have reason to cool our raging motions, our carnal stings, our unbitted lusts.   (1. 3. 320–336)

Most of the traits of character that compete for our adoption are not morally indifferent, but conflict by appealing respectively to our rational or irrational faculties; we are called on, for example, to choose a life

of care (lettuce) or abandon (nettles), purity (hyssop) or voluptuous-
ness (thyme),[1] oneness of purpose or distraction, industry or idle-
ness. These issues do not automatically settle themselves. There is
no such resolution of forces as would naturally result if one of the
contending faculties (reason) did not counterbalance the other
(sensuality). Given the stalemate, neither faculty does the deciding,
but rather, in Milton's phrase, "free will, to her own inclining left /
In even scale." Since, in short, we have "one scale of reason to poise
another of sensuality," a man cannot excuse himself by pleading a
character dominated by an overbalance of sensuality. All dotage is
"voluntary dotage" (4. 1. 27). Every surrender to "a lust of the
blood" is ratified by "a permission of the will" (1. 3. 339–340).

Iago's argument faithfully reproduces an account of free will that
is at least as old as Aristotle's refusal to dispense bad conduct from
punishment when it grows out of the malefactor's disposition.[2]
Catholic teaching, both Roman and Anglican, has inclined to agree
that a man is the principal author of his own personality, or at all
events (granted the astrological theory of personality) that he need
not be the moral puppet of his own ascendant humor.[3] This doctrinal
inclination, however, is offset by a concession that even Aristotle had
been forced to make. There are obviously circumstances, like sleep,
madness, and intoxication, in which reason is no longer at a man's
disposal even though it remains in his possession. "But this is exactly
the state of persons disturbed by emotion; for rages and lustful
desires and the like obviously change the body too, and in some
persons even induce madness."[4] Moreover, Aristotle sees a contrary
implication in his analogy between physical training and the development of virtue or vice. As the very origin of the word testifies,
"moral" character, including the relative force of rational and irrational drives, is intimately linked with disposition or habit, and
hence with what is done to us by social arrangements: "For lawgivers
make citizens good by habituating them to goodness. This is the
object of every lawgiver, and all those who do not do it well are
failures." If moral suasion is to be effective, "it is absolutely necessary
that a disposition to which virtue is congenial should already be

present, one that is fond of the good and intolerant of the base. But it is hard to receive a right upbringing from childhood on without being nurtured by the corresponding laws."[5]

Aquinas too would confine responsibility to occasions when a man not only has his reason but is in a position to use it: "A man resists a motive to sin only by reason, the use of which the devil can hinder completely by moving the imagination and the sensual appetite, as is plain in those who suffer fits. But then, the reason thus bound, whatever a man will do is not ascribed to him as sin." Aquinas, to be sure, insists that "a disposition to be careless makes ignorance itself voluntary and a sin, provided it is ignorance of things one is obliged and able to know."[6] A man must sometimes answer for a debauch that issues in an inadvertent killing. But then it is not the killing so much as the debauch that dictates the degree of moral guilt. By the same token, even if a man somehow consciously chooses to live by an unreflecting habit of mind, the habit itself serves to mitigate his responsibility for the unreflecting harm that results.

Other remarks of Iago's, by the way, betray something of the ambivalence in the traditional attitude to personal responsibility. Desdemona, for example, cannot help succumbing at last to Cassio's charms because "the corrigible authority of our wills" cannot after all invariably control "the blood and baseness of our natures"; "Very nature will instruct her in it, and *compel* her to some second choice" (2. 1. 236–238, italics added); and Iago's whole strategy presupposes that there is indeed "a jealousy so strong / That judgement *cannot* cure" (ll. 310–311, italics added).

The disastrous effect of Cassio's "unhappy brains for drinking" (2. 3. 35) exemplifies the treacherously gradual onset of any disposition "that judgement cannot cure"—in the early stages, a reassuring self-consciousness: "I have drunk but one cup tonight, and that was craftily qualified too, and behold, what innovation it makes here" (ll. 40–42); to be replaced at length by its delusory mirror image: "Do not think, gentlemen, I am drunk. This is my ancient; this is my right hand, and this is my left. I am not drunk now; I can stand well enough, and I speak well enough" (ll. 117–120). The "innovation"—that is, the rebellion—has grown into a coup d'état. Cassio sober and in disgrace is no doubt right when he speaks of his besotted self of a moment since as "so slight, so drunken, and so indiscreet an officer" (ll. 279–280). But the bait of comradeship to which he has risen, from the point of view we have been discussing, is clearly extenuating, as are Roderigo's officiousness (l. 151) and the slow declension of "sensible man," "fool," and "beast" (ll. 310–311) through which the Lieutenant passes on his way to delirium and riot. "Do but see his vice," says Iago. " 'Tis to his virtue a just equinox, / The one as long as th'other. 'Tis pity of him" (ll. 128–130). Iago is venting what the market of popular judgment will bear. Cassio is, perhaps, to blame for his "inordinate cup" (l. 311–312), but the harm he does under its influence is unintentional; he is vicious, and at the same time " 'tis pity of him."

Nor is it absolutely clear, on traditional assumptions, that the cup was any more avoidable than the consequences. According to the philosophy of personal history expounded by Warwick in *II Henry IV*, the record of a man's past contains the "necessary form" of his future; a prediction thus fortified is not merely a guess, but a "perfect guess";

> There is a history in all men's lives,
> Figuring the nature of the times deceas'd;
> The which observ'd, a man may prophesy,
> With a near aim, of the main chance of things
> As yet not come to life, which in their seeds
> And weak beginnings lie intreasured.
> Such things become the hatch and brood of time.[7]

The future is as surely "intreasured" in the past as the bird in the egg; as Iago puts it: "There are many events in the womb of time which will be delivered" (1. 3. 376–378). In the Christian and especially the Calvinist view, if human autonomy must ultimately be circumscribed in this way, the cause is not in the stars but in a divine decree; for it is grace or godliness at least as much as will that makes up the difference between self-control and abandon. Hence the basis for one of Iago's lies: "with the little godliness I have, / I did full hard forbear him" (1. 2. 9–10); with none,

presumably, he could not have forborne at all. And hence also the
untimely truth in Cassio's vinous preachment: "Well, God's above
all; and there be souls must be saved, and there be souls must not
be saved" (2. 3. 105–107). But there is the counterbalancing truth
that souls predestined to damnation are simply receiving their due.
The issue of responsibility, both in the tradition and in the play, is
unresolved. What the play does, at any rate, is to confront us with
the issue. When all is said and done, it may well be that it is not
after all in Roderigo's power to amend.

It will be useful, for our purposes, to examine a further source of
hesitation in the traditional account of responsibility: the psychological
criterion of guilt. And here we must consider a crucial distinction.
For according to a Scholastic-Aristotelian doctrine of wide influence,
anyone who offends against the moral law will exemplify one of two
types of personality, the incontinent and the intemperate or vicious.
Some such dichotomy, as we have already remarked, seems to underlie
the juxtaposition of Claudio and Barnardine in *Measure for Measure*.
The vacillation with which these conditions are traditionally regarded
is painfully reflected in a tendency to condemn them as immoral and
at the same time to talk about them in terms of pathology: "For of
the diseases, incontinence resembles epilepsy, and viciousness dropsy
and consumption."[8] (Hence, as we shall see, the metaphorical
dimension of Othello's seizure.)

The two kinds of men differ, among other things, in the contents
of their moral awareness; and it should be understood that an informed
moral awareness is traditionally thought of as a system of self-evident
truths that answer more or less, in the realm of conscience, to axioms
in geometry: "In conduct the end in view serves as principle, just
as hypotheses are the principles of mathematics. Neither in the latter
sphere nor in the former is reasoning the teacher *of* principles, but
rather a virtue either innate or conditioned of thinking aright *about*
principle."

The incontinent man, then, is in the predicament we have already
touched on, of having an informed conscience but no access to it:
"There is a kind of man who opposes right reason because he is
transported by passion, and whom passion so far masters that he

does not act according to right reason, but not so far that he acquires a tendency to believe that he ought to pursue such gratifications." Emotion goes to the head of the incontinent man; he is "like those who are quickly intoxicated, and by a little wine, and by less than most men." (His infirmity is Cassio's transposed to the mind's inner workings.) We cannot quite allow such a man to disclaim his own behavior, unless we are prepared, by the same standard, to withdraw our praise from the many decent acts that happen likewise to be fueled by emotion: "One ought to be angry with some people and to crave some things, like health and learning." It is more sensible to acknowledge that the incontinent man "is a free agent (for in a way he knows what he is doing and why), but not wicked, for his preference is decent; so that he is half-wicked." One index of the benign and redeemable half is the fact that "every incontinent man has a tendency to repent."[9] The very affliction of such men—the state of being divided against themselves—is also their hope:

> Forthwith therefore commit they the offences with a certaine doubtfull remorse of conscience, and (in a manner) whether they will or no, the which they woulde not doe, unlesse they knewe the things they doe to be ill, but without striving of reason would runne headlong after greedie desire, and then should they not be incontinent, but untemperate, which is much worse.[10]

Intemperance is indeed far worse, because it is, in the specified sense, unprincipled, and hence morally insensate; "for the principles of eligible acts are the ends for which they are eligible. But for one whom pleasure or pain has corrupted principle immediately disappears, along with the awareness that this ought to be the end and the motive of all actions. For viciousness tends to destroy principle." This is not to say that nature has failed to supply the vacuum: "Viciousness distorts the mind subject to it and causes it to lie about the principles of conduct." The products of such lying and distortion are in effect the principles of the unprincipled man.

Moreover, the intemperate man is capable of opinions that agree superficially with those of people endowed with moral awareness:

"Those who deliberately choose what is best and those in whose
opinion it is best do not appear to be the same people, but apparently some are of the opinion that such and such a thing is better,
and because they are vicious deliberately choose what they ought
not."[11] "Deliberate" here presupposes an alternative set of standards.
The intemperate man, in short, can participate correctly in the
ordinary use of moral terms, much as a colorblind person can identify
the red and green traffic lights by relative position. But he uses such
terms not to evaluate but to express opinions about how others
evaluate. Their normative terms are his descriptive. Hence, his
opinion of what is "good" can and does conflict with what he singles
out for his own preference.

> Practitioners in physicke desire and wish in the first place,
> that a man were not sicke at all, but if hee be sicke, that hee
> be not ignorant and senseless altogether of his disease; a
> thing that ordinarily befalleth to all those who be sicke in
> minde: for neither witlesse fooles, nor dissolute and loose
> persons, ne yet those who be unjust and deale wrongfully,
> thinke that they do amisse and sinne; nay some of them
> are persuaded that they do right well.[12]

In this sense the intemperate man is "sicke in minde," for he has no
direct acquaintance with moral distinctions; but his ignorance does
not relieve him of responsibility for what he does.

Unlike the incontinent, the intemperate man is wholly at one with
himself in his wrongdoing, and acts coldly on what serves him for
reason, not primarily on his emotions:

> We should describe as intemperate the man who pursues
> excesses or flees slight pains with little or no desire, rather
> than the man who does so out of a passionate urge. For
> how would the former respond to a vehement longing, or
> the strong pain of a vital need?
> Anyone would think worse of a man if he did a mean thing
> without any urge to do it, or with only a slight urge, than

if he did it on violent impulse; or if he should strike without anger than if he were angry. For what would he do in a passion?

The terror of this possibility is augmented by the fact that, since he acts on his version of principle, and there is no persuading without common assumptions, he cannot be persuaded to repent and is therefore incorrigible, "for the man who cannot repent cannot be cured."[13] We have already observed that in Aquinas's view a sin is not wholly voluntary if the sinner does not know it is a sin. Since the intemperate man, in the intuitive sense, can be so described, one might anticipate his being treated with some leniency. But in fact the state of his reason is precisely what qualifies his sin as deadly.[14] A reason capable of endorsing unreason is clearly a travesty and a handicap; but this is not the end of the intemperate man's misfortunes. He is damned as well.

The distinction we have been examining originates in an attempt to classify attitudes toward the branch of animal impulse that the Scholastics call "concupiscence," the pursuit both of sensual pleasures and (by metaphor) of profit and prestige. But Aristotle set the precedent for making the terms comprehensive by extending them to the other branch as well, the so-called irascible appetite; and it is by this route that the dichotomy comes to be exhibited by the two figures of jealousy that make their appearance in the course of *The Faerie Queene*, one fittingly in the Booke of Temperaunce. The latter has killed his lady in the impetuous belief that she is false:

> Ah God, what horrour and tormenting griefe
> My hart, my hands, mine eyes, and all assayd?
> Me liefer were ten thousand deaths priefe,
> Then wound of gealous worme, and shame of such repriefe.

> I home returning, fraught with fowle despight,
> And chawing vengeaunce all the way I went,
> Soone as my loathed loue appeard in sight,
> With wrathfull hand I slew her innocent.

He is diagnosed by the Palmer as the sort of

> wretched man,
> That to affections does the bridle lend;
> In their beginning they are weake and wan,
> But soone through suffrance grow to fearfull end.

But a motive of hot compulsion can be eliminated, and Phedon is cured. It is a jealousy deliberately embraced, Malbecco's jealousy of cold masochism, that is beyond cure:

> Ne euer is he wont on ought to feed,
> But toads and frogs, his pasture poysonous,
> Which in his cold complexion do breed
> A filthy bloud, or humour rancorous,
> Matter of doubt and dread suspitious,
> That doth with cureless woe consume the hart,
> Corrupts the stomacke with gall vitious,
> Croscuts the liuer with internall smart,
> And doth transfixe the soule with deathes eternall dart.

> Yet can he neuer dye, but dying liues,
> And doth himselfe with sorrow new sustaine,
> That death and life attonce vnto him giues,
> And painfull pleasure turnes to pleasing pain.
> There dwels he euer, miserable swaine,
> Hatefull both to himself and euery wight;
> Where he through priuy griefe, and horrour vaine,
> Is woxen so deform'd, that he has quight
> Forgot he was a man, and Gealousie is hight.[15]

During Othello's extralegal trial of Desdemona both the giving of the *verdict* and the passing of the *sentence* mark recognizable phases in a careful study of Phedon's kind of jealousy. One of Iago's most telling moves in suborning the judge to find against the accused is aimed at Othello's incontinence, or more precisely at that species of it which is traditionally called "impatience"—enslavement of reason by the urge to get rid of pain. (In what follows, the reader should always bear in mind that the "impatience" Iago plays on is simply "incontinence" by a more specific name.) Iago's move is, in fact, quite literally a subornation, though the inducement offered is not cash but a state of mind:

> IAGO.   That cuckold lives in bliss
> Who, certain of his fate, loves not his wronger;
> But, O what damned minutes tells he o'er
> Who dotes, yet doubts, suspects, yet soundly loves!
> OTH. O misery!
> IAGO. Poor and content is rich, and rich enough;
> But riches fineless is as poor as winter
> To him that ever fears he shall be poor.
>
> (3. 3. 167–174)

If, in short, Othello contrives to be certain of Desdemona's infidelity, he will be rewarded with surcease of pain.

Othello's first reaction is to conjure up the desperate fantasy of a transition from doubt to resolve in which, not only is there no interval to suffer through, but "to be once in doubt / *Is* once to be resolv'd" (ll. 179–180, italics added). To dispense either with the interval or with the distinction between doubt and resolve, of course, is to dispense with proof. But it is also to achieve a presumably anesthetic hatred. The price is to resign oneself at the outset; "no, let me know," Iago advises; "and knowing what I am"—that is, a cuckold—"I know what she will be" (4. 1. 73–74)—the concluding hint being left to Othello's vindictive interpretation. Othello has, to be sure, been trapped by a false dilemma; the choice between a blissful certainty of betrayal and a tormenting uncertainty leaves out of account alternatives Iago would prefer his victim not to envisage—the possibility of Desdemona's innocence, for example, and especially the possibility that being certain of betrayal may be no less tormenting than fearing it. A man is said to be jealous when he "wyll suffer none other to be parte taker of his loue," and not merely when he "feareth leste the persone, that he loueth is common to other";[16] so that curing fear will not necessarily cure jealousy.

The trap is a false dilemma, but the bait of the trap is instant relief offered to a temperament that must have it at any price. It is this need that Iago teases to apoplexy by blandly inviting Othello to contemplate an immediate future spent in emotional limbo, "not jealous nor secure" (3. 3. 198): "My lord, I would I might entreat your honour / To scan this thing no farther; leave it to time" (ll. 244–245). Othello already has some notion of the "damned minutes" (l. 169) in which such time would be measured out. He embraces the other horn of the dilemma and elects to "know" Desdemona's guilt. At this point, when he finds that certainty is not after all the promised "bliss," Othello shows just how high a price he is willing to pay for the bliss of ignorance:

> OTH. I had been happy, if the general camp,
> Pioners and all, had tasted her sweet body,
> So I had nothing known.   (ll. 345–347)

Iago manages to avoid the issue of ocular proof by gnawing at the very same weakness in his victim; for the torment of waiting would be only less insupportable than the shock of the kind of certainty such proof would provide. All Iago need do is summon up a tableau:

> OTH. Would I were satisfied!
> IAGO. I see, sir, you are eaten up with passion;
> I do repent me that I put it to you.
> You would be satisfied?
> OTH.   Would! nay, I will.
> IAGO. And may; but, how? How satisfied, my lord?
> Would you, the supervisor, grossly gape on—
> Behold her topp'd?
> OTH.   Death and damnation! O!
> (ll. 390–396)

The thrice-repeated "satisfied" is a mockery, and "satisfaction" chimes twice more in the ensuing exchange, with mounting irony. Ocular proof is a "satisfaction" Othello would gladly forgo, and Iago's bald assertion that such proof is not to be had anyhow provides him with a welcome pretext for devoting himself to easier "satisfactions." Part of the irony, of course, is in the word itself, which can mean contentment, revenge, and proof. The "impatience" (or, generically, incontinence) unmasked by Othello's craving for the former two at the latter's expense, it should be added, is not merely the tendency to flinch from pain; "for when a man gives way to strong and overwhelming pleasures or pains, it is not surprising but forgivable—if he does so with a struggle."[17] But Othello gives way without a struggle.

The cream, perhaps, of the irony we have been considering is that, after he has plainly demonstrated his lack of "patience"—that is, of long suffering—Othello should boast of his potent reserve of that virtue: "I will be found most cunning in my patience" (4. 1. 91); for any other adversity, he protests, "I should have found in some place of my soul / A drop of patience" (4. 2. 52–53). But under the current provocation, even the embodiment of this virtue would lose its nature:

> Turn thy complexion there,
> Patience, thou fresh and rose-lipp'd cherubin,
> Ay there look grim as hell!   (ll. 62–64)

But the virtue in question, according to a venerable homiletic tradition,[18] is the preeminent gift of the Holy Ghost. Cherubs do not turn into demons "grim as hell" unless hell is where they come from.

The steady metamorphosis of Desdemona's *sentencing* into a convulsion of revenge traces the same pattern. Separation or, in ecclesiastical jargon, "divorce from board and bed" is the socially approved sanction against wifely infidelity[19]—the sanction Desdemona seems to have in mind when, on hearing the charge against her, she anticipates "beggarly divorcement" (4. 2. 158) at Othello's hands. Othello's original idea of retribution clearly extends no further:

> If I do prove her haggard,
> Though that her jesses were my dear heartstrings,
> I'd whistle her off and let her down the wind
> To prey at fortune.   (3. 3. 260–263)

But impartiality, in the matter of his verdict, has already yielded to a defect in Othello's powers of endurance, and equity in the awarding of punishment is even more savagely doomed to follow suit:

> If there be cords, or knives,
> Poison, or fire, or suffocating streams,
> I'll not endure it.   (ll. 388–390)

At the peak of Othello's anger, the weapon makes way for the claw: "I'll tear her all to pieces" (l. 431). "I will chop her into messes" (4. 1. 211).

In the sequel Othello reverts to thoughts of poison, significantly to spare himself an ordeal—the possibility of succumbing to a mercy that turns out, on a nearer inspection, to be no more than fondness for the charms of the condemned: "Get me some poison, Iago; this night. I'll not expostulate with her, lest her body and beauty unprovide my mind again" (ll. 216–219). There must be no mercy, it appears, genuine or not; if Othello's mind is not "unprovided"— if it retains what he takes for "providence"—not only the body but the soul should be destroyed:

> Damn her, lewd minx! O damn her! damn her!
>   (3. 3. 475)

> Ay, let her rot, and perish, and be damn'd tonight.
>   (4. 1. 191–192)

> Come, swear it, damn thyself,
> Lest, being like one of heaven, the devils themselves
> Should fear to seize thee; therefore be double damn'd,
> Swear thou art honest.   (4. 2. 35–38)

No doubt Othello could defend what amounts to a moral spasm by pleading the spasm; he has already done so once:

> Now, by heaven,
> My blood begins my safer guides to rule;
> And passion, having my best judgement collied,
> Assays to lead the way.   (2. 3. 204–207)

But as we have already observed, and as a typical Renaissance manual

of honor makes doubly clear, the defense is ambiguous enough to
be construed equally well into an indictment: "Men are not excused by rage or wrath; nor is it allowable in one who is brave,
merciful, or provident that he should suffer himself so over measure
to be transported by rage and by choler."[20]

The satisfaction that Othello sets his heart on is "a capable and
wide revenge" (3. 3. 459) of Italianate disproportion: "O, that the
slave had forty thousand lives! / One is too poor, too weak for my
revenge" (l. 442). The style of his vow is the familiar theatrical
idiom of Senecan diabolism, to be complemented later on by the
obligatory note of cosmic revulsion:

> OTH. Arise, black vengeance, from the hollow hell!
> Yield up, O love, thy crown and hearted throne
> To tyrannous hate! Swell, bosom, with thy fraught,
> For 'tis of aspics' tongues!
> IAGO. Yet be content.
> OTH. O blood, blood, blood!   (ll. 447–451)
>
> Methinks it should be now a huge eclipse
> Of sun and moon, and that th' affrighted globe
> Did yawn at alteration.   (5. 2. 99–101)

But there is a difference, in keeping with Othello's temperament,
between his diabolism and Iago's. At the height of his vindictiveness,
Othello's reason is submerged but not extinguished. A current of
"bloody thoughts" as "compulsive" as that of the Pontic Sea is carrying him toward vengeance "with violent pace" (3. 3. 453–457), but
hate remains for him no other than "tyrannous," vengeance "black,"
its origin hell; and his bosom is swelling not with righteous anger
but with poison—"aspics' tongues." This is far from a glorification.

Iago's diabolism is much nearer to the Senecan model, the priest
and virtuoso of malice who devoutly invokes the "divinity of hell"
(2. 3. 356) and who takes an artificer's delight in the moment of
malign conception: "I have't. It is engend'red. Hell and night / Must
bring this monstrous birth to the world's light" (1. 3. 409–410).
Atreus's enormities too offer this piquant mixture of connoisseurship

and cult: "servatur omnis ordo, ne tantum nefas non rite fiat. saevum scelus iuvat ordinare."[21] There is nothing of such gusto in Othello's "sacred vow" (3. 3. 461); nor is Othello, like Iago, sinning by inciting others to sin:

> When devils will the blackest sins put on,
> They do suggest at first with heavenly shows,
> As I do now.   (2. 3. 357–359)

It is Iago, and not Othello, who is the devil's vicar:

> OTH. I look down toward his feet; but that's a fable.
>   If that thou be'st a devil, I cannot kill thee. . . .
> IAGO. I bleed, sir, but not kill'd.
>   (5. 2. 286–289)
> Will you, I pray, demand that demi-devil
> Why he hath thus ensnar'd my soul and body?
>   (ll. 301–302)

The satanic troth-plighting of the climactic scene—"OTH. I am bound to thee forever"; "IAGO. I am your own forever" (3. 3. 213, 479)— is Iago's masterpiece, not Othello's; though it has not always been clearly understood that this is precisely what makes it doctrinally unwarranted to see Iago as the devil, not to say an abstraction of malice: "The devil always tempts in order to harm, by casting headlong into sin, and therefore is it said that his peculiar function is to tempt; for even if sometimes the tempter is a man, he is acting as the devil's minister."[22] For purposes of temptation, a concrete agent of the devil will do as well as the principal, and an abstract malice will not "do" at all.

Othello's reason at this point is not extinct. He retains his humanity. But the grasp loosens when he begins to see in the symmetry of the *lex talionis*—"Thy bed, lust-stain'd, shall with lust's blood be spotted" (5. 1. 36)—the very different symmetry of justice:

> IAGO. Do it not with poison; strangle her in the bed,
>   even the bed she hath contaminated.

OTH. Good, good; the justice of it pleases; very good.
(4. 1. 220–223)

Even here, Othello's claim, if it is a passing delusion, is not beyond
the pale. Vindictiveness, as Emilia's reasoning illustrates, is a reflex
of ordinary moral imperfection:

> Why, we have galls, and though we have some grace,
> Yet have we some revenge. Let husbands know
> Their wives have sense like them. . . .
> Then let them use us well; else let them know,
> The ills we do, their ills instruct us so.
> (4. 3. 93–95, 103–104)

A worldly moralist will even venture to endorse this bit of casuistry:
"keeping no fayth with her, hee [the husband] muste not looke that
shee should keepe promise with him; for as the saying is, Hee that
doeth not as hee oughte, must not looke to be done to as he would."[23]
But the impulse exists to be repudiated, as Desdemona repudiates it:
"Heaven me such uses send, / Not to pick bad from bad, but by
bad mend" (4. 3. 105–106). And there can be nothing more
ominous than the conversion of that impulse into a chronic state, and
thence into a principle of conduct.

The scriptural metaphors for this process are the hardening and
blinding of the heart, and through centuries of commentary their
spiritual significance is notorious:

> Blinding and hardening have two senses, whereof the one
> is the movement of a man's mind fixed in evil and averted
> from the light of God; and thus far God is not the cause of
> blinding and hardening, even as He is not the cause of
> sin. The other is the withdrawal of grace upon which it
> follows that the mind is not enlightened of God unto up-
> right seeing, and the heart of man not made tender unto
> upright living; and thus far is God the cause of blinding
> and hardening.[24]

In a penumbral phase between hardening and blinding one sees the right and wills the wrong; *video meliora proboque—deteriora sequar.* In that phase Claudius is capable of seeing that his offense is rank, but not of praying (*Ham.* 3. 3. 36–37), and Macbeth of seeing his "hangman's hands," but not of saying "Amen" (*Mac.* 2. 2. 28–29). It is far from reassuring, then, that Othello should be arrested in mid-frenzy by the discovery that "my heart is turn'd to stone; I strike it, and it hurts my hand" (4. 1. 192–193).

If Othello's behavior, up to the point of his vow, is plainly symptomatic of incontinence, Iago's is intemperate throughout. In the theological sense, there is blindness as well as hardness in his virtual erection of malice into an ideal of conduct. For Iago such an ideal is "gain'd knowledge" that he would "profane" if he did not pursue it to his "sport and profit" (1. 3. 390–392), and it is clear that in large measure the sport is what dignifies the profit. Iago might well say, with Volpone, that he glories more in "cunning purchase" than "glad possession"; what he does say, after a night spent in engineering Cassio's dismissal, is that "pleasure and action make the hours seem short" (2. 3. 385). Happiness is activity in accordance with *virtú.* Virtue, on the other hand, including the Christian virtue of forbearance, is "small beer" (2. 1. 161). Iago's characteristic outlook, in short, is not cynical; he recognizes that "honest" intentions exist and are sometimes carried out, but he thinks that they are the contemptible fruits of intellectual mediocrity. He reserves his admiration for those who, like himself, have "some soul" (1. 1. 54).

The tenacity of this outlook is somewhat obscured by the fact that the society whose language Iago cannot help using has preempted the normative terms in which he might have expressed his aberrant approval or disapproval, and he is consequently reduced to inconsistent makeshifts, sometimes using those terms as neutral descriptions, sometimes adapting them to his own scale of value:

> You shall mark
> Many a *duteous* and knee-crooking *knave*
> That, doting on his own obsequious bondage,
> Wears out his time, much like his master's ass,

For nought but provender, and when he's old, cashier'd.
Whip me such *honest knaves*.

(1. 1. 44–49, italics added)

Here "duteous" and "honest" simply describe a pattern of conduct, whereas "knave" has been appropriated to a perverse norm. In the use of "knave," Iago indulges an urge to break the monopoly of the decent on the vocabulary of approval, much as do Macbeth and his lady when they misappropriate the normative use of "man" (*Mac.* 1. 7. 49, 3. 1. 103, 3. 4. 58–59, 99). Iago is, to be sure, a facile hypocrite; he is familiar enough with the nuances of ordinary moral discourse to mimic ordinary moral perception:

> Though in the trade of war I have slain men,
> Yet do I hold it very stuff o'th' conscience
> To do no contriv'd murder.   (1. 2. 1–3)

> She is of so free, so kind, so apt, so blessed a dis-
> position, she holds it a vice in her goodness not
> to do more than she is requested.

(2. 3. 324–327)

But his characteristic use of words that conventionally express moral value is simply, as with "duteous" and "honest," to ticket the conduct he writes off as "small beer" so that he may include it in his calculations:

> So will I turn her virtue into pitch,
> And out of her own goodness make the net
> That shall enmesh them all.

(2. 3. 366–368)

> And many worthy and chaste dames even thus,
> All guiltless, meet reproach.   (4. 1. 47–48)

In the same way, when he promises to abuse Cassio to the Moor "in the rank garb" (2. 1. 315), the rankness is obviously rather to the credit of the garb than otherwise. Iago's nearest approach to a sincere judgment with which his audience can sympathize is his remark that Cassio "hath a daily beauty in his life / That makes me ugly" (5. 1. 19–20). But he has talked about his competitive disadvantage to Cassio once before and appears to be doing so here; Cassio outshines him in appeal to others, not to Iago. The disadvantage is in any case not absolute but comparative, and not moral but esthetic. Iago is gauging public taste in order to determine whether his rival is worth putting out of the way.

Iago's principled assent to evil, by theological standards we have already considered, furnishes him with impeccable credentials for damnation, and this blatant fact gives us a new measure of his intemperance. For Iago is acquainted with the doctrine that certain men are denied a donation of saving grace (2. 3. 105–108); he is evidently aware that such privation has unpleasant consequences— "I do hate him," he says of Othello, "as I do hell-pains" (1. 1. 155) —and he knows enough about *attritio*, the carnal dread of such consequences, to caricature it with sarcastic effect:

> OTH. If thou dost slander her and torture me,
>   Never pray more; abandon all remorse;
>   On horror's head horrors accumulate;
>   Do deeds to make heaven weep, all earth amaz'd;
>   For nothing canst thou to damnation add
>   Greater than that.
> IAGO.   O grace! O heaven forgive me!
>   (3. 3. 368–373)

Yet he buoyantly acknowledges that hell and night are playing midwife to his designs (1. 3. 409–410), and his homage to the "divinity of hell" (2. 3. 356) is almost gay. Indeed, we are given some grounds for wondering whether he has even put two and two together:

> CAS. For mine own part . . . I hope to be saved.
> IAGO. And so do I too, Lieutenant.
>   (2. 3. 109–112)

Does he in fact entertain such a hope? Or is he resigned, and indifferent? In either case—presumption or despair—he is suffering, not only from moral insensibility, but from the spiritual torpor or disengagement known to theologians as *accidia*. If to be "honest" and "blessed" is, in the traditional view, to be fully awake, Iago is being presented to us as a somnambulist.

His choice of victim is probably to be interpreted in this light. One of the motives he alleges is hatred, and we have no reason to doubt his word; but at no point does that hatred rise in vehemence of expression above the perfunctory level of the two terse allusions in his soliloquies: "I hate the Moor" (1. 3. 392); "I endure him not" (2. 1. 297). His more voluble expressions to Roderigo cannot be taken very seriously, since the faltering "snipe" must in any case be reassured that he has in Iago a passionate ally against the Moor; thus Iago does not so much confide as protest:

> Rod. Thou told'st me thou didst hold him in thy hate.
> Iago. Despise me if I do not.   (1. 1. 7–8)

> I had told thee often, and I re-tell thee again and again,
> I hate the Moor.   (1. 3. 372–373)

"I do hate him as I hate hell-pains," he announces at another point; but as we have observed, the ancient is remarkably nonchalant on the subject of hell pains.

Iago syntactically dissociates his hatred from mention of his main grievance against the Moor (1. 3. 392ff),[25] and this is fully in keeping with the Scholastic view that "hatred can arise both from anger and from envy, but arises more immediately from envy"; and that envy in turn is "sadness concerning a neighbor's good regarded as one's own ill, and as tending to impair one's good."[26] A tradition originating in the treatise on envy in Aristotle's *Rhetoric* has it that the emotion is directed only at those who are near in place and rank, and on the accession of goods that bring honor and glory.[27] As a colleague Othello is available, he already immeasurably outshines (and hence impairs) his ancient, and he has but lately made a match by which, "if it prove lawful prize, he's made forever" (1. 2. 51). Iago's notion of self-love is the ability to "distinguish betwixt a benefit and an injury" (1. 3. 313), and while he is avowedly not so impractical as to value repute for its own sake (2. 3. 268–272), he is by the same token too practical to belittle what it can do for a man. To someone ready to regard a neighbor's honor as a personal insult, Othello's very being is now an insult incarnate.

By such logic, Iago's success in preventing Othello from being "made forever" will be the making of Iago: the ambush of Cassio, he promises his henchman, "makes us, or it mars us" (5. 1. 4); "this is the night," he gloats just before Desdemona's murder, "that either makes me or fordoes me quite" (5. 1. 128–129). Iago is in quest of aggrandizement, symbolic and perhaps, by successive promotions, even literal, at his General's expense. "Were I the Moor, I would not be Iago. / In following him I follow but myself" (1. 1. 57–58).

In addition to his hatred, Iago has a grievance, and here we should expect to find some passion:

> I do suspect the lusty Moor
> Hath leap'd into my seat; the thought whereof
> Doth, like a poisonous mineral, gnaw my inwards,
> And nothing can or shall content my soul
> Till I am even'd with him.
>
> (2. 1. 304–308)

Iago's craving for being "evened" is implacable, but this in itself is inconclusive; in an intemperate man a little passion goes a long way. The crux in this regard is the exact weight of "gnaw my inwards." But that would seem to depend on the sensitivity of the inwards being gnawed, and the wry insouciance of "leap'd into my seat" does not suggest much tenderness. Iago is restating the cool resolve of his earlier speech:

> And it is thought abroad that twixt my sheets
> He has done my office. I know not if't be true;
> Will do as if for surety.   (1. 3. 393–396)
> But I, for mere suspicion in that kind,

Mere suspicion does not, in the second version, ripen into "surety"; Iago still merely suspects, and knows not if't be true. He promised, however, to pursue his revenge "*as if* for surety," and we may infer that the "as if" on which he will act is morally equivalent to the effects of the "poisonous mineral" in the restatement, just as the mock-delicate brutality of "twixt my sheets . . . done my office" anticipates the tone of impassive contempt in Iago's later periphrasis.

There is, then, no growth between soliloquies in the vehemence of Iago's resentment; indeed, there is little sign of vehemence at all—though of course this is not to say that there is no resentment. Emilia herself bears witness that Iago is not improvising the suspicion:

> Some such squire he was
> That turn'd your wit the seamy side without,
> And made you to suspect me with the Moor.
> (4. 2. 145–147)

She is, to be sure, under the impression that Iago has long since granted the absurdity of the "squire's" charge; but Iago is adept in conveying false impressions.

One thing, at all events, that Iago cannot be resenting is the supposed fact that he has been discarded from "where either I must live or bear no life" (4. 2. 58). The point of the shopworn little satire with which he entertains Desdemona is not bitterness but a callous ennui:

IAGO. Sir, would she give you so much of her lips
    As of her tongue she oft bestows on me,
    You'd have enough.
DES.   Alas, she has no speech.
IAGO. In faith, too much;
    I find it still, when I have list to sleep.
    Marry, before your ladyship, I grant,
    She puts her tongue a little in her heart,
    And chides with thinking.
EMIL.   You have little cause to say so.
IAGO. Come on, come on, you are pictures out of door,
    Bells in your parlours, wild-cats in your kitchens,

Saints in your injuries, devils being offended,
Players in your housewifery and housewives in your beds.
(2. 1. 101–113)

Whether Iago truly finds his wife shrewish and frigid, or merely thinks it witty to say so, it is clear that one does not use a pearl richer than all one's tribe as the butt of a well-practiced vaudeville turn. We are later permitted an intimate view of the emotional sterility behind the harlequinade:

EMIL. Do not you chide; I have a thing for you.
IAGO. A thing for me? It is a foolish thing—
EMIL. Ha!
IAGO. To have a foolish wife.   (3. 3. 301–304)

And the quality of life here reflected, as we might expect, is of no very recent date; " 'tis not a year or two shows us a man," Emilia has reason to assure her mistress;

They are all but stomachs, and we all but food;
They eat us hungerly, and when they are full
They belch us.   (3. 4. 103–106)

Since Iago's resentment is not warranted by the value he attaches to what he has lost, it would seem more satisfactory to refer it to the same habit of mind by which pure hatred is traditionally explained. If envy is the poison in Iago's "poisonous mineral," then the truth of the gossip and the value of the alienated wife are irrelevant, for the essential provocation is the simple nearness of the person envied. That nearness has been enough, from Iago's point of view, to dim his luster, and more than enough, as the event proves, to have caused it to be "thought abroad" that Iago has been outmanned and outwitted. If he does not cherish his wife, he cherishes his wit most abundantly—the "gain'd knowledge" of the rules of "sport" that lead to "profit." And a name for wit, like good name in general, will have sufficient utilitarian value in his eyes to infect him with the hate that traditionally attends on envy. The whole point of his revenge is clearly to turn the tables in this sense, by exhibiting

Othello in the posture of being "led by th'nose / As asses are" (1. 3. 407–408)—by "making him egregiously an ass" (2. 1. 318).

Iago, moreover, suspects the truth of what is "thought abroad," and for one who is intemperately vindictive—that is, vindictive on principle and by sober preference—the mere fact of a theft regardless of the property stolen and the resentment aroused, is enough to legitimate revenge.

One may wonder, perhaps, how the vaunted wit could have entertained such a suspicion in the first place. But if we discount Iago's success in making an ass of Othello as heavily assisted by the latter's susceptibilities, there is very little evidence that Iago's "gain'd knowledge" of human nature is as trenchant as he claims. Our glimpse of Cassio's tawdry life with Bianca—the life in which Iago sees "a daily beauty"—does not tempt us to agree with him. That Desdemona loves Cassio, he judges at one point, "is apt and of great credit" (2. 1. 296)—an obtuseness compounded by the fact that in Iago's vocabulary "apt" is nearer to "true" than to "probable": "I told him what I thought, and told no more / Than what he found himself was apt and true" (5. 2. 176–177). To be sure, he makes amends elsewhere for his misjudgment of Desdemona, classing her among "worthy and chaste dames" (4. 1. 47) and observing that

'tis most easy
Th'inclining Desdemona to subdue
In any honest suit.   (2. 3. 345–347)

But his record of accuracy is mediocre, and not least mediocre, as should by this time be clear, in his simplistic ascription to Othello of "a constant, loving, noble nature" (2. 1. 298). Indeed this faint obtuseness is one of the touches Iago inherits from his prototype in Cinthio, who first imagines that "Disdemona" has rejected his advances "because she was on fire with the Lieutenant," and then belatedly acknowledges "the chastity that he knew the Lady observed."[28] Both Iago and his prototype are marked here by a symptom of intemperance, the same inanition of sympathetic insight as disables the amoral Oswald in *King Lear* from grasping the design in his lord's preferences: "What most he should dislike seems pleasant to him, / What like, offensive" (4. 2. 9–10).

By his own account, then, Iago fixes on Othello as victim out of pure hatred—hence envy—and out of what passes in him for sexual jealousy, the jealousy of the intemperate rather than the incontinent man. Those who choose to dismiss Iago's testimony in preference for the hypothesis of a destructive urge directed against mankind in general, glorious and inglorious alike, have still to explain how a general urge can be said to confine itself to a particular object. If they contend that for a creature like Iago talk of cause has no meaning, they must give up their talk of "destructiveness" and "floating hatred" as well.[29] Nor is it easy to see why the soliloquizing Iago should be lying about his motives either to himself or to his audience. It can hardly be because he is "an essentially conscienceless person trying to get by among consciences";[30] by the normal convention of soliloquy, there do not happen to be any consciences in attendance to "get by" among. Iago's justifications, moreover, are clearly not of the kind that would help him to pass muster in any case. He himself characterizes his plans as "knavery" (1. 3. 400, 2. 1. 321)—an honorific in his own lexicon, but a term of opprobrium to such consciences as he might conceivably wish to appease. What remains is that Iago is not appeasing consciences; he is following one. And the conscience he is following, however aberrant, is his own. The intemperate man is a city that has bad laws and abides by them; his bad conduct is not fortuitous, as it would be were he a city with no laws at all.

Othello may well say, on deputing Iago to kill on his behalf: "Now art thou my lieutenant" (3. 3. 478). In the radical sense, Iago has indeed become Othello's moral lieutenant—his surrogate, the man who holds his place. Othello's tragedy, in fact, is that the metaphoric relation of lieutenancy is symmetrical; that if Iago shares Othello's place, Othello has inevitably come to share Iago's. Hence the ultimate menace of Iago's assurance that in following the Moor he follows but himself (1. 1. 58).

The coup de grace to Othello, in his long spiritual death, will be the acquisition of an alien moral sensibility and its principles. Othello will find himself called on to kill Desdemona, not by rage as formerly, but now by his notions of manhood and honor—notions that turn the gentleman's code on its head: "Slaying of wives is a heathenish manner; nor is it a thing honest . . . or honorable to use violence against a woman, or against any person of little strength."[31] Cinthio's Moor, like Othello, sees his manly honor in a very different light: "I will hale her soul out of her body, for I should hold myself no man did I not take from the world this wretch." But the essential unmanliness of his plan is reflected in his first requirement for carrying it out: "Departing thence he set himself to thinking how he should do the woman so to die, and with her his Leader of Squadron, as that he might not have the blame of her death." The Moor, says Cinthio, is possessed by "fear of the inviolable justice of the lords of Venice."[32] Faced with the possibility of being found out *flagrante delicto*, Shakespeare's "valiant Moor" cuts the same inglorious figure:

> Still as the grave. Shall she come in? Were't good?—
> I think she stirs again. No. What's best to do?
> If she come in, she'll sure speak to my wife.
>
> > (5. 2. 94–96)
>
> Soft; by and by.—Let me the curtains draw.
>
> > (l. 104)
>
> Why, how should she be murd'red? . . .
> You hear her say herself, it was not I.
>
> > (ll. 126, 128)

In executing Desdemona Othello conceives himself to be fulfilling the demands of justice as well as honor, and once again his notion of those demands is a travesty. Othello is indulging himself with the same abusive privilege as Brabantio was offered by the Duke:

> the bloody book of law
> You shall yourself read in the bitter letter
> After your own sense. (1. 3. 67–69)

Othello is not only taking the law into his own hands but interpreting it arbitrarily—reading it after his own sense. And what is far graver, he is applying the ultimate penalty sanctioned by law to a crime that, no matter how the law regarded it, is by no means ultimate. He is reading the bloody book in the bitter letter. And this new conception of judicial fairness offers us a quintessence of the moral perversion we have already variously encountered in other plays. The act of murder that Hamlet's conscience comes to approve in deference to "Heaven ordinant," that the maundering Lear longs for as the course of justice and equity, that Angelo and Isabella take for justice, "set down so in heaven" if not "in earth," here becomes for a tragic hero the object of a deliberate choice.

According to a Terentian tag much in use among sixteenth-century theorists of equity, the extreme of justice is the highest injustice— *summum ius summa iniuria*[33]—and it is to this highest injustice that Othello dedicates himself in the name of its opposite. For Othello, the truth of the verdict guarantees the validity of the sentence, and we join him in this confusion only at the risk of missing the point of his final confrontation with Desdemona. "I did proceed," as he explains to Emilia, "upon just grounds / To this extremity" (5. 2. 138–139). But even were Desdemona guilty, there would be no such grounds; extremity is as incompatible with justice as it is with the love that Othello continues to protest.

Indeed, the perverted act of justice is at the same time a perversion of love, which Othello manages to equate with necrophilia: "Be thus when thou art dead, and I will kill thee / And love thee after" (ll. 18–19). But Desdemona will not be thus when she is dead, as Othello admits:

> If I quench thee, thou flaming minister,
> I can again thy former light restore,
> Should I repent me; but once put out thy light,
> Thou cunning'st pattern of excelling nature,
> I know not where is that Promethean heat
> That can thy light relume.   (ll. 8–13)

The best he can do is to secure the corpse from vandalism:

> Yet I'll not shed her blood,
> Nor scar that whiter skin of hers than snow,
> And smooth as monumental alabaster.
>
> (ll. 3–5)

This will have to do; for the hypothetical repentance he mentions (l. 10) turns out to reflect no hesitancy about the justice of what he is about to do: "O balmy breath, that dost almost persuade / Justice to break her sword" (ll. 16–17). The sword belongs to Justice, and it remains unbroken. Othello has been apprehensive about facing Desdemona "lest her body and beauty unprovide my mind" (4. 1. 217–218), but his new commitment to "justice" is proof against his regret for the physical allure he will no longer be able to "smell . . . on the tree" (5. 2. 15). And he reserves for himself a measure of consolation. He will kill Desdemona first and love her after.

The arch-necrophilist of the poetic imagination is death, and even for death such love is a perversion. "That death's unnatural," says Desdemona, "that kills for loving" (l. 42)—unnatural, she means, as a return for love; but especially unnatural, in the context of a would-be executioner's kisses, as an expression of love. The hero is undergoing a poetic as well as a moral metamorphosis, for it is Othello as well as Death "that kills for loving"; the person fuses with the personification.

On the other hand, it is a commonplace of Christian doctrine that all divine acts, even retribution, emanate from the divine love, whose handiwork, as Dante says, includes the gate of hell. This paradox furnishes Othello with a satisfying means of reconciling love with his own act of justice: "This sorrow's heavenly; it strikes where it doth love" (ll. 21–22). The analogy, of course, is blasphemous. In disobedience to scriptural warning, Othello presumes to imitate divine justice. Divine mercy, which it is his Christian duty to imitate, he leaves to heaven:

> DES. Talk you of killing?
> OTH.   Ay, I do.
> DES.   Then Heaven
>   Have mercy on me!

OTH.   Amen, with all my heart!
DES. If you say so, I hope you will not kill me.
OTH. Hum!   (ll. 33–36)

OTH.   Thou art to die.
DES. O heaven, have mercy on me!
OTH.   I say, amen.
DES. And have you mercy too!   (ll. 56–59)

And here it is important to note that the situation as Othello conceives it—the putting to death of a woman taken in adultery—has a special Christian resonance. It is above all others the situation that typifies the superseding of the bloody book of law. The pursuit of retributive justice by fallen man is a pharisaical act and an offense to conscience: "He that is without sin among you, let him cast the first stone. . . . And they which heard it, being convicted by their own conscience, went out one by one, beginning at the eldest, even unto the last" (John 8 : 7, 9).

When Othello is not delegating this duty to God, he is parodying it. Thus the sublime of his "mercy"—this apparently without conscious irony—is to get his "cruelty" over with as soon as possible:

Not dead? not yet quite dead?
I that am cruel am yet merciful;
I would not have thee linger in thy pain.
So, so.   (ll. 85–88)

—an access of "mercy," by the way, that immediately follows the first sounds of Emilia's knocking. Nor does this exhaust Othello's fund of the preeminent judicial virtue. Justice to Desdemona is mercy to others: "Yet she must die, else she'll betray more men" (1. 6). As the appeal to the common welfare would lead us to suspect, Othello's model for the ethics of solemn execution is civil law, the very law that Renaissance jurists are most careful to distinguish from the justice embodied in the law of nature and conscience; he is, at any rate, acting on principle, and no longer exclusively driven by a vengeful anger that admittedly comes from "the hollow hell" (3. 3. 447). And his model restrains him from doing his worst:

> If you bethink yourself of any crime
> Unreconcil'd as yet to Heaven and grace,
> Solicit for it straight. . . .
> I will walk by.
> I would not kill thy unprepared spirit; . . .
> I would not kill thy soul.   (5. 2. 26–32)

Othello is not practicing mercy, which is available to him only in the form of a pardon. He is pushing severity to its absolute limit. The respite he grants is that of the headsman and not the judge.

And it seems to have an ulterior purpose; Othello wants to hear Desdemona confess: "Sweet soul, take heed, / Take heed of perjury; thou art on thy deathbed" (ll. 50–51). It is clearly a confession and not a denial that interests Othello; he is not hoping to be dissuaded, for he leaves no way for Desdemona to dissuade him:

> Therefore confess thee freely of thy sin;
> For to deny each article with oath
> Cannot remove nor choke the strong conception
> That I do groan withal. Thou art to die.
> (ll. 53–56)

On the contrary, his mounting annoyance at being refused a confession is the key to why he wants one:

> DES.   I never did
> Offend you in my life; never lov'd Cassio
> But with such general warranty of heaven
> As I might love; I never gave him token.
> OTH. By heaven, I saw my handkerchief in's hand.
> O perjured woman! thou dost stone my heart.
> And makes me call what I intend to do
> A murder, which I thought a sacrifice.
> (ll. 58–65)

Othello is moved not by second thoughts but by frustration. If an execution is to be a sanctified act—"a sacrifice"—it is not enough that the punishment be just; the hearts of the participants, both executioner and victim, have to be "prepared" (l. 31). By refusing to tell the truth, Desdemona has tainted her own heart and hardened Othello's, thereby turning "sacrifice" into "murder." By spoiling Othello's ritual, she has done violence to his conscience—the same depraved instrument that has defined itself at the beginning of the scene.

The horror of Othello's metamorphosis is the more disturbing as the playwright succeeds in making us parties to the strangulation it leads up to. The trap has been carefully set. For it has gradually been borne in on us that Desdemona's wifely conduct is deficient in a respect that would have seemed even more serious to Jacobeans than it does to us; she is tactless, and tactless to an exasperating degree. Even under more favorable circumstances her notion of domestic advocacy would be disastrously self-defeating:

> My lord shall never rest;
> I'll watch him tame, and talk him out of patience;
> His bed shall seem a school, his board a shrift;
> I'll intermingle everything he does
> With Cassio's suit.   (3. 3. 22–26)

OTH. Not now, sweet Desdemon; some other time.
DES. But shall't be shortly?
OTH.   The sooner, sweet, for you.
DES. Shall't be tonight at supper?
OTH.   No, not tonight,
DES. Tomorrow dinner, then?
OTH.   I shall not dine at home;
    I meet the captains at the citadel.
DES. Why, then, tomorrow night; on Tuesday morn;
    On Tuesday noon, or night; on Wednesday morn.
    I prithee, name the time, but let it not
    Exceed three days.   (ll. 55–64)

From the Renaissance point of view, this is not mere nagging. It is arrogant folly: "as that glasse is nothing worth, which makethe a sad countenance seeme joyfull, or a joyfull, sad: so that woman is a foole, who seeing her husband merry, pouteth or loureth, or seeing him pensive, sheweth her selfe pleasaunte: And therefore let her be resolved to frame her selfe to the thoughts of her husbande, and to judge things sweete or sowre, according to his taste."[34]

As matters stand, of course, the folly is suicidal—though Desdemona is clearly not to blame for what she does not know, or for a suspicion already fully formed, and capable of being inflamed by such flimsy indications. Yet the danger her vice is edging her nearer to, and the torture to which, however unwittingly, it subjects Othello, tend to jar against the unreserved sympathy she might otherwise claim:

> OTH.   Fetch't, let me see't.
> DES. Why, so I can, sir, but I will not now.
>   This is a trick to put me from my suit.
>   Pray you, let Cassio be receiv'd again.
> OTH. Fetch me the handkerchief; my mind misgives.
> DES. Come, come;
>   You'll never meet a more sufficient man.
> OTH. The handkerchief!
> DES. I pray, talk me of Cassio.
> OTH. The handkerchief!
> DES.   A man that all his time
>   Hath founded his good fortunes on your love,
>   Shar'd dangers with you—
> OTH.   The handkerchief!
> DES. In sooth, you are to blame.
> OTH. Zounds!   (3. 4. 85–97)
>
> LOD. Is there division 'twixt my lord and Cassio?
> DES. A most unhappy one. I would do much
>   T'atone them, for the love I bear to Cassio.
> OTH. Fire and brimstone!
> DES.   My lord?

OTH.   Are you wise?
DES. What, is he angry?
LOD.   May be the letter mov'd him;
   For, as I think, they do command him home,
   Deputing Cassio in his government.
DES. Trust me, I'm glad on't. (4. 1. 242–249)

In the face of clear evidence that her solicitude is somehow hurting
Cassio's cause, Desdemona persists in expressing it volubly.

And the crowning indiscretion comes opportunely, on the appearance in Othello of a cold and twisted righteousness that threatens
to repel sympathy altogether. At her moment of greatest danger,
Desdemona treats Othello to still another expression of solicitude for
Cassio. Ironically, it is the most forgivable of her outbursts:

DES. O! my fear interprets. What, is he dead?
OTH. Had all his hairs been lives, my great revenge
   Had stomach for them all.
DES. Alas! he is betray'd and I undone.
OTH. Out, strumpet! weep'st thou for him to my face?
                         (5. 2. 73–77)

We have, to a degree, been drawn into the horror of Othello's relapse
into passion. And from the esthetic standpoint, Othello has been
spared the ultimate disfigurement of murder in cold blood, though he
is far from being redeemed; Aristotle asks rhetorically what an intemperate man would do if he fell into a rage, and we have been
given the answer.

Othello has shown himself willing in principle to treat adultery
as a capital crime, and to take up the first stone. Such intemperance
and spiritual pride, as we have observed, are well-known plague
signs of damnation, and not to know they are is part of the reason
why. Othello does not know they are; but he has a reason for
anticipating the worst:

   O, I were damn'd beneath all depth in hell
   But that I did proceed upon just grounds
   To this extremity.   (ll. 137–139)

The mortal sin, for Othello, if there is one, is not the sentence but the verdict, and when the verdict is set aside, he concedes that his soul has been "ensnared" (l. 302), and that Desdemona's innocence will rightly deny him entry into heaven:

> when we shall meet at compt,
> This look of thine will hurl my soul from heaven,
> And fiends will snatch at it.   (ll. 273–275)

He accordingly embraces his fate with ardor:

> Whip me, ye devils,
> From the possession of this heavenly sight!
> Blow me about in winds! roast me in sulphur!
> Wash me in steep-down gulfs of liquid fire!
>   (ll. 277–280)

Here it is wholly superfluous to point out the likelihood that the mortal sin of despair, made irrevocable by suicide, will result in damnation; and not enough to point out that Othello's frame of mind is indeed a form of despair. The relevant question is *what* form, for we have been given two alternatives that must be rejected. Othello's is not the apathetic despair of Iago, or the embittered renunciation of grace hypothetically attributed to Brabantio:

> Did he live now,
> This sight would make him do a desperate turn,
> Yea, curse his better angel from his side,
> And fall to reprobance.   (ll. 206–209)

Othello's final desperate act, like his killing of Desdemona, or for that matter, of the turbaned Turk in Aleppo (ll. 352–355), is a usurpation of divine justice. The Moor appoints himself a minister of that justice, as Despaire nearly succeeds in persuading Red Crosse to do:

> Is not his law, Let euery sinner die:
> Die shall all flesh? what then must needs be donne,
> Is it not better to doe willinglie,
> Then linger, till the glasse be all outronne? . . .

> Then gan the villein him to overcraw,
> And brought vnto him swords, ropes, poison, fire,
> And all that might him to perdition draw;
> And bad him choose, what death he would desire:
> For death was due to him, that had provokt Gods ire.[35]

Othello's despair, then, is not a cue for musings about eschatology. It directs our attention to a theme that has occupied us throughout the final scene: the perversion of Othello's sense of justice.

Perhaps the most evil flowering of that perversion is the mad logic behind Othello's dying gesture: "I kiss'd thee ere I kill'd thee: no way but this, / Killing myself, to die upon a kiss" (5. 2. 358–359). The essence of punitive justice, for Othello, is retaliation in kind; as Desdemona's death was preceded by a kiss from Othello, so it is fitting that her murderer should die after kissing Desdemona. This from the man who has just now declared himself unfit even to look at Desdemona's face (ll. 277–278). Othello's kiss, then, is very far from embodying "the discovery, at the cost of death, of a truth which man could have had simply by being open to it."[36] It is instead the symbol of a mind that is incapable of discovery because it is now shut up forever in its own falsehood. That mind ends by turning a gesture of love into an act of justice; and once again both the love and the justice are irredeemably perverse.

Whatever the otherworldly judgment on Othello's actions, it is clear that they have grown directly and inescapably out of ingrained traits of personality. They do not conform to the model of responsibility drawn up at the outset by Iago. But then, that model is in some respects distinctly uninviting, not to say implausible. To hold a man responsible for the birth and persistence of his own character is to hold that the character is ultimately distinct from the man— to hold, in short, that the man is at bottom characterless. But a freedom that reduces the human essence to a faceless energy or void is hardly the kind of freedom that could ever be thought of as a notable ingredient in human dignity. If the "I" in Iago's declaration "I know my price" (1. 1. 11) has no essential character, it is hard to see how it could have a "price" either.

Iago takes great pride in his capacity for self-love and challenges a place among those who "keep their hearts attending on themselves" (l. 51), but in his view a man has sufficiently proved that capacity when he can "distinguish betwixt a benefit and an injury" (1. 3. 313–314). The self that is reaping the benefit apparently need not be so distinguished, and indeed, if it is to be free, it cannot be; determinate form, conceived as a principle of authentically personal choice, is inconsistent with Iago's version of freedom. For the radically free man Iago aspires to be, even more than for the chronically vicious man he is, a true self-love is, in the nature of the case, beyond reach. "Having nothing in them worth befriending, they feel nothing friendly toward themselves."[37]

In conformity with this view of will, Iago delightedly affirms an independence of restraint far deeper than that of the most adroit hypocrisy—not merely "I am not what I seem" but "I am not what I am" (1. 1. 65). The equivocation on "am" that makes the paradox involves two uses of the copula, identity and predication: the self is not to be *equated with* the qualities it happens to *have;* in scholastic terms, its existence is prior to its essence. To say, "I am not what I am," then, is virtually to appropriate the self-bestowed name of God in Exodus (3. 14), "I am *that* I am."[38] It is not surprising that the freedom Iago expounds bears some resemblance to the kind of free will suggested by that name, especially to theologians of "voluntarist" persuasion: an uncircumscribed will, one that is prior to essence, cannot be confined to good, or any other character, and yet it would be blasphemous to think of it as capable of evil; the alternative recourse is that options become "good" when the divine will determines on them, and for no other reason. To that will all competing options are indifferent. "Good" means divinely enacted, permitted, or decreed; "bad" means divinely rejected or forbidden. To suppose moral distinctions intrinsic is to make the "goodness" of God dominate His will, and hence to fall, as Adam did, by presuming on one's reason:

Man made a total defection from God, presuming to imagine that the commandments and prohibitions of God

were not the rules of Good and Evil, but that Good and
Evil had their own principles and beginnings.

For God, who can command a murder, cannot command
an evill, or a sinne; because the whole frame and Government of the world being his, he may vse it as he will.

A human will that is free in this sense would be pure spontaneity
equally inclined to "good" or to "evil"—that is, obedience or disobedience to the divine sovereign: "Free will is impartial with
respect to choosing well or ill; wherefore it is impossible that free
will should be a predisposition."[39] If the human will were itself
sovereign, of course, it would control the use of these empty labels,
and could interchange them at random:

> DES. Beshrew me, if I would do such a wrong
>   For the whole world.
>   EMIL. Why, the wrong is but a wrong i'th' world; and
> having the whole world for your labour, 'tis a wrong in
> your own world, and you might quickly make it right.
>
> (4. 3. 78–83)

As applied to man, this view of freedom has always been uncomfortable doctrine. It is hard to see how one can take responsibility
for conduct that does not originate in one's own character; or how
matters are improved by substituting for bondage to character an even
more bewildering bondage to inner chance; and the central tradition
in Christian thought has been hard put to it to reconcile its view of
will as rational appetite and evil as essentially irrational with the
obligatory thesis *malitia est quoddam voluntarium.*[40] Moreover, the
repugnance of vesting God with a constitutional impartiality with
respect to good or evil, and of declaring good or evil empty labels, is
clear enough when the same judicial caprice is exercised by God's
vicar, the demigod of civil order:

> Thus can the demigod Authority
> Make us pay down for our offense by weight
> The words of Heaven: on whom it will, it will;
> On whom it will not, so; yet still 'tis just.[41]

Bianca may well deny her moral inferiority to a woman who we know thinks nothing of condoning adultery on the part of an adulteress who owns the world:

> EMIL.   O fie upon thee, strumpet!
> BIAN. I am no strumpet, but of life as honest
>   As you that thus abuse me.
> EMIL.   As I? Fie upon thee!
>   (5. 1. 121–123)

If theology is not to slander divine justice by reducing it to mere improvisation, it has to allow, with Hooker and his mentors, that there are rational criteria of justice, and that the divine will is free because it is by nature responsive to such criteria.[42] The devotional tradition has been even less reluctant to speak of the bondage of God's will to what is highest in His nature: "Ye, for trouth, Loue bond the allmyghty god so fermely that he myght no thyng do but as loue gaf hym leue."[43] The key to freedom, human or divine, is the existence of standards independent of will and authority, and Emilia redeems her earlier laxity when she defies all mere imperatives, whatever the source, to stand by justice: "Let Heaven and men and devils, let them all, / All, all, cry shame against me, yet I'll speak" (5. 2. 221–222). By unmasking Iago's free will of moral indifference, and by allowing us to witness Othello's new "justice" in action, the play forcibly demonstrates that the freedom "to plume up my will / In double knavery" (1. 3. 399–400) is bondage in disguise, and that the choice between justices is far from indifferent.

A theology of the sovereign will is familiar to us from other plays we have considered. That is the kind of God Hamlet supposes to have exempted him from the general application of a law of charity. And it is the kind of God Whose mercy Claudio recognizes as the model for the judicial caprice of the "demigod Authority." The dismissal of autonomous moral criteria that goes with such a theology has also met us in several versions: the "honor" to which Hamlet and Troilus subscribe, the ordinances of Hamlet's God, the legalism of Angelo and Isabella, Edmund's worship of his own instincts. Perhaps the most schematic rendition of such an "ethic" in Shakespeare's canon is the interchangeableness of the operative words in the Weird Sisters' doggerel: "Fair is foul and foul is fair" (*Mac.* 1. 1. 11). For the morally dead (like Iago and Edmund, Othello and Macbeth) whose awareness has so far degenerated that the Weird Sisters' formula adequately describes it, there is indeed "nothing serious" in human life (*Mac.* 2. 3. 98), least of all their own moral death; a life lobotomized in this way must indeed become a "tale /Told by an idiot" (5. 5. 26–27). In *Othello* as in *Macbeth* we are, I think, meant to find in the contrast between the stage-flat unreality of such a consciousness and the full dimensionality of our own an adequate rebuttal to the theory of morals that would reduce the latter to the former. That Othello, once Iago has had his will of him, could never appreciate that rebuttal is a measure of the curse in their vow of mutual bondage (3. 3. 213, 479).

There is a striking if partial resemblance between the tragedy of Othello and that of Hamlet. Failure or inability to love betrays both heroes into a sterile quest for insight by circumstantial evidence. Both men hold up the poisonous fruits of that quest as justification for a course of action—revenge—that their consciences at least initially reject. And both men, but particularly Othello, show us in their decline that the mind to which voluntarism is a genuinely plausible account of moral experience is a mind that labors under a terrible privation, a form of unintelligence at least as crippling to thought as the stupidity Iago dreads. But here an important difference asserts itself. Othello's abortive career as a police magistrate, unlike Hamlet's as chief inspector, is counterbalanced by a demonstration, in the person of Desdemona, that love is not only a real possibility but (as insight into the worth of another mind) the sole path to the very kind of truth Othello is benightedly hunting for. Like *Lear*, the present play affirms the authenticity of intrinsic value in the process of affirming the love that enables us to perceive it.

The acts of will by which Othello destroys himself have been free neither by Iago's test nor by its rationalist alternative. Those acts exemplify human weakness tested beyond its meager endurance by a suffering that offers no very consoling vision of what suffering does to man—a suffering that is not purgative but morally disfiguring and that disfigures the tortured as surely as the will to inflict it does the torturer. By our sympathy with Othello in the long process of his moral dissolution, we come to recognize that malice or vindictiveness is itself an affliction, and an affliction to which anyone may succumb. For after the Fall, incontinence is not so much a vice as it is the human condition, and to be spared its worst consequences is a precarious gift of circumstance or grace. Like moral perception, sympathetic imagination is vindicated in *Othello* by being exercised, this time in the interest of doing an exacting justice to a mind incapable of either sympathy or justice. If Iago in himself is beneath pity and worthy only of fear and loathing, the Iago in his victim claims the more difficult response. Toward the citizens of hell, says Dante, pity lives when it is safely dead.[44] The unique achievement of *Othello* is that it makes it possible to disagree with such a view. If, in short, tragic discovery and transcendence are denied to the Moor, they are thereby made available to us.

Epilogue

THE OBJECT of this book has been to consider the thematic inter-weaving, in certain reflective plays of Shakespeare, of two speculative issues that tend to complicate each other in human experience: whether moral distinctions are intrinsic, and whether there is knowl-edge of minds other than one's own—the problems, in short, of justice and trust, or sympathy. I have singled out the plays under dis-cussion because of the clarity with which each seems to me to develop a distinct and characteristic attitude toward these issues, although in two instances the attitudes are not, I believe, unique in the Shake-spearean canon; the contrasting positions I ascribe to *Measure for Measure* and *Othello* seem to me to hold true, respectively, of *Troilus and Cressida* and *Macbeth* as well.

These contrasts are by no means offered as evidence of an evolution in the playwright's thought or as materials for his intellectual biog-raphy; I have not followed chronology in arranging the sequence of studies, and though I have argued that *Troilus and Cressida,* for in-stance, succumbs to the very challenge that *King Lear* later answers triumphantly, and thus is logically prior to the later play, I do not mean to suggest that the two plays could never, in point of content, have been written in the reverse order. It is a commonplace that a lifetime's thinking may meander, often without any unbreakable promise of its destination, and sometimes without any destination. I have mentioned an interweaving or mutual complication of themes, and a final word is in order here about how, in general, I take this to occur in each play.

In *Hamlet* a man embraces the possibility of violating a dictate of conscience in response to an alternative—and extrinsic—sanction of conduct. His only problem in justifying action, at first, is to contrive a diagnostic means simply of convicting or acquitting a suspected evildoer. His concern with the knowledge of other minds, then, is ominously superficial; indeed, it is not with minds so much as with appearances—with reconstructing the past behavior of his suspect and predicting the future. His failure to settle on a satisfactory alternative to conscience, however, leads him to apply the same diagnostic arts to detecting quite another sort of arcane behavior—the command of a sovereign will he identifies, in the end, as the ultimate datum of conscience. The play as a whole, on the other hand, gives us ample reason to recognize that the hero's sagacity, especially in the last instance, is delusory, and that his tracing of ethical principles to mere sovereignty is not only delusory but perilous.

In *Measure for Measure* we encounter similar delusions and perils, but no hint that a reassuring corrective is available. A vice-regent committed to a policy of judicial severity revives a law enjoining a ludicrously inordinate punishment. His principal critic pleads, not, as one might suspect, that the law is inherently unjust, but (*faute de mieux*, it seems) that a particular application of the law happens to be unmerciful. The ultimate success of this appeal to mercy, once more, is disturbingly vitiated by the concurrent and total failure of a rational standard of penal justice to assert itself, and we are left with an uneasy sense of the possibility that in the supernatural no less than the natural order, mercy by free gift is simply the obverse of justice by fiat.

So much for the peril. As for the delusion: it is clear almost from the outset that the vice-regency is a diagnostic test of its unwitting occupant's integrity. The diagnostician is one and the same with the supposedly absent ruler, a man whose shortcomings in both capacities are borne in on us in the course of the play. The morally questionable ruse by which he hopes to inspire his vice-regent to an act of sympathetic imagination fails because it turns on a disastrous misreading of the vice-regent's likely reaction—in short, because of a failure of the sympathetic imagination. This failure is coupled with much faltering of moral purpose. The ruler condemns a prisoner he pronounces unprepared, to an execution he pronounces damnable, yet is dissuaded from this proceeding not only because it is damnable but because it is less expedient than an alternative that suddenly presents itself. And he admits to having inflicted on his subjects

fourteen years of demoralizing permissiveness, yet in the end cheer-
fully ushers back the old regime, letting off a foiled murderer and
seducer with a reprimand, and linking him in misalliance with a lady
whose devotion to her betrothed has been so outraged that its con-
tinuance is not merely unjustified but perverse. These facts cannot,
I think, be denied or minimized simply because they appear to be out
of keeping with the spirit of an occasion on which the play was
performed. On the contrary, they invite us to revise our estimate
of the moral complexity that could be tolerated in a Christmas entertainment given before a royal audience.

In *King Lear* two men fail in prudence, wisdom, and trust, thereby
falling easy victim to cruel enemies. In the course of their ordeals
both enjoy illuminations that are insufficient to justify those ordeals,
but are sufficient to show the authenticity of the values being
illuminated. The knowledge of other minds that is the chief medium
of illumination is no longer merely prudential or behavioral, no
longer a matter of extrapolating from present appearances to past or
future, but rather of radical insight or compassion, of passing from
appearances to reality. Since the entire point is to show that intrinsic
values are not invalidated by defeat, we are not to expect and do not
get any intimation of a providential order insuring the ultimate victory
of those values. The apparent disorder in effect hypothetically concedes the premise of *Troilus and Cressida;* the affirmation of value,
in effect, denies its conclusion. It may be noted here that in two ways
King Lear is markedly untragic. Its collision of good and evil is
purest melodrama, and it atypically suspends belief in cosmic order;
even in the *Prometheus*, where that order is on trial, we repeatedly
see the danger of swallowing the martyr's testimony whole, and look
forward to the revelation in the sequel of the Διὸς ἁρμονία that is
not even here quite submerged. *Lear*'s departures from the pattern
of tragic affirmation are marked but indispensable, I think, to achieving its own kind of affirmation.

In *Othello* a man fails a test of sympathetic insight, falling into a
headlong suspicion that belies his professions of love. Certain of
having been betrayed but unable to bear the ocular proof required
at once by simple justice and by the finality of his contemplated

response, he embraces the flimsiest of indirect evidence, and with it a code of retribution that would be a travesty of justice even were the evidence conclusive. The last phase of the hero's degeneration is a twisting or extinguishing of moral sense recognizable as *excaecatio*, the blinding of the reprobate, a disease of the soul from which the only protection is grace. This and other cues tend to discourage any self-righteous hatred of the depraved in the play and to promote a special and difficult kind of pity. As the rejoinder to voluntarism in *King Lear* is a vision of human dignity, so here the same persuasion is refuted by a vision of its consequences to the human spirit. In both plays the insight that matters is granted not to the hero but to the audience, and the moral posture fostered by that insight is not judgment but sympathy.

In our scientific age, refutation by vision or self-evident truth has largely lost its credit, and in the main with reason, though perhaps not entirely so. Perhaps it is a case of the boy who cried wolf, and the only self-evident truths that have genuinely been discredited are the ones that have been called so in vain. It is at least suggestive that a staunchly positivistic thinker of our day finds it necessary to support his social proposals by appeal to what a more benighted age would have called the *consensus gentium:* "Let us agree, to start with, that health is better than illness, wisdom better than ignorance, love better than hate, and productive energy better than neurotic sloth."[1] The blithe confidence of this expectation that there are values that need only be affirmed to elicit rational agreement is surrendered, I think, as a lost innocence in *Measure for Measure* and earned back as sublime and painful experience in *King Lear*.

Notes

Introduction

1. Roy W. Battenhouse, *Shakespearian Tragedy: Its Art and Its Christian Premises* (Bloomington, Ind., 1969).

2. Roland Mushat Frye, *Shakespeare and Christian Doctrine* (Princeton, N.J., 1963), p. 36.

3. *Certaine Sermons or Homilies*, Scholars' Facsimiles and Reprints, ed. Mary Ellen Rickey and Thomas B. Stroup (Gainesville, Fla., 1968), pp. xif.

4. Eleanor Prosser, *Hamlet and Revenge* (Stanford, Calif., 1967), p. 185.

5. *Measure for Measure*, The Arden Shakespeare, ed. J. W. Lever (London, 1965), p. lxxiii.

6. Augustine, *Ad Simplicianum* 1. q. 2 (Migne, *PL* 40. 6. 118), *De correptione et gratia* 14 (*PL* 44. 10. 943), *Ad Simplicianum* 1. q. 2 (*PL* 40. 6. 119), *De correptione* 12 (*PL* 44. 10. 940).

7. Augustine, *De peccatorum meritis* 2. 6 (Migne, *PL* 44. 10. 155). Translation mine.

8. *Summa Theologica* 1. 23. 6, ibid. ad 3, 1. 23. 5, ibid. ad 3. Hereafter cited as *STh*.

9. *Ham.* 3. 3. 68–69.

10. Augustine, *Contra duas epistolas Pelagianorum* 1. 3 (Migne, *PL* 44. 10. 553), *De gratia et libero arbitrio* 1. 15 (Migne, *PL* 49. 10. 899).

11. Frye, *Shakespeare and Christian Doctrine*, p. 106.

12. John Calvin, *Institutes of the Christian Religion* 2. 3. 4. I quote here and throughout the translation by Ford Louis Battles in The Library of Christian Classics, vols. 20 and 21 (Philadelphia, 1960). Hereafter this work will be cited as *Inst.*

13. *Inst.* 2. 2. 12.

14. *Inst.* 2. 3. 4.

15. Quoted by Frye, *Shakespeare and Christian Doctrine*, p. 251.

16. *Shakespeare and Christian Doctrine*, p. 252.

17. *Shakespeare and Christian Doctrine*, p. 158.

18. *Inst.* 2. 4. 6, 7.

19. *Inst.* 2. 5. 2, 5.

20. *STh* 1–2. 10. 4 ad 3.

21. *STh* 1–2. 22. 4 ad 3.
22. *Shakespearian Tragedy*, p. 223.
23. *STh* 1–2. 77. 3 ad 3.
24. Ibid., art. 1.
25. *Shakespearian Tragedy*, p. 226.
26. *Shakespeare and Christian Doctrine*, p. 158.
27. L. C. Knights, *An Approach to Hamlet* (Stanford, Calif., 1961), p. 81.
28. Harry Levin, "Evangelizing Shakespeare," *Journal of the History of Ideas* 32 (1971): 310.
29. John Holloway, *The Story of the Night* (London, 1961), pp. 18f.
30. *The Story of the Night*, pp. 18, 11.
31. *The Story of the Night*, p. 180.
32. Ernest Schanzer, *The Problem Plays of Shakespeare* (New York, 1963), pp. 5f.
33. *The Problem Plays of Shakespeare*, p. 7.
34. *The Story of the Night*, p. 153.
35. D. G. James, *The Dream of Learning* (Oxford, 1951), p. 27.
36. *The Dream of Learning*, p. 83.
37. *The Dream of Learning*, p. 78.
38. *The Dream of Learning*, p. 2.
39. Jonathan R. Price, "*Measure for Measure* and the Critics: Towards a New Approach," *Shakespeare Quarterly* 20 (1969): 187.
40. Maynard Mack, *King Lear in Our Time* (Berkeley, Calif., 1965), p. 117.
41. George C. Herndl, *The High Design: English Renaissance Tragedy and the Natural Law* (Lexington, Ky., 1970), p. 6.
42. Clifford Leech, "The 'Meaning' of *Measure for Measure*," *Shakespeare Survey* 3 (1950): 67.
43. Allan H. Gilbert, "The More Shakespeare He, in *Shakespearian Essays*, ed. Alwin Thaler and Norman Sanders (Knoxville, Tenn., 1964), p. 61.

CHAPTER ONE

"I Know My Course": Hamlet's Confidence

1. Cf. *De ratione dicendi ad Herennium* 4. 63sqq. My source for all quotations from Shakespeare will be the New Cambridge Edition, *The Complete Plays and Poems of William Shakespeare*, ed. William Allan Neilson and Charles Jarvis Hill (Cambridge, Mass., 1942).
2. *AYL* 3. 2. 387–403. The point of Rosalind's mockery is that there are no unequivocal "marks" (*notae*) of lovesickness.

3. Cf. Diogenes Laertius 9. 72; Cicero *Academica* 1. 44, 2. 32.

4. *The Complete Poems of Sir John Davies*, ed. A. B. Grosart (London, 1876), 1: 19.

5. *Elegantiarum e Plauto et Terentio libri duo, Publilii Syri sententiae*, ed. Erasmus and Fabricius (1581), sent. 169.

6. Cf. 4. 7. 109.

7. *Elegantiarum*, sent. 327; cf. sent. 311.

8. Cf. Tommaso Campanella, *La Città del Sole e Poesie*, ed. Adriano Seroni (Milan, 1962), p. 64: "Il mondo è un animal grande e per-fetto. . . . Se ignoriamo il suo amor e 'l suo intelletto, / né il verme del mio ventre s'assottiglia / A saper me."

9. See *Plotini Enneades cum Marsilii Ficini interpretatione*, ed. Friedrich Creuzer and Georg Heinrich Moser (Paris: Didot, 1855), which supplies Ficino's scholia as well as his translation. For the cosmic sisterhood see *Ennead* 4. 3. 7, 8, and especially 6.

10. See Ficino's scholia ibid., at 4. 4. 6, 16; 6. 4. 12.

11. Ibid., scholium at 4. 4. 4.

12. *Bartas His Divine Weekes and Words*, trans. Joshua Silvester (1605), pp. 280f. Cf. Plotinus, ibid., Ficino's scholium at 4. 4. 12 ("pleni-tudine [rationum seminalium] res futuras anticipat in praesentibus"), 33, 39.

13. See *The Sermons of John Donne*, ed. Evelyn M. Simpson and George R. Potter (Berkeley, Calif., 1962), 10 : 82f. Cf. *Letters to Severall Personages by John Donne*, ed. Charles Merrill, Jr. (New York, 1910), p. 94. For original sources see Aquinas *STh* 1, q. 57, a. 4 and Duns Scotus *Quaestiones in libros Sententiarum* 2, distinctio 9, q. 2, ad 1; 4, d. 10, q. 8 ad 3. It is, of course, highly unlikely to say the least that Shakespeare was directly acquainted with the literature of this controversy. However, the prestige and currency of lore about angels during his lifetime are notorious. On the general problem, cf. Bembo's celebrated affirmation in Castiglione's *Courtier* 4. 57. "I fisionomi al volto conoscono spesso costumi e talora i pensieri degli uomini." But it is a mistake to appraise it without reference to the same speaker's bitter acknowledgment in 2. 29: "negli animi nostri sono tante latebre e tanti recessi, che impossibil è che prudenza umana possa conoscer quelle simulazioni, che dentro nascose vi sono." To be sure, Erasmus, the apostle of humanism, draws a happy moral from the parallel between the method of the natural theologian and that of the physiogno-mist: "Ev. Credisne Deum esse? FA. Maxime. Ev. At nihil minus videri potest quam Deus. FA. Videtur in rebus conditis. Ev. Idem videtur animus ex actione" (Erasmi *Colloquia*, ed. Cornelius Schrevel [Amsterdam, 1693], p. 399). But Saint Paul, an apostle of somewhat higher standing, draws from the same parallel a moral that is both authoritative and considerably less happy (1 Cor. 2 : 11).

14. *Ethica Nicomachea* 1170^{b}5–12; cf. 1157^{a}30sq., 1157^{b}4sq. Hereafter cited as *Eth. Nic.*

15. Ibid., 1155^{b}26sq., 1165^{b}10sq.; Cicero *Laelius* 92.

16. *Complete Poems*, 26. What normally passes for self-knowledge in the rational soul is a humble inference from the nature of its own processes; as with other things not directly observable, "the work the touchstone of the nature is" (ibid., p. 35). Serious people seek the friendship of the judicious, Aristotle tells us (1159^{a}22sq.), precisely to confirm their opinion of themselves: "They are gratified because they put their trust in the judgment of those who pronounce them good."

17. *Ars amatoria* 618, *Remedia amoris* 497sq. Translation mine.

18. *Patrologia Latina* 26. 363 (cf. Ps. 24). Harvey typically associates Jerome with Menander as authorities for the "Ulyssean" insight that a lie is preferable to a destructive truth. See *Gabriel Harvey's Marginalia*, ed. G. C. Moore Smith (Stratford-upon-Avon, 1913), pp. 118f. Cf. Erasmus *Colloquia*, p. 473.

19. *H5* 2. 4. 38.

20. *Sir John Harington's translation of Orlando Furioso*, ed. Graham Hough (Carbondale: Southern Illinois University Press, 1962), p. 39.

21. Plutarch, *Moralia*, trans. Philemon Holland (London, 1911), p. 47.

22. *TN* 1. 2. 48–51, 53; 3. 4. 403f.

23. Cf. L. C. Knights, *An Approach to Hamlet* (Stanford, Calif., 1961), p. 13: Shakespeare's "main interest seems to have centered on the deceived, and a question that he asks with some insistence is how men come to make false or distorted judgments about other persons or about the world at large—what it is in their own natures that makes them capable of being deceived." But this is to reckon, like the Prince, without (*a*) the intrinsic deceptiveness or ambiguity of some appearances, (*b*) the crucial difference between "other persons" and "the world at large" as objects of knowledge—i.e., between transcending and extrapolating experience.

24. Harry Levin, *The Question of Hamlet* (New York, 1959), p. 54. For a more minute discussion of Hamlet's poem see the exchange of correspondence with the present writer in *PMLA* 90 (1975).

25. *Mac.* 1. 3. 107, 123–126. Eleanor Prosser, *Hamlet and Revenge* (Stanford, Calif., 1967), p. 113. Cf. ibid., p. 112. Cf. also Roy W. Battenhouse, *Shakespearian Tragedy: Its Art and Its Christian Premises* (Bloomington, Ind., 1969), p. 238.

26. Jasper Heywood, trans., *Seneca His Tenne Tragedies*, ed. *Thomas Newton anno 1581* (London, 1927), p. 57.

27. Prosser, *Hamlet and Revenge*, pp. 129, 131.

28. Prosser, *Hamlet and Revenge*, p. 140.

29. Cf. Knights, *An Approach to Hamlet*, p. 45.

30. The translation, in the *antiqua versio*, of Aristotle's *antipeponthós*

(*Eth. Nic.* 1132^b21) is *contrapassum* (vengeance). For divine right of vengeance, cf. Dante's use of *contrapasso*, *Inferno* 28. 139–142. According to Aristotle *contrapassum* (measure of pain for measure of pain) can be accommodated to neither branch of justice, distributive or commutative. Cf. Prosser, *Hamlet and Revenge*, pp. 13, 70, 81, 94; Battenhouse, *Shakespearian Tragedy*, pp. 239f, 244f; L. C. Knights, *An Approach to Hamlet*, passim; Victor H. Strandberg, "The Revenger's Tragedy: Hamlet's Costly Code," *South Atlantic Quarterly* 61 (1966); H. S. Wilson, *On the Design of Shakespearian Tragedy* (Toronto, 1957), pp. 44f.

31. Prosser, *Hamlet and Revenge*, p. 137.

32. John Donne, *Biathanatos* (1646), p. 83.

33. For references and discussion see chap. 3.

34. *H5* 2. 2. 174–181. Cf. Prosser, *Hamlet and Revenge*, p. 81: "As God's vice-regent on earth [*H5* 2. 2] he [Henry V] is the appointed voice to pronounce punishment, to be the agent of God's revenge. None the less, Shakespeare carefully develops the scene to insist that if there is a 'sacred duty' in such a case, it is not to inflict revenge on the man but to aid in the salvation of his soul."

35. *Meas.* 4. 3. 71ff.

36. Cf. Battenhouse, *Shakespearian Tragedy*, p. 254: "Hamlet's interpreting it[Gertrude's remarriage] as an act of sheer sensuality, however, is now driving her to feel shame." But Horatio tersely confirms the wifely impiety of the haste (1. 2. 174–181). Cf. Prosser, *Hamlet and Revenge*, pp. 124f. Most important, to say that Hamlet ascribes Gertrude's consent to sensuality is not to read what he says, which is that in Gertrude "sense is apoplex'd" (3. 4. 73). He ascribes her failure to honor her husband with a fitting period of mourning, incidentally to the temptation of the devil (ll. 76–77), essentially to her will (the appetite that implements reason [l. 88]), and instrumentally to a corrupted reason that "panders will" (l. 88).

37. *Eth. Nic.* 1109^b4–12. For Aquinas's comment see Sancti Thomae Aquinatis *In decem libros ethicorum Aristotelis ad Nicomachum expositio*, ed. P. Fr. Angelo M. Pirotta (Turin, 1939), ad locum.

38. Prosser, *Hamlet and Revenge*, pp. 196, 198, 194.

39. Knights, *An Approach to Hamlet*, pp. 65, 13.

40. Roland Mushat Frye's observations on Hamlet's plan for ministering to Gertrude avoid this pitfall of sentimental unfairness to the prince. See *Shakespeare and Christian Doctrine* (Princeton, N.J., 1963), pp. 149f, 154f, 174, 248.

41. Rom. 14 : 4, Deut. 32 : 35.

42. Battenhouse adumbrates this point, but then loses its bearing in a thicket of numerology (*Shakespearian Tragedy*, p. 261).

43. Hugh of Saint Victor, *PL* 175. 44; Ambrose, *PL* 14. 377, 378.

44. Agrippa d'Aubigné, *Les Oeuvres complètes*, ed. Réaume, de Caussade, and Legouez (Paris, 1873–1892), vol. 4 (1877), p. 245.

45. Bartas, p. 380.

CHAPTER TWO
Revenge, Honor, and Conscience in Hamlet

1. Cf. Harold S. Wilson, *On the Design of Shakespearian Tragedy* (Toronto, 1957), pp. 44f: "Hamlet, in his overwrought excitement and for the moment, accepts the obligation imposed by the ghost without trying to understand what warrant he has for so doing. Later on, Hamlet will try to understand that warrant."

2. Aristotle *Rhet.* 1382ᵃ14sq.; Aquinas *STh* 1–2. 29. 4, 78. 4 ad 3, 46. 6 ad 1. Translations mine.

3. *Eth. Nic.* 1100ᵃ18–21, 1101ᵃ22sq., 1101ᵇ5–9. Cf. Pindar *Ol.* 8. 77–80.

4. *Sir John Harington's translation of Orlando Furioso*, ed. Graham Hough (Carbondale, Ill., 1962), p. 178.

5. Cf. Eleanor Prosser, *Hamlet and Revenge* (Stanford, Calif., 1967), pp. 153f. It is instructive in this connection to contrast Pyrrhus's ironic pose, as his sword "seem'd i'th' air to stick" (2. 2. 501) with Hector's sincere forbearance, as he hangs his "advanced sword i'th' air, / Not letting it decline on the declin'd" (*Tro.* 4. 5. 188–189). Unlike Pyrrhus, Hector typifies the mind that is not "vindicative" (l. 105), not a worshiper of "the venom'd vengeance" (5. 3. 47). Pyrrhus's travesty of this kind of temper is not only a negative example but an ironic reminder of possibilities Hamlet ignores.

6. *The Question of Hamlet* (New York, 1959), pp. 141–164.

7. For a different view see Levin, ibid., p. 147.

8. Aristotle *Rhet.* 1382ᵃ8–11. Translation mine.

9. All biblical quotations are taken from the Geneva Bible.

10. *The Works of the Learned Sir Thomas Brown, Kt.* (London, 1686), vol. 2 (1685), p. 31. (See Kenelm Digby's "observation," p. 78.)

11. A number of critics have, like Roy W. Battenhouse, perceived the importance of Hamlet's "coming to see in his adversary Laertes a mirror of his own cause" (*Shakespearian Tragedy* [Bloomington, Ind., 1969], p. 231). Cf. Prosser, *Hamlet and Revenge*, p. 216; Victor H. Strandberg, "The Revenger's Tragedy: Hamlet's Costly Code," *South Atlantic Quarterly* 61 (1966): 102f.

12. Giovanni Battista Possevino, *Dialogo dell'honore* (Venice, 1565), pp. 500, 503sq., 515, 521.

13. *IH4* 1. 2. 92–93.

14. Ibid., 3. 2. 147–152.

15. "Fu Bradamante quella che t'ha tolto / quanto onor mai tu guadagnasti al mondo." Translation mine; Harington's version diverges from the original at this point.

16. John Donne, who does not scorn it, reminds us in two separate places that "all honors from inferiors flow," and that God Himself, Who is the fountain of intrinsic value, has only such honor as His creatures grant Him. See *Poems*, ed. Grierson (Oxford, 1912), 1 : 218, 263. Cf. *AWW* 2. 1. 31ff.

17. Prosser senses a fault in Hamlet's principle of honor but locates it mistakenly in the concrete application (*Shakespeare and Revenge*, p. 210). On the contrary, it is its abstractness from moral substance that is reprehensible. D. G. James correctly locates the fault in the principle but somehow finds that the practice is alien to Hamlet (*The Dream of Learning* [Oxford, 1951], pp. 56f).

18. There is, however, a difficulty that ought to be faced; for in his initial formulation Hamlet puts these alternatives somewhat more darkly: "to suffer / The slings and arrows of outrageous fortune, / Or to take arms against a sea of troubles, / And by opposing end them." The alternative to *generic* suffering, one might argue, is *generic* acting; so that the taking of arms in the third line can hardly suggest a *specific* action, let alone one so drastic and so far from constructive as suicide. The weakness of this argument is that Hamlet does not in fact speak of suffering in general, but suffering fortune; and in the Elizabethan view the only alternative to suffering fortune is ending life. Indeed, active men suffer fortune with an even more conspicuous inevitability than passive, for though fortune's purview is the whole sublunary sphere, her name denotes par excellence the mutable condition of all human *affairs*; to resist her is to suffer her obstreperously. "Ending one's troubles," if it is to mean a valid alternative to "suffering fortune," must be equivalent to "ending one's life." To be sure, it does not necessarily follow that "opposing one's troubles," likewise, is equivalent to "opposing one's life"; one may happen to die by unsuccessfully opposing one's troubles in the hope of surviving. But by the same token one may happen to realize this hope, and survive. Hamlet, however, speaks of *ending* his troubles, not of *happening* to end them; he is, after all, assessing the comparative "nobility" of effectual choices, not of contingent events that are beyond choice and hence cannot ennoble; this would be especially true of the series "opposing and ending," which, besides being a candidate for the title of superior nobility, can hardly exemplify the "suffering of fortune" to which it is the *alternative*. "Ending one's troubles," in short, is not the inadvertent result but the purpose of "opposing" them. "Troubles," therefore, must be literal and not metonymy for the things that trouble one; what is being opposed is, not the occasions of

"heartache" and the weariness of life, but the weary life itself. As has till very lately been assumed, the alternative to suffering fortune is dying by choice, or suicide. But this question is, in the most regrettable sense, academic; the bare bodkin Hamlet mentions in due course is unequivocal, and he does not appear to have changed the subject.

19. See *S. Aureli Augustini De Civitate Dei*, ed. J. E. C. Welldon (London, 1924), 1 : 37, 39.

20. Ecclus. 14 : 6. Cf. Lactantius *Patrologia Latina* 6. 407.

21. Cf. *Cym.* 3. 4. 78ff.

22. Cf. L. C. Knights, *An Approach to Hamlet* (Stanford, Calif., 1961), p. 80: "It does not matter that in Hamlet's mind the thought of suicide merges with the thought of killing the king." This will not do, for two reasons: (*a*) "merges" is inaccurate; they are compared in "nobility"; (*b*) to say that the comparison does not matter is to assume that Shakespeare played dice with his universe; the playwright is entitled to a presumption of innocence on this score. There is a special reason why theological connections deserve careful study in this play. It is brought out very forcefully by Roland Mushat Frye in *Shakespeare and Christian Doctrine* (Princeton, N.J., 1963): "As we have so often noticed in our analysis of Shakespearian speeches, it is Hamlet who seems most aware of the full range of Christian doctrine" (p. 234). Cf. ibid., p. 161. On suicide see ibid., pp. 25, 25n14, 26n15.

23. Cf. Frye, *Shakespeare and Christian Doctrine*, p. 152: "Yet there is a more frightful state than that of guilt-inspired fear. . . . At that point, a man's conscience no longer makes a coward of him because his conscience is dead."

24. See Roy W. Battenhouse, *Marlowe's Tamburlaine* (Nashville, Tenn., 1941), pp. 171, 133; and Ariosto *Orlando Furioso* 17. It is interesting that one of the texts adduced by Erasmus to illustrate the concept fits Claudius far better than Hamlet: "Fortassis illud est quod ait Job cap. xxxiv. *Qui regnare facit hypocritam, propter peccata populi.*" See *Colloquia*, ed. Schrevelius (Amsterdam, 1693), p. 133. The scourgeship of Claudius, in view of Hamlet's mission, would add a particularly mordant irony to the play; vengeance on the Scourge, all the authorities agree, is reserved to God alone.

25. See G. R. Elliott, *Scourge and Minister: A Study of Hamlet* (Durham, N.C., 1951), p. 122, and Fredson Bowers, "Hamlet as Minister and Scourge," *PMLA* 70 (1955): 740–749.

26. These two possibilities must be eliminated. If Hamlet is thinking of either as a crime for which heaven has punished him, then we should be forced to give up the thesis that he never repents his dedication to vengeance. For the earlier possibility—the sparing of Claudius at prayer— there is a specious case; a little before his talk of being a scourge Hamlet

rebukes himself, and is rebuked by the ghost, for being dilatory. But the language fits his interview with his mother very well and his conduct in the earlier scene not at all. At the moment of the ghost's interruption Hamlet's only positive effort is being directed toward his mother. He is thus, from the ghost's point of view, clearly "laps'd in time and passion" with regard to his principal assignment, which is now hardly more than a "blunted purpose." His reason for sparing Claudius, on the other hand, bespoke, not a blunted, but a newly whetted purpose; it was no lapse in passion but the sublime of hatred to add Claudius's immortal soul to the bill of execution.

One may, however, invoke the principle of parsimony and contend that Hamlet regards the murder of Polonius both as a sign that the *intention* thereby frustrated was contrary to the will of heaven and (in consequence) as a punishment for that intention, guilt being punished by guilt. But the point to be proved, we must remember, is not that Polonius's accidental death might be taken as such a sign, but that Hamlet in fact so takes it. And this requirement is all the more pressing because the sign in question is ambiguous; heaven's substitution of Polonius could as easily arise from a positive desire to kill Polonius—to punish "this with me," as Hamlet puts it—as from a check to some unfitness in Hamlet's choice of a time and place for revenge. The two motives, to be sure, are not incompatible, but either of them alone would be sufficient, and Hamlet mentions only the former; moreover, the only ground for repentance he mentions is the killing of Polonius. It is very odd in any case, if what is being punished is a particular crime, to repent of the punishment and pass over the crime without a word. It would be doubly odd if the crime were a phase, indeed the voluntary phase, of the same repented act. But the latter oddity, at least, need not trouble us; for Hamlet shows no sign at all of thinking that heaven frowns on his choice of an occasion for revenge.

There is, however, good reason to think that Hamlet ought to reach this conclusion, whether he does so or not. For in the orthodox view the only retributive act that might escape the imputation of sin against the Holy Ghost was one that was not essentially retributive at all: a solemn public execution under the law or by arbitrament of arms, enacted not to satisfy a grudge but to restore the common weal. By leaping at the arras Hamlet acts damnably, as private assassin rather than public executioner. If Hamlet's model is a Harry Richmond, "exacting public justice in battle" (Bowers, "Hamlet as Minister and Scourge," p. 744), he seems totally unaware of the fact, a circumstance that is particularly strange in view of Laertes' impulsive and successful appeal to public militancy. Laertes' storming of the castle and attempted usurpation, of course, are illegal—"antiquity forgot, custom not known." Hamlet, on the other hand, has not only the right to be a Richmond but also a political reserve at least equal to Laertes';

such is "the great love the general gender bear him" that Claudius could not proceed publicly against him for fear the proceedings "would have reverted to my bow again / And not where I had aim'd them." The facilities for a public vengeance are obviously available, but Hamlet does not avail himself of them. The issue does not arise for him. Hamlet can hardly think himself condemned to the status of scourge for breaking a law of privacy with which he is clearly unacquainted.

27. Bowers, "Hamlet as Minister and Scourge," p. 743.

28. Ibid., p. 745.

29. Claudius reveals his plan in soliloquy rather than dialogue after dismissing R and G (4. 3. 57–59); cf. Prosser, *Hamlet and Revenge*, p. 204. Moreover, once they lose Hamlet to the pirates R and G would hardly bother to deliver Claudius's letter if they knew what was in it.

30. *De Civitate Dei*, pp. 36sq., 42. Hereafter cited as *Civ. Dei*.

31. Roland H. Bainton, "The Immoralities of the Patriarchs according to the Exegesis of the Late Middle Ages and of the Reformation," *Harvard Theological Review* 23 (1930): 39–49.

32. Prosser, *Hamlet and Revenge*, pp. 70, 94, xi; cf. H. S. Wilson, *On the Design of Shakespearian Tragedy*, pp. 44f.

33. Philip J. Ayres, "Degrees of Heresy: Justified Revenge and Elizabethan Narratives," *Studies in Philology* 69 (1972): 465.

34. Ibid.

35. Ibid., p. 470.

36. Ibid., p. 463.

37. "Mine Own John Poins," ll. 37–42. For a medieval parallel see *Purg.* 1. 71.

38. *Hamlet and Revenge*, p. 111.

39. *Hamlet and Revenge*, p. 178.

40. *Hamlet and Revenge*, p. 237.

41. For a discussion of Hamlet's initial response to the ghost, and of Prosser's contrary interpretation (*Hamlet and Revenge*, pp. 140f), see the previous chapter.

42. Cf. Prosser, ibid., p. 225: "Extreme provocation coupled with his shock at Ophelia's death is surely sufficient to account for a momentary release of emotion." The question is what sort of emotion is released, and here the word *shock* is obfuscatory. If a sudden access of ostensible grief reinforces Hamlet's "extreme provocation" instead of dissipating it, something important has been disclosed about the quality of his "grief."

43. Cf. Battenhouse, *Shakespearian Tragedy*, p. 229: "Hamlet's final duel with Laertes . . . is fought as an exhibition of swordsmanship for the sake of personal glory."

44. *Hamlet and Revenge*, p. 227.

45. *Hamlet and Revenge*, p. 234.

46. *Hamlet and Revenge*, p. 235.
47. *Shakespearian Tragedy*, p. 244.
48. *Hamlet and Revenge*, p. 106.
49. *Shakespearian Tragedy*, p. 293.
50. *Inf.* 3. 6, 20. 29f, 33. 150.
51. *Shakespearian Tragedy*, p. 251.
52. *Laws* 1. 2. 3. See also chap. 3n30.

CHAPTER THREE
Pain, Law, and Conscience in Measure for Measure

1. For a characteristic denial that the comedy involves us in any such emergency, cf. R. A. Foakes, *Shakespeare, the Dark Comedies to the Last Plays: From Satire to Celebration* (Charlottesville, Va., 1971), chap. 2. It is possible that Foakes's extreme position is simply a justifiably violent reaction to the old fad of interpreting *MM* as Christian tropology or homily; cf. Roy W. Battenhouse, "*Measure for Measure* and the Christian Doctrine of Atonement," *PMLA* 61 (1946): 1029–1059; G. Wilson Knight, *The Wheel of Fire* (London, 1949); S. L. Bethell, *Shakespeare and the Popular Dramatic Tradition* (New York, 1949); R. W. Chambers, *The Jacobean Shakespeare and Measure for Measure* Annual Lecture of the British Academy, 1937 (London, 1938). The similar attitude reflected in Josephine Waters Bennett's *Measure for Measure As Royal Entertainment* (New York, 1966) seems also to have been negatively inspired by the same fad.

As for the approach of the present chapter, a straw in the wind may be the following criticism of D. L. Stevenson's *The Achievement of Shakespeare's Measure for Measure* (Ithaca, N.Y., 1966) by Michel Grivelet ("And Measure Still for Measure: sur quelques études récentes," *Études Anglaises* 21 [1968]: 70): Stevenson "n'accorde pas non plus toute l'attention qu'elles méritent à une série d'études . . . sur la notion d'équité." See ibid. for references.

2. *The Fourth Part of the Institutes of the Laws of England*, 4th ed. (London, 1669), p. 290.

3. "That which is called common right in 2E.3 is called common law in 14E.3, and in this sense it is taken where it is said, ita quod stet recto in curia, ita legi in curia" (*The Second Part* [London, 1797], 1 : 56). "When an act of Parliament is against Common right and reason, or repugnant, or impossible to be performed, the Common law shall controll, and adjudge such act to be void. . . . Some statutes are made against Common law and right" (8 Co. Rep. 118, in *The Sixth (to Eleventh) Part of the Reports of Sir Edward Coke* (London, ?1658), p. 758; the title

motto reads, "Neminem oportet esse legibus sapientiorem. Non aliunde floret res publica quam si legum vigeat auctoritas"). On the ultimacy of common law as to clemency, cf. Sir Thomas Smith, *De re publica Anglorum*, ed. L. Alston (Cambridge, 1906), p. 61. For the statement about the identification of common law with the "higher law," see Edward S. Corwin, *The "Higher Law" Background of American Constitutional Law* (Ithaca, N.Y., 1955), p. 24.

4. Quoted in W. S. Holdsworth, *A History of English Law* (London, 1927), 1 : 207n7. Cf. *The Second Part*, 1 : 56: " 'Discretio' est discernere per legem quid sit justum"; "ubi non est scientia [*sc.* legum] non est conscientia" (*Fourth Part*, p. 79). "Judicia sunt tanquam juris dicta" (*Second Part*, p. 360).

5. *Fourth Part*, p. 66. Cf. "Interest rei publicae res judicatas non rescindi" (*Second Part*, p. 360), and the Duke's jeremiad at 3. 2. 237–239: "Novelty is only in request, and it is as dangerous to be aged in any kind of course, as it is virtuous to be inconstant in any undertaking."

6. "Quod non apparet non est, et non apparet in isto casu ante judicium" (*Second Part*, p. 479).

7. Cf. John Calvin, *Institutes of the Christian Religion*, trans. John Allen (Philadelphia, 1936), 1 : 399, 401, 295.

8. *The Advancement of Learning* (New York, 1930), p. 211.

9. Alexander M. Bickel, "Civil Rights Boil Up," *New Republic*, 8 June 1963, 11a.

10. Cf. Ernest Schanzer, *The Problem Plays of Shakespeare* (New York, 1963), p. 116: "It is Escalus who in this play illustrates the *via media* between the two excesses [laxity and severity] in the administration of justice." But this is to disregard the fact that Escalus endorses Angelo's severity and fails to see a "remedy" for it (2. 1. 296–299).

11. According to J. W. Lever (*MM* [The Arden Shakespeare] [London, 1965], p. lxvii), Angelo's judicial error in administering a legal prescription of death for fornication is to think that "no extenuating circumstances need be considered." But this argument gratuitously assumes the justice of the prescription itself, and thereby illustrates the seductiveness of Angelo's basic error (if it is one) that the law itself, being axiomatic, is beyond criticism. Cf. Schanzer's equivalent remark about Claudio's offense that "a proper regard for its circumstances should have earned him the judge's pardon" (*Problem Plays*, p. 78; also ibid., p. 116).

12. Two useful surveys of equitable jurisprudence in Shakespeare's day and of the evidence (collected long ago by Judge Phelps of Baltimore) for a topical reference in the play to current disputes about Chancery have been published in *Shakespeare Quarterly* 13 (1962): Wilbur Dunkel, "Law and Equity in *Measure for Measure*," pp. 277–285, and J. W. Dickinson, "Renaissance Equity and *Measure for Measure*," pp. 287–297.

13. Sancti Thomae Aquinatis *In decem libros ethicorum Aristotelis ad Nicomachum expositio*, ed. P. Fr. Angelo M. Pirotta, O.P. (Turin, Italy, 1943), nn. 1028f, 1044. Cf. n. 1056: "operari ea quibus accidit esse injusta non est idem ei quod est per se facere injustum."

14. Ibid., nn. 333, 381, 1214f, 1248. Cf. also n. 1123.

15. Cf. *Ethicorum expositio*, nn. 905, 1087; "Necessaria est post legem latam sententia judicum per quam universale dictum legis applicatur ad particulare negotium." This vein of judicial empiricism can be traced in part to the tradition of classical equity; cf. A. P. d'Entrèves, *Natural Law* (London, 1951), pp. 29f, 49. For *summo iure contendere* in Erasmus and Roman law as literal, not as constant, adherence to the substance of law, see Guido Kisch, *Erasmus und die Jurisprudenz seiner Zeit* (Basel, Switzerland, 1960), pp. 10, 62–67, 118f, 159. For natural equity and avoidance of *summo iure contendere* as accommodation of law to specific differences in case (and by implication to individual differences), see ibid., pp. 4, 11n, 129f.

16. Quoted in Holdsworth, 5 : 235. In 1605 the civilian Cowell complains in the following terms of his common law rivals: "statutorum cortici et particularibus rerum judicatarum exemplis mordicus adhaerescentes universalem juris naturalis rationem suavemque *epieikeian* nihil morantur" (quoted ibid., p. 21n4). The use of "universal" and "particular" here betrays a certain apriorist legalism on Cowell's own part: but the hostile attitude of the contemporary common lawyer to "sweet equity" is well attested. By way of qualification, however, it should be noted that Coke himself, in defining the judicial role of Parliament, seems to ascribe to it "a species of equity jurisdiction in individual cases which, while it may seem often to invade the rights of those immediately affected, was apparently controlled by the motive of vindicating the rights of others" (Corwin, *The "Higher Law,"* p. 56).

17. See Sir Paul Vinogradoff, "Reason and Conscience in 16th-Century Jurisprudence," *Law Quarterly Review* 24 (1908): 373–84, esp. 382.

18. *Compendium theologiae* 121; *Ethicorum expositio* n. 952.

19. *Ethicorum expositio* n. 384.

20. Ibid., n. 1089.

21. Roscoe Pound, Intro., *The Individualization of Punishment*, by Raymond Saleilles, trans. Rachel Jastrow (Boston, 1913), p. xiv.

22. Epilogue, *Third Part*. On the issue of penal severity and obsolescence, contrast *Digesta* 1. 3. 25, 32.

23. *Of the Laws of Ecclesiastical Polity* (published ca. 1593, reissued 1604), 1. 10. 12. Cf. Alberici Gentilis *Regales disputationes tres* (1605), Disp. prima, "De potestate regis absoluta," cited in d'Entrèves, p. 68.

24. *Il Principe* 26. 3. Cf. *Istorie fiorentine* 5. 8, and Livy 9.

25. Edward J. White, *Legal Antiquities* (Saint Louis, Mo., 1913), p. 195.

26. *Second Part*, p. 179.

27. *The Sermons of John Donne*, ed. R. Potter and Evelyn M. Simpson (Berkeley, Calif., 1959), 4 : 272.

28. *Biathanatos* (1646), pp. 92, 93f, 95.

29. *Biathanatos*, p. 23f; Aquinas *STh* Suppl. 3. 94. 1 and ibid. ad 3.

30. Lever suggests (*MM*, p. lxvii) that according to Claudio the "demi-god authority" "rightly" emulates the divine jurisprudence of Rom. 9 : 15, and does so by "exacting vengeance and dealing measure for measure." But clearly the subject of Paul's text and Claudio's paraphrase is arbitrariness in the distribution of justice and mercy.

31. *Ethicorum expositio*, nn. 1336, 1409, 1423, 2151.

32. Norman N. Holland, "*Measure for Measure:* The Duke and the Prince," *Comparative Literature* 11 (1959): 16–20. A highly seasoned account of Machiavelli's views was available to Shakespeare in the English translation (1602) of Innocent Gentillet's "Anti-Machiavel" (1576). Cf. Allan H. Gilbert, "The More Shakespeare He," in *Shakespearian Essays*, ed. Alwin Thaler and Norman Sanders (Knoxville, Tenn., 1964), p. 50.

33. *Il Principe*, ed. Luigi Rosso, after Mario Casella (Florence, 1931): "li principi debbano le cose di carico fare sumministrare ad altri, quelle di grazia a loro medesimi" (19. 7). Also 19. 1, 17. 2–3, 8. 8, 20. 6, 21. 2.

34. *Il Principe* 18. 5.

35. H. B. Charlton, *Shakespearian Comedy* (London, 1938), p. 254; W. W. Lawrence, *Shakespeare's Problem Comedies* (New York, 1931), p. 121; Schanzer, *Problem Plays*, pp. 100, 117ff.

36. D. L. Stevenson's perception ("Design and Structure in *Measure for Measure:* A New Appraisal," *ELH* 23 [1956]: 256–278) of the rottenness at the core of Isabella's chastity seems to me unexceptionable: "She plays a grim game with a man facing the axe, hinting, hesitating, but not quite telling, how he may escape death" (p. 277). But his theory that she finally achieves the equity only accidentally accorded her at the outset fairly trumpets its weakness: "Her subsequent rôle *as a kind of pander . . .* represents her first *surrender* to a more measured, less absolute, mercy" (p. 277, italics added). Lever suggests that in acting as a go-between Isabella "is being reeducated in the function of virtue as an active force in the world" (*MM*, p. lxxxii). This reeducation continues at the denouement when "grief and revenge" drive her to the length of "exposing herself to public shame" (ibid.), a "humiliation" that is the "necessary psychological purge" of her morbid aversion to shame (ibid., p. xcv). If this is so, why is her response to purgation, as Lever concludes, "not very

different in tone from the simulated rhetoric in which . . . she had previously denounced Angelo" (ibid.) ? It is neither persuasive nor reassuring to be told that this counterinstance to Lever's theory is to be numbered among "the basic defects of the play" (ibid, p. xciv). In the same vein of "reeducation," Mariana's insistence that she craves "no other, nor no better man" (5. 1. 431) is supposed to show us that "she has converted infatuation into a selfless love that is truly charitable" (ibid., p. lxxxiii). But charity toward Angelo is not only not entailed by wishing to have no other man, but entirely inconsistent with wishing the man she has no better. (On charity in this connection see Aquinas *STh* 2–2. 27. 2, 1 2. 26. 4.).

37. *Second Part*, p. 658.

38. Holdsworth, 5 : 201; Sir James Fitzjames Stephen, *A History of the Criminal Law of England* (London, 1883), 2 : 222ff.

39. Cf. Elizabeth Marie Pope, "The Renaissance Background of *Measure for Measure*," *Shakespeare Survey* 2 (1949): Isabella's "act [defending Angelo] is not natural; it is not [as the Duke has carefully pointed out] even reasonable: it is sheer, reckless forgiveness of the kind Christ advocates in the Sermon on the Mount" (p. 79). This argument gratuitously presupposes that the mercy advocated by Christ is "reckless" or at odds with the laws of nature and reason, the basis of equitable punishment. But it is a commonplace of Christian ethical theory that knowledge of men's duty "no less to love others than themselves," and hence to abstain "from all violence," can penetrate by "degrees of discourse the minds even of mere natural men" (Hooker *Laws* 1. 18. 7; cf. Aquinas *STh* 1–2. 100. 2 ad 1; Augustine *Civ. Dei* 9. 5). Since equitable punishment, the fruit of such "discourse," is traditionally described as corrective and hence as the judicial form of requiting evil with good, it is hard to detect in Isabella's deprecation of punishment for Angelo, who is to say the least in some need of correction, the authentic spirit of the injunction to return good for evil. Pope considers that, since among her Renaissance authorities "no one advocates showing leniency to . . . serious or hardened criminals," the prevailing theory was marred by "a certain failure to pull the concepts of mercy and retaliation together" (p. 75), a "disturbing discrepancy between the concepts of religious mercy and secular justice" (p. 80). But these equations of "secular justice" with "retaliation" and of "mercy" with "leniency" are, not to belabor the present argument, inconsistent with the theory they purport to represent. It is very little to Isabella's credit that they are indeed the basis of her plea on Angelo's behalf. For an argument similar to Pope's see Madeleine Doran, *Endeavors of Art* (Madison, Wis., 1964), p. 368.

Schanzer (*Problem Plays*, pp. 102f) speaks of the "legalism" of Isabella's brief for Angelo, but in his analysis of the points that chiefly reveal it limits himself to strictures that are themselves legalistic: (*a*) he fails to question Chambers's assertion, in support of Isabella, that Claudio's "capital offence" is "a postulate of our story"; the injustice in Angelo's allowing the law to take its course, according to Schanzer, is simply that the judge thereby broke his promise; (*b*) he acquiesces in Chambers's judgment that Angelo's attempted liaison with Isabella is a crime "not in act, but in thought"; according to Schanzer, Angelo's actual crime in connection with Isabella is defined by the nature of his office: "his gross abuse of his judicial powers."

40. Cf. W. W. Lawrence, *Problem Comedies*, pp. 116f: "The pardon of a repentant villain and his union to a heroine was a commonplace in Elizabethan drama, and would certainly have been readily accepted by a contemporary audience." Also ibid., p. 113: "But the complete repentance and forgiveness of the villain is a common dramatic convention." It is question-begging to assume that Angelo, who never shows awareness of his perverse legalism, has undergone complete repentance.

41. *FQ* 5. 1. 7, 10. 2.

42. Cf. Aquinas *STh* 1. 21. 3 ad 2.

43. *MV* 4. 1. 199f.

44. The simile seems to be an imitation of passages from book 6 of Palingenius's *Zodiacus vitae*. See the translation by Barnaby Googe (London, 1576), especially p. 87, the passage beginning "An Ape (quoth shee) and jesting stock is man to God in skye," p. 91 ("O Monkey, learne to bridle well"), and (for the source of "glassy essence"), p. 86 ("like the brittle breaking glass").

45. See *The Essayes of Montaigne*, trans. John Florio (New York, 1933), p. 524.

CHAPTER FOUR

King Lear *and the Meaning of Chaos*

1. Contrast Aquinas *In Ethicam Nicomacheam expositio* n. 1028: "Ea enim quae sunt naturalia apud nos sunt quidem eodem modo ut in pluribus, sed ut in paucioribus deficiunt"; and the above quote from John Donne, *Biathanatos*, p. 35.

2. Aquinas contends that physical suffering is *privatio corporeorum bonorum* (*STh* 1. 48. 6).

3. Professor Heilman's philosophical analysis illustrates the *petitio principi* involved: "Yet the tragedy as a whole affirms the preeminence of order; the paradox of tragedy is that order comes out of a world wracked by disorder, that chaos proves order. There cannot be a breach in nature unless there is nature" (*This Great Stage* [Baton Rouge, La.,

1948], p. 91). The great thing, of course, is to tell the breach from the observance, chaos from order (i.e., bad order from good), without resorting to verbalism.

4. According to Maynard Mack (*King Lear in Our Time* [Berkeley, Calif., 1965], p. 106), the play asks, among other abstract questions: "To what extent have our distinctions of degree and status, our regulations by law and usage, moral significance? . . . To what extent are they simply the expedient disguises of a war of all on all, wherein humanity preys on itself (as Albany says) 'like monsters of the deep'?" But in the first place the moral significance of institutions as such or of particular institutions is hardly in serious question if, as Mack goes on to argue on the play's behalf, "institutions are necessary if society is to exist at all; but as the play here eloquently points out [4. 6. 169–170] . . . they are not enough" without "mutual humility and compassion" (ibid., pp. 108f). To say that something is not enough by itself to achieve an end to which it is only a partial means is not to impugn its utility or its "moral significance." There is nothing in Mack's argument or in the lines he quotes to suggest that institutions ever fail men, but merely that men sometimes fail both institutions and each other. Secondly, moral generalizations about a predatory "humanity" can hardly be the concern of a play that presents humanity, in Mack's phrase, as "a moral spectrum (beastly behavior and angelic)" (ibid., p. 101). In *King Lear* men sometimes fail each other— and sometimes not. For an argument anticipating Mack's see Arthur Sewell, *Character and Society in Shakespeare* (Oxford, 1951), pp. 110, 117.

On Albany's speech cf. also Roland Mushat Frye, *Shakespeare and Christian Doctrine* (Princeton, N.J., 1963), p. 129: "What concerns us here is Albany's concern for a predatory humanity [*Lr.* 4. 2. 46–50]. It was a commonplace among authorities on ethics that where power was disjoined from order and law, man would be reduced to an animal-like existence." This collocation is misleading. The danger Albany foresees is not that the British alone will be corrupted, viz., by being forced or allowed to vent their criminal impulses, but that men everywhere will be scandalized by the failure of Goneril and her associates to meet with miraculous punishment. Such failure will suggest, in Albany's view, that crime really lacks what he takes to be its distinguishing mark: the gods' displeasure. That this is in fact Albany's meaning is witnessed by the ironic fulfillment of his fear in the anarchic sentiments expressed earlier by the second and third servants of Cornwall (3. 7. 99–102).

5. Edmund Spenser, *FQ* 5, Prologue 4; Pierre de Ronsard, *Mascarades* (1564).

6. 1. 1. 1–6. If Shakespeare had wished us to think of political indiscretion here he would not have blurred the issue. As Roy W. Battenhouse well argues: "How could an audience know what would have

happened in England had Cordelia received her intended share, the central and 'more opulent' third of territory?" (*Shakespearian Tragedy: Its Art and Its Christian Premises* [Bloomington, Ind., 1969], p. 279).

7. In *This Great Stage* Heilman maintains that Lear's fallacy at the beginning of the play is "the introduction of irrelevant quantitative standards" (p. 290), a failure in particular to understand that love "cannot be quantified" (p. 162). This line of argument, it seems to me, is seriously mistaken and is based on a personal and rather implausible prejudice. Love, like other feelings, obviously can and does admit of varying degrees of intensity; Goneril neither profanes nor misrepresents it by relying on this fact. Indeed the embattled truth that moral distinctions, of degree as well as kind, are real, intrinsic, and inalienable, is one of the play's most important contentions. We may, for example, assume that Cordelia actually does, as Goneril only pretends to, love Lear more than eyesight and no less than life. And this even though it would of course be a mockery for her to say so; not because such an answer would be wrong in principle, but because Lear has put his question in the form of a bribe, so that what would in content be a valid way of professing love is branded in effect as a mercenary solicitation.

8. Heilman's argument in this connection is twofold: (*a*) "Lear himself paves the way for the breakup of the organic order . . . by making contractual relationships basic" (p. 218). But Heilman himself has persuasively argued that Lear's status is "something that he as an aged king has earned" (p. 108); Lear has *already* discharged his responsibilities and now expects to come into his rights. Moreover, to pass on the vital business of ruling to abler hands is not obviously irresponsible. In any case, Lear's lack of a prior right to deference as a king would not invalidate either his claim to the deference promised him by "contractual relationships," or his right to filial respect. (*b*) "Goneril and Regan subject him to the same kind of indefensible deprivation to which he has subjected Cordelia" (p. 167). "Their failure of imagination is in effect exactly comparable to his own" (ibid.; cf. p. 195). There is no analogy at all between Lear's principles in dealing with Cordelia and those of his wicked daughters in denying him his hundred men; at least, Heilman's arguments do not give us a clue to any. Lear does, as the critic contends, appeal to the sanctity of the contract, maintaining in effect that Cordelia has failed to fulfill her side of the filial bond and thus released him from his. But Goneril and Regan, on the contrary, clearly repudiate their side of the abdication agreements. Nor is their attitude toward the number of Lear's retainers equivalent to Lear's own prior emphasis on what Heilman calls the "quantification of symbols." The daughters, like Heilman, are insisting that the number of retainers does *not* matter, whereas Lear continues to insist that it does, and rightly: for in this case the

"quantification," for better or worse, is surely an integral part of the symbol; one valet does not mean the same as a troop of attendants.

9. 3. 4. 107–113. Cf. Jan Kott, *Shakespeare Our Contemporary*, trans. Boleslaw Taborski (Garden City, N.Y., 1964), p. 154. But Kott makes no attempt to show that the play as a whole is designed to encourage agreement with Lear on the absurdity of unaccommodated man.

10. Heilman (p. 108) thinks that Lear's retinue is morally necessary because it symbolizes "the gratuity in excess of need, the dignity, the honor, which distinguishes man from animal." Cf. ibid., p. 175. That a gratuity in excess of need distinguishes man from animal is precisely the view that Lear must and does unlearn.

11. "I will keep her ignorant of her good," says the deus ex machina in *MM*, "To make her heavenly comforts of despair, / when it is least expected" (4. 3. 114–115). It is significant that this self-appointed deity is depicted as a fallible man who fully and mistakenly expects his ruse to result in a pardon for Claudio. In *King Lear*, too, "divine" justice is the work of men, a kind of immanent Providence. Lear appeals to the rich to renounce their conspicuous waste: by agreeing to redistribution they will be showing, not themselves, but the heavens to be more just. And so with Edgar's facsimile of divine intervention.

12. In this sense Edmund's self-inflicted wound (2. 1. 35–36) is a malign inversion of Gloucester's unfeigned suicidal impulse, just as Edmund's liaisons with the pelican daughters burlesque Cordelia's charity, and his dying exultation in their love Lear's dying epiphany of Cordelia. For patience as a Gift of the Holy Ghost, see Rosamond Tuve, *Allegorical Imagery* (Princeton, N.J., 1966), p. 166. See also Aquinas *STh* 2–2. 136. 3; Augustine *Civ. Dei* 4. 9. Cf. Shakespeare, *TN* 2. 4. 117f., *Lr.* 2. 4. 274, *Oth.* 4. 2. 63.

13. Cf. Phyllis Rackin, "Delusion As Resolution in *King Lear*," *Shakespeare Quarterly* 21 (1970): 31: "What Edgar says, of course, is literally a lie, although symbolically true." Two of these symbolic truths are interpreted ibid. Neither interpretation seems quite acceptable: (*a*) Gloucester "has been saved by a miracle—the miraculous devotion of the son he has repudiated." But it is Gloucester's life, not the motive of the act that preserves it, that is described in the text as a miracle. (*b*) "What is more, there is a very important sense in which the gods do here 'make them honours / Of men's impossibilities,' for 'men's impossibilities' need not mean what superstitious Gloucester probably takes it to mean, 'things impossible to men, done by the gods, who thus acquire honours.' 'Men's impossibilities' can also mean 'things impossible to men, done by men, with the result that the gods acquire honours.' " But in the second version "things done by men" are clearly possible to them only when they are granted the help of the gods. The latter in any case can hardly "acquire

honours" for accomplishments with which they have nothing to do. On either figurative interpretation, then, Edgar's speech remains an unsubstantiated claim of divine intervention. The commentator has failed to derive from that speech a statement about Gloucester's survival that we can accept as, by the speaker's standards at least, "perfectly true."

14. This "art of our [moral] necessities" that "can make vile things precious" (3. 2. 70–71) is an inversion of the economic theory of value with which the play had begun.

15. For the Fool as utilitarian aphorist and representative of "everyday common sense" see Wolfgang Clemen, *The Development of Shakespeare's Imagery* (New York, 1957), pp. 143f.

16. The classical analogy of the hellish wheel, of course, is Ixion's *rota*, on which the King of the Lapiths, like Lear, is punished by being forced to pursue and run away from himself at the same time (*volvitur Ixion et se sequiturque fugitque*). See Ovid *Met.* 4. 461. Ixion was the father of the Centaurs; but so is Lear, who characterizes Goneril and Regan as follows: "Down from the waist they are centaurs, / Though women all above" (4. 6. 126–127). It is tempting to see Lear as an Ixion, doomed on the wheel of his madness and torment to find himself in his very flight from reality, the begetter of unnatural children who turn against him and his kind as the Centaurs turned against the Lapiths.

17. See Heilman, p. 142. Cf. Maynard Mack, *King Lear in Our Time*, p. 113. Cf. also D. G. James, *The Dream of Learning* (Oxford, 1951), pp. 113f. James's failure to recognize in Cordelia's and Edgar's "spiritual perfection" the *imitatio Christi* is apparently chargeable to a false inference from his own remark that in *King Lear* "Shakespeare set himself to divest his play of any framework of Christian belief and deliberately denied himself any occasion for its expression" (ibid., pp. 120f). That neither the setting nor any event or utterance in the play strictly entails Christian belief does not mean that its characters cannot exemplify an abounding charity.

18. G. E. Moore, *Philosophical Studies* (New York, 1922), pp. 268f. Cf. Ralph Cudworth, *Immutable Morality*, 1. 2. 1, 2 in *The True Intellectual System of the Universe*, etc. (Andover and New York, 1838), 2 : 373f. For the quotations from Aquinas immediately following, cf. respectively *STh* 1. 19. 10, ibid., 5, *CG* 3. 97; *STh* 1. 19. 7 ad 4; ibid., 2. 94. 5 ad 2.

19. *Expositio super symbolum Apostolorum*, cap. 14.

20. *De jure belli*, Prolegomena 2. See also ibid., 1. 1. 10. Cf. John Milton, in *The Doctrine and Discipline of Divorce*, bk. 2, chapter 4: "God hath created a righteousness in right itself, against which he cannot do. So David, Psalm cxix. *The testimonies which thou hast commanded are righteous and very faithful; thy word is very pure, and therefore thy*

servant loveth it. Not only then for the author's sake, but for its own purity." See *Milton's Prose,* ed. M. W. Wallace (Oxford, 1949), p. 221. Virtue, if not its own reward, is its own justification. Cf. James, *The Dream of Learning,* p. 125. For the neutrality of *Lear* as to theodicy cf. Mack, *King Lear in Our Time,* pp. 62f. To his credit Battenhouse on occasion finds himself able to say but little more: "Appropriately they [Edgar's triumph and Cordelia's martyrdom] have a quality of paradox and enigma, lest by consoling unambiguously they dissolve the tragic frame" (*Shakespearian Tragedy,* p. 275). But this is to admit that their consolation is ambiguous.

21. A. C. Bradley, *Shakespearean Tragedy* (New York, 1955), pp. 204, 217, 429n29, 259, 228 respectively. Cf. also: "Thus the world in which evil appears seems to be at heart unfriendly to it. . . . The world reacts against it violently and in the struggle to expel it is drawn to devastate itself" (pp. 242f.; cf. p. 37). The notion of a cosmic moron, in his anxiety to perform first aid on a scratch, frenetically reaching for carbolic acid instead of iodine, conveys no very exalted idea of moral order. With such friends, the goodness and nobility in the world stand in very little need of enemies. Battenhouse's eschatological arguments are more ingenious but equally unsatisfactory. Lear, for example, is "learning the truth of how *this* world goes, the world of 'this great stage of fools.' . . . He is thus being made apt for a new 'stage' in another world" (*Shakespearian Tragedy,* p. 292). The reasoning is faulty here. To be sure, Lear's use of the demonstrative "this" suggests a presupposition that there are stages other than the one that now concerns him; and his talk of a *figurative* stage implies that he knows of *literal* ones. But neither the demonstrative nor the metaphor strictly entails the speaker's belief in another *figurative* stage, viz., heaven. Nor is Lear's "aptness" for a better world a sign that there is one.

22. In Aquinas, "second causes" are immediately provided for by God's wisdom, as are all things; see *Compendium* 130–131.

23. D. G. James recognizes that "the old Lear is not entirely transfigured in the new one we see in Act V" (*The Dream of Learning,* p. 98), but the critic maintains at the same time that he finds in Lear a growing sense that "the source of his daughters' evil is in himself" (ibid., p. 93). Quoting a passage in which Lear calls Goneril "a disease that's in my flesh, / Which I must needs call mine" (2. 4. 225–226), James argues that Lear's sense of being the source of his daughters' evil "mitigates his strong anger and causes him to desist from judgment" (ibid., p. 94), for, he notes, Lear goes on to say: "But I'll not chide thee; / Let shame come when it will, I do not call it" (2. 4. 228–229). This interpretation cannot stand: (*a*) Lear nowhere says in the passage that his flesh is the "source" of its own disease, or that his blood is the "source" of its

own corruption, or that his will is the "source" of either the disease or the corruption. (*b*) the adversative "but" shows that what precedes (Lear's shame at having in his flesh or "corrupted blood" [l. 228] the disease called Goneril) is an impediment rather than an encouragement to forbearance; he will not chide Goneril *despite* the fact that she shames him. Lear is saying he has reason (which he resolves to overlook) to reproach Goneril—not himself—for the disease she is to him. (*c*) In a later passage the crazed Lear does admit that flesh is the source of "pelican daughters" and thereby deserves the "judicious punishment" meted out when "discarded fathers," like Tom, "have thus little mercy on their flesh" (3. 4. 74–77). But the punishment that is praised as judicious here is the mercilessness of discarded fathers toward their own flesh, not (as James implies, ibid., p. 94) the mercilessness toward one such father of the storm on the heath. Having blamed his flesh, Lear carefully dissociates himself from it. It is not Lear but his flesh that is undeserving of Lear's mercy, and it is well to recall that in the earlier passage Lear's flesh includes Goneril (2. 2. 224). There is no suggestion here of forbearance toward Lear's daughters or of any acknowledgment on Lear's part of moral (as opposed to genetic) involvement in their evil.

Maynard Mack believes that there is a "strong undertow of victory in the play which carves on those same chalk walls [of Dover] Lear's 'new acquist' of self-knowledge and devotion to Cordelia, the majesty of his integrity and endurance, the invincibleness of his hope" (*King Lear in Our Time*, p. 87). But Lear's self-knowledge, as far as it is to include a rejection of primitive *do ut des*, is incomplete; his devotion to Cordelia is renewed even before the worst of his ordeal; his majesty or authority (witness Kent) has never left him; and his endurance is no match for grief, for by Mack's own account Lear's final hope marks the victory of anesthesia not only over suffering (ibid., p. 116), but also over consciousness itself in its struggle to master the fullness of "tragic knowledge" (pp. 112ff). Victory so equivocal in its gains and so exorbitant in its cost is surely Pyrrhic.

24. William R. Elton, *King Lear and the Gods* (San Marino, Calif., 1966), p. 37.

25. Cf. e.g., *Inst.* 3. 2. 42, 24. 8.

26. See W. K. Ferguson, *The Renaissance in Historical Thought* (Cambridge, 1948), p. 47. For the quotation from Carpenter see Elton, *King Lear and the Gods*, p. 22. See also *The Mirror for Magistrates*, ed., Lily B. Campbell (Cambridge, 1938), p. 67 (Baldwin's epistle) and *The Defence of Poesie* (London, 1595), sig. D4ᵛ. Cf. Dante *Paradiso* 4. 67sgg.

27. John Calvin *Commentaries*, ed. and trans. Joseph Haroutunian and Louise Pettibone Smith, Library of Christian Classics, vol. 23 (Philadelphia, 1958), pp. 261f; *Inst.* 1 : 208. For a different interpretation of Providence

in the Christian tradition, see C. A. Patrides, *The Grand Design of God* (London, 1972).

28. *Inst.* 1 : 211; *Comm.*, p. 282.
29. *Comm.*, p. 281.
30. Ibid.
31. Elton, *King Lear and the Gods*, p. 29. Henceforth the pages of this book will be cited parenthetically in the body of the text.
32. *Inst.* 2 : 902.
33. *Inst.* 1 : 51f, 68f.
34. F. C. Copleston, S.J., *Aquinas* (London, 1955), p. 131.
35. *Inst.* 1 : 273f.
36. See, respectively, *Summa contra gentiles* 1. 4; *STh* 1. 22. 2 ad 2; *Compendium Theologiae* 102. Cf. also *STh* 1. 47. 1.
37. *Enneads* 3. 2. 8. All translations from Plotinus are by the present writer, and are based on the edition of Emile Bréhier (Paris, 1925).
38. See respectively *Enneads* 2. 2. 7 and 3. 2. 6.
39. *Enneads* 3. 2. 15.
40. Ibid.
41. See *Consolatio Philosophiae* 4. pr. 6 (translation mine) and *Of the Laws of Ecclesiastical Polity*, ed. Roland Bayne (London, 1925), 1 : 153f.
42. Battenhouse supplies an otherworldly interpretation of what Lear sees: "Yet now Kent beholds Lear reading in this dead body a sign (a spirit instead of a letter), by which Lear can *almost see* the higher miracle of her coming to him with life—to 'redeem all sorrows / That ever I have felt' " (*Shakespearian Tragedy*, p. 290, italics added). This interpretation ignores the clear indication in the preceding lines that the breath the rejoicing Lear thinks he detects is simply the life whose continued residence in "a dog, a horse, a rat" filled the despairing Lear with indignation.
43. Beaumont and Fletcher, *Philaster*, 3. 1. 228–231.
44. *STh* 1, 2. 79. 3; ibid., ad 1.
45. *De defectu oraculorum* 67. Translation mine.
46. See Colucii Salutati *De laboribus Herculis*, ed. B. L. Ullman (1947), 1 : 85. Translation mine.
47. See, respectively, *Of the Progresse of the Soule*, ll. 425f, 429ff; *The Knight's Tale*, ll. 1303–1312, 1251–1260; *Inferno* 14 : 46–66; *De morbo Gallico* 3. 295–301 (translation mine); Michael Hadrianides ed. *Petronii Satyricon* (Amsterdam, 1669), "Ad lectorem."
48. *Inst.* 1 : 16.
49. *Essays in Divinity*, ed. Evelyn M. Simpson (Oxford, 1952), p. 82.
50. See, respectively, *Eth. Nic.* 1175^{a}18sq., *Rhetorica* 1362^{b}26sq., *Eth. Nic.* 1170^{b}1sq., *Paradise Lost* 2. 146–151.
51. *Inst.* 1 : 181.

52. See *STh* 1. 104. 4, 1. 62. 3.
53. Hooker *Laws*, 1 : 177; Aristotle *Met.* 1006ᵃ6–9.
54. *Erasmi Colloquia*, ed. Cornelius Schrevel (Amsterdam, 1693), p. 474.
55. *King Lear in Our Time*, p. 112.
56. Ibid., p. 117.
57. Ibid., p. 117 and passim.
58. Ibid., p. 117.
59. Ibid., p. 117.
60. Ibid., p. 117.
61. Ibid., p. 114.
62. Ibid., p. 113.

CHAPTER FIVE
Love and Responsibility in Othello

1. Andreas Capellanus, *De amore*, ed. Amadeu Pagès (Castelló de la Plana, 1930), pp. 64, 141 (for the quoted phrase). Translation mine.
2. *Eth. Nic.* 1123ᵇ1sq.
3. Aquinas *STh* 2–2. 162. 3; 1–2. 77. 4 ad 1.
4. *Eth. Nic.* 1166ᵃ24sq., 1168ᵇ25–34.
5. *The Civile Conversation of M. Steeven Guazzo*, trans. Pettie and Young 1581 and 1586 (New York, 1925), 2 : 17.
6. Baldassare Castiglione, *The Book of the Courtier* (London, 1928), pp. 31f.
7. Giambattista Giraldi Cinthio, *Hecatommithi* (Venice, 1608), p. 316.
8. *The Essayes of Montaigne*, trans. Florio (New York, 1933), pp. 560, 563; *Erasmi Colloquia*, ed. Cornelius Schrevel (Amsterdam, 1693), p. 549. Translation mine.
9. *Essayes of Montaigne*, p. 572. Roland Mushat Frye, *Shakespeare and Christian Doctrine* (Princeton, N.J., 1963), p. 182: "Here [*Oth.* 3. 3. 155ff] Iago is merely elevating to the level of poetry an analogy which was repeatedly used in connection with a good name and the slanderer. Calvin gives similar expression to this popular thought: 'For if a good name is more precious than all riches [Prov. 22 : 1], we harm a man more by despoiling him of the integrity of his name than by taking away his possessions.'" Calvin's thought is not equivalent to Iago's at all. A good name may be more precious than all riches without being the immediate jewel—i.e., the essential dignity—of the soul. That immediate jewel, for Calvin and for Macbeth when he knows he has lost it (*Mac.* 3. 1. 68), is justice or saving grace.
Frye goes on to argue in a similar vein: "Reputation is indispensable to

leadership, it is what the leader leaves behind him in the world, and Cassio [*Oth.* 2. 3. 262ff] may merely be expressing a proper regard for his own good name" (ibid., p. 183). Cassio goes considerably beyond this. To say that only one's reputation will survive one, the rest being bestial, is to deny the immortality of the soul. Cassio's regard for his good name in this passage is notably less than proper.

10. Castiglione, *Book of the Courtier*, pp. 94, 36.

11. Andreas Capellanus, *De amore*, p. 143. Cf. Marsilio Ficino, *Commentarium in Convivium Platonis*, ed. Raymond Marcel (Paris, 1956), pp. 143f.

12. Jean-Pierre Boon, "La théorie évolutive des 'Essais' de Montaigne," *PMLA* 83 (1968): 300n19; G. Wilson Knight, *The Wheel of Fire*, 5th ed. (New York, 1957), p. 107.

13. Andreas Capellanus, *De amore*, p. 138. Cf. Ficino, *Commentarium*, pp. 142, 192.

14. Castiglione, *Book of the Courtier*, p. 271. Othello proves to lack this virtue. Cf. Harold S. Wilson, *On the Design of Shakespearian Tragedy* (Toronto, 1957), p. 63. As we shall see in the following chapter, Wilson here oversimplifies the traditional account of the autonomy of reason.

15. Guazzo, p. 28. It is hard to see the relation between what happens in act 3, scene 3 and Robert B. Heilman's contention, in *Magic in the Web* (Lexington, Ky., 1956), p. 61, that Othello there "adopts a technique of rigorous verification." Such a technique, had Othello adopted it, would surely have exonerated Desdemona.

16. Virgil K. Whitaker, *The Mirror up to Nature* (San Marino, Calif., 1965), p. 245.

17. *Sonnets* 116, 56; *TN* 2. 4. 100, *Tro.* 3. 2. 22f, 2. 169f. Cf. Ficino, *Commentarium*, pp. 252, 192.

18. Guazzo, p. 23. Cf. Ficino, *Commentarium*, p. 153.

19. Whitaker, *Mirror up to Nature*, pp. 244f.

20. *Enneads* 3. 5. 1. 24–30, 40–44.

21. Edmund Spenser, *An Hymne of Beavtie* 197–206. Cf. Ficino, *Commentarium*, p. 158; see rest of passage for grounds of "similitude," e.g., astral, demonic, temperamental, educational.

22. *Colloquia*, p. 746. Translation mine.

23. *STh* 1–2. 22. 3; Leone Ebreo, *Dialoghi d'amore*, ed S. Caramella (Bari, Italy, 1929), 3 : 50, quoted in Giuseppe Saitta, *Il pensiero italiano nell'umanesimo e nel Rinascimento* (Bologna, 1950), 2 : 104; sonnet 116.

24. Whitaker, *Mirror up to Nature*, p. 246. Cf. Ficino, *Commentarium*, pp. 177, 144.

25. *FQ* 6, proem 5.

26. Whitaker, *Mirror up to Nature*, p. 246.

27. Ovid *Ars amatoria* 3. 397; Augustine *De trinitate* 10. 2. 4.

28. *STh* 1–2. 3. 4; Paul Oskar Kristeller, *The Philosophy of Marsilio Ficino* (Gloucester, 1964), p. 259. Cf. Ficino, *Commentarium*, pp. 176, 201, 209, 226. Cf. Aristotle *Metaphysica* 1072ª26–30.

29. Castiglione, *Book of the Courtier*, p. 303.

30. Guazzo, pp. 21, 7; *Hymne of Beavtie*, ll. 231–238. Cf. Ficino, *Commentarium*, p. 206.

31. Quoted in Chilton Latham Powell, *English Domestic Relations 1487–1653* (New York, 1917), p. 105.

32. Giambattista Giraldi Cinthio *Hecatommithi*, p. 315.

33. *STh* 1. 114. 2. Dame Helen Gardner seems to ignore this truism of the Christian outlook in setting up her dichotomy: "A view which sees in *Othello* the tragic sense that there is something in the very nature of our temporal existence that defeats our highest human needs and aspirations, and that 'to live your life is not so simple as to cross a field,' seems more adequate to Shakespeare's play than an attempt to find the root of the disaster in flaws in Othello's nature that made him an easy prey to Iago" ("*Othello:* A Retrospect, 1900–67," *Shakespeare Survey* 21 [1968]: 10). But these alternatives do not exclude each other. According to the received wisdom of Shakespeare's age it is in the very nature of our temporal existence to have flaws that make us an easy prey to corruption and thereby defeat our highest human needs and aspirations.

34. See *Purgatorio* 11. 2.

35. Guazzo, p. 23.

36. I quote from *Beaumont and Fletcher*, ed. F. E. Schelling (New York, 1917).

37. *FQ* 3. 11. 1, 10. 56, 55; Capellanus, *De amore*, p. 151sq.; Cinthio *Hecatommithi*: "finalmente fu da parenti della Donna, com'egli meritava, vcciso" (p. 321).

38. Whitaker, *Mirror up to Nature*, p. 248.

39. Cinthio *Hecatommithi*, p. 314.

40. Whitaker, *Mirror up to Nature*, p. 251.

41. Guazzo, pp. 26f, 25; *The Catechism of Thomas Becon*, ed. John Ayre (Cambridge, 1844), p. 334; *The Whole Works of the Right Reverend Jeremy Taylor*, ed. Reginald Heber (London, 1822), 11 : 325.

42. Whitaker, *Mirror up to Nature*, p. 259.

43. We have been assuming that the happiness hypothetically affirmed in " 'twere now to be most happy" is Othello's marital "content" (ll. 193, 198), "comfort" (ll. 194, 209), or "joy" (l. 199). But on this assumption the hypothesis "if it were now to die" is otiose in substance (given that the present moment is Othello's happiest, it is so whether he dies forthwith or not) and formally undermines Othello's tribute to his

"comfort" by making the latter depend on a condition contrary to fact ("if it were now to die"). The following paraphrase would avoid these objections: If I died now, I should be very happy to do so, for I fear that continued life can offer no comfort to match the present. In this reading the condition, being causal, is not otiose; and since the happiness referred to is not the "comfort" of love for Desdemona, Othello is not consciously damning the latter with faint praise.

44. *Rom.* 2. 6. 9–15, 2. 121f; cf. Horace, *Carmina* 1. 13; Donne, "Lovers infinitenesse."

45. For a different view see Hilda M. Hulme, "The Spoken Language and the Dramatic Text," *Shakespeare Quarterly* 9 (1958): 380f.

46. Benvenuti de Rambaldis de Imola, *Comentum super Dantis Aldigherij Comoediam*, ed. J. P. Lacaita (Florence, 1887), 4 : 24.

CHAPTER SIX
Justice and Responsibility in Othello

1. For hyssop cf. Num. 19 : 18, Lev. 14 : 1–4, Exod. 12 : 22, Ps. 51 : 5ff, 9; for thyme (and honey) cf. Virgil *Ecl.* 7. 17, Aen. 1. 436; Horace *Car.* 4. 2. 29, *Ep.* 1. 3. 21; Ovid *Met.* 15. 80. Iago's thesis should not be mistaken for Pelagianism. In its double "thus," Iago's opening remark is ambiguous enough to be consistent with the Calvinist view that "it is not from creation but from corruption of nature that men are bound to sin and can will nothing but evil" (*Inst.* 2. 5. 1); man sins not by divine compulsion but by self-inflicted necessity (ibid., 2. 3. 5). Iago, however, goes on to clarify his intention, which is simply to declare the will immune from coercion by appetite. Such immunity in turn does not rule out, though of course it does not imply, a Calvinist perversity of will. Indeed, Original Sin often expresses itself in the will's perverse resistance to the natural appetite for good: "the power of free choice is not to be sought in such an appetite, which arises from inclination of nature rather than from deliberation of mind" (ibid., 2. 2. 26). That the will, however perverted, is immaterial and hence not necessitated by bodily appetite is a commonplace of Elizabethan psychology. Cf. Hooker, *Laws,* 1. 7. 3. Original Sin regularly consists in the innate neglectfulness of human wills, but not always by the stubborn pursuit of appetite. For the English Church, this defect consists, not in men's inability to practice the cardinal virtues without divine assistance—to triumph over lust—but in the equivalence of even such formally virtuous acts to sin, "forasmuch as they spring not of faith in Jesus Christ" (Article 13). Cf. *Inst.* 3. 14. 2. It is precisely Roderigo's ability to carry through a formally virtuous act, not

his ability to save his soul thereby, that Iago is defending in the present speech.

If Iago must be acquitted of Pelagianism, he is by the same token guiltless of the Neopelagianism associated with the Jesuit theologian Luis de Molina. The latter charge is pressed energetically by Daniel Stempel in "The Silence of Iago," *PMLA* 84 (1969): 252–263, notably on the grounds of what he supposes (p. 254) to be a "fundamental difference" between Iago's notion of a will bound neither to lust nor to reason and Hooker's, of a will by definition subject exclusively to reason or the show of reason. But Stempel apparently fails to note that Hooker finds it necessary to qualify the latter definition lest "any man think that this doth make any thing for the just excuse of iniquity." The ultimate cause of sin is not after all an erring reason: "There is not that good which concerneth us, but it hath evidence enough for itself, if Reason were diligent to search it out. Through neglect thereof, abused we are with the show of that which is not" (*Laws* I. 7. 7). The error of reason that seduces the will to sin is itself occasioned by an initial error of will (viz., neglect or, in Hooker's gloss, *segnities*) that presumably cannot in turn be referred (without incurring an infinite regress and the very excuse Hooker means to disallow) either to reason or to the show of reason. The passage I quote from Aquinas should suffice to show that Hooker's qualification simply clinches the Thomistic account of free will as essentially unconditioned.

2. *Eth. Nic.* Translation mine.

3. Aquinas, *In decem libros Ethicorum Aristotelis ad Nicomachum expositio*, ed. A. M. Pirotta, O.P. (Turin, Italy, 1934), note at 1114^a of *Eth. Nic.*; *STh* 1–2. 78. 2.

4. *Eth. Nic.* 1147^{a}11–17.

5. *Eth. Nic.* 1103^{b}3sqq., 1179^{b}29–32; cf. 1103^{a}17sq.

6. *STh* 1–2. 80. 3, 76. 3, 76. 4.

7. *2H4* 3. 1. 80–88.

8. *Eth. Nic.* 1150^{b}32sqq.

9. *Eth. Nic.* 1151^{a}16–19, 20–24, 3sqq.; 1111^{a}30sq.; 1152^{a}15sqq., 1150^{b}30sq.

10. Castiglione, *The Book of the Courtier*, trans. Hoby (New York, 1948), p. 269.

11. *Eth. Nic.* 1140^{b}16–20, 1144^{a}34sqq., 1112^{a}8–11.

12. Plutarch, *The Morals*, trans. Philemon Holland (London, 1603), p. 313.

13. *Eth. Nic.* 1110^{b}28–32, 1148^{a}17–22, 1150^{a}27–30, 22.

14. *STh* 2–2. 36. 3.

15. *FQ* 2. 4. 28f, 34; 3. 10. 59f.

16. Thomas Cooper, *Bibliotheca Eliotae* (London, 1559), s.v. *zelo* and *zelotes*.

17. *Eth. Nic.* 1150^b6sqq. Cf. Brents Stirling, "Psychology in *Othello*," *Shakespeare Association Bulletin* 19 (1944): p. 137.

18. Rosemond Tuve, *Allegorical Imagery* (Princeton, N.J., 1966), pp. 96f, 166.

19. Chilton Latham Powell, *English Domestic Relations 1487–1653* (New York, 1917), pp. 8, 72.

20. Giambattista Possevino, *Dialogo dell'onore* (Venice, 1565), p. 273.

21. Seneca, *Thyestes* 689, 715.

22. *STh* 1. 114. 2. A metaphorical Iago to represent Othello's vice would be superfluous. What needs external representation is not the formal cause of Othello's passion but the efficient. On Othello's diabolism cf. Robert H. West, *Shakespeare and the Outer Mystery* (Lexington, Ky., 1968), p. 122: "Othello's exchange of oaths with Iago . . . is no literal witch's pact, for it lacks the necessary circumstance that the human party to it know that he is dealing unreservedly with the Adversary and so act not just sinfully but in deliberate despite of God." It is not clear (*a*) in what sense Othello can be held ignorant of an ultimate commitment he specifically acknowledges and (*b*) in what clause of his implacable vow Othello has concealed a reservation.

23. *The Civile Conversation of Master Steeven Guazzo*, trans. Pettie and Young (New York, 1925), p. 25f.

24. *STh* 1–2. 79. 3.

25. "I hate the Moor; / And it is thought abroad" (italics added). In *Magic in the Web* (Lexington, Ky., 1956), p. 31, Robert B. Heilman gratuitously assumes that the "and" is Iago's way of subjoining the cause of his hate and concludes from the unfitness of the conjunction for this purpose that Iago's jealousy is a rationalizing afterthought. The normal use of "and," however, would seem to indicate that the jealousy is not causally subordinate to the hate in the first place, but rather co-ordinate with it as a joint motive for Iago's plotting.

26. *STh* 2–2. 34. 6 ad 3; 36. 1.

27. *Ars rhetorica* 1388^a6sq.

28. Cinthio *Hecatommithi*, pp. 315, 317.

29. See Heilman, *Magic in the Web*, pp. 36, 40. Stempel ("The Silence of Iago") in dismissing the motives avowed by Iago, apparently fails to see that the very avowing of a motive, or sufficient condition, of choice unwittingly undermines any claim Iago might have to the unconditional freedom of will affirmed in his speech to Roderigo. Nor is an explanatory reference to such a motive, or ultimately to Iago's distorted principles, ruled out by the celebrated passage Stempel quotes (p. 263^b) from

Augustine, in which we are discouraged from seeking an efficient cause for an evil act of will (*Civ. Dei* 12. 7. A-B). As is clear from the preceding chapter, Augustine's subject here is the Fall of the angels, and (by extension) that of man as well; hence his dilemma: "unde fieri potest, ut natura bona, quamuis mutabilis, antequam habeat uoluntatem malam, faciat aliquid mali, hoc est ipsam uoluntatem malam?" Since the prelapsarian state of the creature cannot be implicated in the Fall without compromising the beneficent Creator, it remains that the Fall must be entirely uncaused and gratuitous. No such qualm inhibits us from referring the actual sins of Adam's issue either to Original Sin or to the spiritual deformities to which that sin gives rise. Cf. Robert H. West, *Shakespeare and the Outer Mystery*, p. 106f. West's dismissal of habit or predisposition is too hasty. If a will is constitutionally averse to goodness, then the slightest provocation is enough to explain the greatest enormity.

30. Heilman, *Magic in the Web*, p. 35.

31. Possevino, *Dialogo dell'onore*, p. 294.

32. Cinthio *Hecatommithi*, pp. 319, 318, 320.

33. The original verse (*Heautontimorumenos* 4. 5. 48) is "Dicunt, ius summum saepe summa malitiast," with a variant "iniuriast" in some MSS. Cicero *De officiis* 1. 10 quotes it in the form later current. By *ius summum* Terence apparently means any legal quibbling, but in the sixteenth and seventeenth centuries the tag was used to mean severity of penal "justice" (as opposed to "equity"). Thus for More's "quidni merito summum illud ius summa vocetur iniuria?" Ralph Robinson has "why maye not this extreme and rigorous justice wel be called plaine injurie?" The subject is capital punishment for theft. Cf. *The Jew of Malta* 3. 2. 152f.

34. Guazzo, p. 37. See Margaret L. Ranald, "The Indiscretions of Desdemona," *Shakespeare Quarterly* 14 (1963): 127–139. Mrs. Ranald's inference from Desdemona's indiscretion to her "partial responsibility for the tragic action of the play" seems to me misleading for reasons set forth above.

35. *FQ* 1. 9. 47, 50.

36. Heilman, *Magic in the Web*, p. 193.

37. *Eth. Nic.* 1166[b]17sq.

38. Heilman, *Magic in the Web*, p. 256, mentions a similar suggestion made by William Maginn. Iago's paradox occurs at least twice elsewhere in the Shakespearean canon: *Rom.* 1. 1. 187 and *TN* 3. 1. 53.

39. *The Works of Francis Bacon*, ed. Spedding, Ellis, and Heath (Boston, 1861), 14 : 51; John Donne, *Biathanatos* (1646), p. 37; *STh* 1. 83. 2.

40. Aquinas, *Ethicorum expositio*, note at 1113[b] of *Eth. Nic.*

41. *MM* 1. 2. 124–127.

42. Richard Hooker, *Of the Laws of Ecclesiastical Polity* (New York, 1925), 1 : 152f.

43. *Tretyse of Loue*, ed. John Hurt Fisher, EETS (London, 1951), p. 5. Cf. Dionysii Areopagitae *De divinis nominibus* 4. 10. 708B.

44. *Inferno* 20. 28–30. Cf. West, *Shakespeare and the Outer Mystery*, p. 107.

Epilogue

1. B. F. Skinner, "Freedom and the Control of Man," *American Scholar* 25 (1955–1956): 51.

Index